BUSINESS SYSTEMS IN
EAST ASIA

BUSINESS SYSTEMS IN EAST ASIA

Firms, Markets and Societies

Richard Whitley

SAGE Publications
London • Thousand Oaks • New Delhi

First published 1992, Reprinted 1994
First paperback edition 1994

SAGE Publications Ltd
6 Bonhill Street
London EC2A 4PU

SAGE Publications Inc
2455 Teller Road
Thousand Oaks, California 91320

SAGE Publications India Pvt Ltd
32, M-Block Market
Greater Kailash - 1
New Delhi 110 048

British Library Cataloguing in Publication data
Whitley, Richard
  Business Systems in East Asia: Firms, Markets and
    Societies
  I. Title
  338.7095

  ISBN 0-8039-8739-0

  ISBN 0-8039-8740-4 (pbk)

Library of Congress catalog card number 92-050229

Typeset by Mayhew Typesetting, Rhayader, Powys
Printed in Great Britain by J.W. Arrowsmith Ltd, Bristol

Contents

For Barbara

Preface and Acknowledgements

The impetus for this book came from the experience of setting up the Citicorp Doctoral Programme in Management Studies at Hong Kong University in 1988 and the associated opportunity to learn more about the leading economies and ways of doing business in East Asia. It quickly became apparent to me that there are major differences between these economies which can only be explained in terms of their histories and institutional divergences. This made East Asia seem an ideal location for exploring the links between social institutions and forms of economic organization in market economies. Accordingly, I began to collect material on leading firms and patterns of market organization during my stay in Hong Kong and have been able to obtain further information on subsequent visits to the Far East since 1988.

As will be clear from this book, the bulk of the analysis is based on secondary material, although I have benefited from the field-work and archival research conducted by PhD students at the University of Hong Kong, particularly that undertaken by Judith Nishida. I am, therefore, very grateful to Citicorp for generously funding the new Doctoral Programme and the associated Visiting Professorship in Management Studies and to the Institute for Economic Culture at Boston University, directed by Peter Berger, which largely funded later visits. The hospitality of Hong Kong University is also a pleasure to acknowledge, especially that of the Department of Management Studies and its head Gordon Redding and the considerable help given by many members of its staff. In many respects, Gordon Redding provided the prime precipitating factor for this book through his own research on the Chinese family business, and I have benefited greatly from his detailed knowledge of business organizations and practices in East Asia. Finally, I am also greatly indebted to Lynn Dalton, who has ably coped with the many revisions and changes that have been carried out and produced the final version.

Additionally, I am grateful for the comments and suggestions of participants at the Ninth European Group for Organization Studies Colloquium in Berlin, at a seminar held at the Ecole Polytechnique in 1989, at a European Science Foundation Workshop at Netherlands Institute for Advanced Studies in Wassenaar in 1991 and at conferences and seminars held at Lancaster University,

London Business School and Warwick University where this material has been presented.

R. D. Whitley
Manchester, November 1991

1
The Comparative Analysis of Business Systems

The relative decline of the United States in the world economy since 1970 and the concomitant rise of Japanese firms in many sectors have encouraged growing interest in the comparative analysis of business organizations, as well as reinforcing doubts about the general applicability of US management theories and practices. Whereas many discussions of market economies used to assume that they were all basically the same, there is now an increasing awareness of the variety of institutional arrangements found in different market economies and of their influence on firm structure and behaviour (see, for example, Granovetter, 1990; Maurice et al., 1986). In particular, the development of highly successful Japanese companies with distinctive characteristics has emphasized the close interconnections between social institutions and effective managerial practices, so that organizational forms and strategic choices can no longer be adequately understood in isolation from their institutional contexts. Rather, it is becoming widely accepted that different kinds of business environments generate different kinds of managerial structures which are equally successful in world markets (for example, Dore, 1983; Lincoln, 1990).

The variety of effective forms of business organization and their interdependences with key institutions, such as the state and the financial system (cf. Cox, 1986; Zysman, 1983), imply that a single economic rationality or logic of efficiency is inadequate to explain the development of successful managerial structures and processes in market economies. Equally, a single set of abstract and general contingencies cannot be held to 'explain' variations in organizational structures in all contexts when it is clear that authority relations, control mechanisms and the division of tasks in leading organizations are closely connected to the institutional contexts in which they operate, as illustrated by European comparisons and the Chinese family business (Lane, 1989; Maurice et al., 1980, 1986; Redding, 1990; Sorge and Warner, 1986). Thus, a key task in organizational analysis is to understand how different kinds of business organizations and economic rationalities develop and become effective in different institutional contexts. In this book I develop a framework for comparing such differences across societies on the basis of analysis of the very different, yet equally successful, forms of business organization that have become established in Japan, South Korea, Taiwan and Hong Kong as a contribution to this task. The major variations in the organization of these market economies, and of dominant economic agents in them, make them an especially appropriate focus for the comparative analysis of business systems and their success over the past 40 years demonstrates the importance of this analysis for management and organization studies.

The significance of differences between forms of business organization and economic rationalities is, of course, contested by those who adhere to the tenets of what might be termed 'economic rationalism', be they neo-classical or transaction cost economists, population ecologists or contingency theorists of organizations. Despite their considerable differences, all these groups of economic rationalists believe that competitive markets select efficient forms of business organizations and destroy inefficient ones. While they might accept that patterns of industrialization and social institutions can vary significantly, they none the less claim that underlying market pressures ensure that the firms which survive by competing successfully in international markets will converge to the same efficient structure, practices and strategic decisions which 'fit' particular technology and market imperatives. Thus, even if firms vary between industries – either because of transaction costs, technology or market structure – they are constrained to follow the same basic 'recipe' within each industry (cf. Spender, 1989; Stinchcombe, 1965) if they are to survive, because efficient structures and practices will drive out inefficient ones.

This presumption of market determinism and the irrelevance of social institutions, except perhaps as influences on micro-social beliefs and attitudes (cf. Child, 1981), has been challenged by a number of critics adhering to various forms of cultural or institutional relativism. Although differing considerably on a number of issues, they share a commitment to the social embeddedness of economic activities (Granovetter, 1985) and the socially constituted nature of firms and markets (Baker, 1987). Economic efficiency and success, in this view, are socially constructed and so vary across significantly different social contexts. Thus, the hypostatization of an asocial, general economic and/or managerial rationality which determines efficient structures and practices for co-ordinating and directing economic activities irrespective of institutional differences is strongly rejected by cultural/institutional relativists (cf. Brossard and Maurice, 1976; Mizruchi and Schwartz, 1987; Orru, 1991; Sorge, 1983).

The differences between these two broad intellectual positions stem as much from the significance they attribute to the socially constructed nature of firms and markets as from their acceptance or denial of its validity. While economic rationalists may accept that firms are complex social organizations whose structure and activities reflect the diverse conceptions and values of their owners and/or managers as well as other employees, they consider competitive pressures to be so strong that efficient forms of business organization and 'rational' strategic choices quickly dominate market economies irrespective of cultural and institutional variations. Thus differences in beliefs, preferences and expectations are essentially irrelevant to economic outcomes in this view. Conversely, cultural and institutional relativists regard differences in social conventions, rationalities and moral codes to be so strong across societies that they generate highly distinctive forms of successful business organization and practices which are specific to their context. Variations in institutional contexts are seen here as directly affecting the nature of market processes and how economic success is achieved so that the sorts of business structures and practices that become established, and remain dominant, in a particular context reflect the specific features of that context.

How the significance of the socially constituted nature of firms and markets is evaluated is clearly tied to conceptions of markets and competitive processes as well as to the theoretical objectives being pursued and the level of analysis adopted. Students of 'perfect' markets in equilibrium obviously do not need to concern themselves overly with social institutions and variations in firm behaviour, although they do need to deal with the difficulties of combining perfect competition with perfect knowledge, as Richardson (1960) has demonstrated. However, once it is agreed that markets are imperfect and firms do matter as economic actors, then a number of consequences follow for the comparative analysis of business organizations. In particular, where firms and markets are mutually constitutive, the beliefs and rationalities of economic actors necessarily affect economic outcomes, so that who controls firms, and how they gain such control, helps to determine efficient managerial structures and practices. However, the extent to which, and ways in which, dominant social institutions in particular social collectivities generate sharply distinct forms of business organizations vary, and there is no overwhelming reason to presume that each 'culture' or nation state necessarily possesses its own unique business system. These points will now be elaborated as the prelude to outlining what is meant by the comparative analysis of business systems and what it involves.

The Socially Constructed Nature of Imperfect Markets

Accepting the pervasiveness of uncertainty in market economies and the interdependence of firms' activities as economic decision makers, so that they can be conceived neither as atomistic price takers nor as omnipotent price makers, leads to three major consequences for organizational analysis. First, firms' actions collectively determine economic outcomes, and so how strategic decisions are taken affects their subsequent success. Second, where major institutions vary considerably between business environments, so too do 'rational' and 'efficient' managerial structures and practices. Third, since social systems are 'open' systems, and so social structures and relations can change endogenously as well as exogenously, market processes and outcomes can alter as a result of learning and changes in preferences. Thus previously 'efficient' and 'rational' actions may cease to be effective.

The pervasiveness of uncertainty and disequilibrium in market economies means that firms, as economic actors with delegated control over human and material resources (Whitley, 1987), make investment, production and distribution decisions in ignorance of their competitors' decisions and future demand. Typically, they rely on knowledge of previous behaviour and judgement (Leifer and White, 1987). Since market outcomes are the result of the totality of firms' decisions and consumers' responses, they both vary according to current knowledge and judgements and also depend on previous understandings and judgements about market behaviour. How the dominant coalitions of firms perceive their own and competitors' capacities and interests thus affects market outcomes, especially those of the larger and more powerful firms. The interdependence of firms' activities and their uncertainty about future actions mean that the results of their decisions are dependent on how they interpret 'what is going on' (cf. Taylor, 1985) and cannot be reduced to a single, external, system logic. If dominant coalitions change their understandings and priorities, their actions will change and so will market outcomes. Thus 'rational' and efficient structures and practices are dependent on, and vary according to, currently dominant beliefs, priorities and ways of making judgements.

Economic rationalists assume that these can be ignored because markets necessarily follow an overall system logic irrespective of economic actors' particular decisions. This assumption can only be justified if they can show how markets pervaded by uncertainty, and constituted by firms of varying economic power, are compelled to follow such a system logic. This would involve identifying both the mechanisms by which such compulsion would be achieved together with the circumstances in which they would generate such consequences. In the absence of such a demonstration, it seems best to conclude that market processes and effective decisions are dependent on the rationalities and judgements of firms' dominant coalitions.

The second major consequence, the significant effects of variations in businesses' institutional contexts on what constitutes efficient and rational managerial practices, has two components. First, dominant institutions structure the paths by which particular business owners and managers with particular qualifications, backgrounds and experiences achieve control over major economic entities and so the ways in which they understand the business world and set priorities (cf. Gunz and Whitley, 1985). Second, the institutional context structures they ways in which critical components of the business environment impinge upon firms' activities and their outcomes. Thus, for example, major differences in the structure and operations of the political system in different states affect firms' willingness to undertake long-term investments and their dependence on state agencies in making decisions. What is 'rational' strategic behaviour therefore varies according to the role of the state in different market economies (cf. Cawson et al., 1987; Cox, 1986; Grant et al., 1987; Okimoto, 1989; Zysman, 1983).

Similarly, variations in the nature of the financial systems between European countries have affected relationships between banks and industrial companies so that the management of financial risks together with the use of financial management skills and financial accounting methods vary considerably between major enterprises in these societies (Horovitz, 1980; Scott, 1987). Thus, 'efficient' firms in Britain have to adapt to the more active 'market for corporate control' (Lawriwsky, 1984) and separation of financial institutions from industry (Ingham, 1984) in ways that do not apply to many continental firms operating within credit-based financial systems. Because business environments vary in many important respects between countries, then, so too do 'efficient' management structures and practices. Beliefs and systems that work well in one context will not be so effective in others where important institutions operate quite differently. This means that the contrast between technical and institutional sectors drawn by Meyer and Scott (1983: 140–1) in their analysis of organizational isomorphism is misleading, since market efficiency is institutionally constructed (Orru et al., 1988; Orru, 1991).

Finally, the open nature of social systems means that markets and firms can change as the result of learning and altered perceptions thus modifying the efficacy of previously successful structures and practices. Open systems in this sense are those which do not generate invariant empirical regularities (Bhaskar, 1979: 57). They violate both the intrinsic and extrinsic conditions for closure, that is, for the production of constant conjunctions of events. In Sayer's terms (1984: 112, cf. Bhaskar, 1975: ch. 2), the intrinsic condition for closure requires that 'there must be no change or qualitative variation in the object possessing the causal powers if mechanisms are to operate consistently'. For example, the spring in a clockwork mechanism must not suffer from metal fatigue if it is to produce regular movement. The extrinsic condition for closure requires that 'the relationship between the causal mechanism and those of its external conditions which make some difference to its operation and effects must be constant if the outcome is to be regular'. For example, changes in public opinion due to independent factors may alter the effectiveness of a political pressure group's campaigns irrespective of its own cohesion and strategy, and so it cannot be said to operate in a closed system.

Social systems are open because they can develop emergent properties and powers as a result of reinterpretations of social and material realities which alter the nature of the social world. The meaningful and concept-dependent nature of social relations and institutions means that internal learning and changing perceptions as a result of external events can alter human understandings to the extent that actions and relationships alter significantly and system outcomes become quite different. Thus, when enough people in an organization change their perception of what is going on and redefine its nature, its structure and procedures will alter. While, then, much managerial effort is devoted to establishing and maintaining relatively closed systems which produce approximate regularities, such closure is always contingent upon employees' beliefs and values remaining sufficiently stable and acquiescent to continue to generate the desired outcomes in a regular manner. As a result, previously effective managerial structures and practices may produce different outcomes if perceptions change, and those which worked in one situation will not do so in contexts where interpretations and rationalities are quite different. Particular strategies and control systems, then, generate varied results in distinct contexts and cannot be presumed to function effectively in all institutional environments. The more meaning systems and rationalities differ and change, the less transferable will any particular economic logic or set of managerial practices be between them.

These three points together imply that market processes and the outcome of firms' decisions vary significantly between their institutional contexts and depend, inter alia, upon the beliefs, priorities and understandings of those responsible for controlling and directing economic resources. It is, however, important to note here that the degree of such variation depends upon the extent to which particular institutional contexts and managerial rationalities are both internally cohesive and also sharply distinct from one another. Where, for example, institutional pluralism within a number of nation states is quite high, and there are strong institutional similarities between them, as in many Anglo-Saxon countries, it is likely that firms' dominant coalitions will have a variety of perceptions of effective managerial policies and practices within each country, especially perhaps between industries, and yet share some beliefs about, say, financial prudence and the importance of financial accounting procedures, across national boundaries. Conversely, where institutional pluralism is low and cultural homogeneity is high within nation states, and dominant institutions vary considerably between them, we can expect quite distinctive managerial rationalities and practices to become established in different states and to generate separate forms of business organization. Thus, the extent to which distinctive ways of organizing and directing firms characterize individual nation states – or any other unit of analysis – depends on their internal homogeneity and external differences.

Bearing this point in mind, the socially constructed nature of imperfect markets means that differences in how dominant coalitions of firms develop and reproduce themselves will result in different managerial structures and practices becoming established in particular market sectors and economies. It also means that different institutional contexts will encourage different forms of business and market organization to become established so that particularly cohesive and distinctive contexts will be characterized by quite distinctive kinds of firms and ways of organizing relations between them. Relatedly, of course, where these institutional contexts undergo substantial changes, so too will the distinctive characteristics of firms and markets that have developed interdependently with them. Thus, different kinds of business and market organization develop and dominate different market economies as a result of major variations in social institutions and constitute distinctive business systems.

These systems are particular ways of organizing, controlling and directing enterprises that become established in different contexts; they reflect successful patterns of business behaviour and understandings of how to manage economic activities that are reproduced and reinforced by crucial institutions. The comparative analysis of business systems is therefore concerned with the processes by which different kinds of business and market organization become established in particular contexts, dominate them and change as a central part of the sociological analysis of business structures in market economies.

This approach is similar in certain respects to the study of organizational isomorphism developed in the 'institutional' school of organizational analysis (for example, DiMaggio and Powell, 1983; Meyer and Scott, 1983; Scott, 1987; Zucker, 1987). Here, organizations in the same sector of society are seen as adopting similar forms and practices as a result of institutionalized conventions and 'rules of the game'. Just as Stinchcombe (1965) suggested that organizations follow the dominant pattern established when an industry first developed, the institutionalists argue that schools, public television stations, hospitals and other organizations in the USA follow the pattern set by the most successful and legitimate organization in their particular field to demonstrate their correctness and modernity. This mimetic isomorphism is considered especially strong in fields where the standards of organizational success and effectiveness are ambiguous (DiMaggio and Powell, 1983), although Fligstein (1985) has discussed the spread of the multi-divisional corporate form in similar terms.

Most of the organizations studied by the institutionalists have been non-profit-making and there has been a tendency to regard isomorphism among privately owned businesses as primarily technical and competitive in nature rather than 'institutional' (Meyer and Rowan, 1977). This is despite the general assumption that powerful economic agents' beliefs and conceptions affect organization structures and practices (Scott, 1987). Indeed, some proponents of the institutionalist approach suggest that the search for institutional legitimacy and imitation of fashionable procedures necessarily lead to technical inefficiency, even though the nature of 'efficiency' is clearly institutionally dependent, as argued above (cf. Meyer and Rowan, 1977; Zucker 1987).

The comparative analysis of business structures and practices proposed here shares the institutionalists' view that integrated and strong institutional environments encourage isomorphism between organization structures and practices, so that differences between these environments lead to differences in organizational forms. Rather than drawing a distinction between technical and institutional isomorphism, though, it focuses on the ways that different institutional environments generate different kinds of technically efficient business systems so that equally effective forms of business organization become similar within them but quite different between them. Social institutions, in this view, are key phenomena in the constitution of different competitive orders and should not be counterposed to market efficiency (cf. Fligstein and Dauber, 1989; Orru et al., 1988).

The Nature of Business Systems and their Comparison

In advocating a comparative analysis of ways of organizing economic activities, more than the cross-national study of micro-organizational phenomena is being proposed. In addition to this recognition of the national variability of many attitudinal and similar phenomena, it is important to be aware of the differences in what Richardson (1972) has called the 'organization of industry' between institutional contexts. These variations concern patterns of relations between firms and the extent to which they specialize in particular competences and activities. They thus focus on differences in market organization and the relations between markets and hierarchies in different contexts. As Imai and Itami (1984) have emphasized, there are considerable differences between Japanese and United States firms in terms of both their internal structures and their interconnections in variously organized markets. These differences arise from the particular institutional environments in which successful firms developed.

Variations in market organization between institutional contexts have important implications for the nature of firms and their internal organization. Differences in the scope and intensity of connections between firms are related to differences in the sorts of activities they co-ordinate and their competitive strategies. The widespread use of 'relational contracting' between Japanese companies, and their common membership of inter-market business groups which exchange information and resources (Clark, 1979; Dore, 1986; Futatsugi, 1986), for example, enable them to specialize in particular activities and competitive capacities at lower risk levels than could firms in Anglo-Saxon societies (cf. Yoshino and Lifson, 1986: 37–50). The nature of firms as authoritative co-ordinators of economic activities, then, is interdependent with the ways in which they are organized as 'industries' and are embedded in reciprocal obligation networks which vary across institutional environments. These variations are also related to differences in authority structures and control systems, as the example of Japanese employment practices and employer–employee commitment indicates (Clark, 1979: 221–2). Indeed, the dominant pattern of authoritative co-ordination and control in different business systems is not, I suggest, fully comprehensible without considering how firms developed as particular economic decision-making units and their connections with business partners and competitors.

Distinctive business systems, then, are particular arrangements of hierarchy–market relations which become institutionalized and relatively successful in particular contexts. They combine preferences for particular kinds of activities and skills to be co-ordinated authoritatively with variations in the degree of discretion exercised by managers from property rights holders and in the ways in which activities are co-ordinated. They also exhibit differences in the extent and manner in which activities are co-ordinated between economic actors. Thus the nature of firms as quasi-autonomous economic actors, their internal structures and their interdependences are all interrelated and differ significantly between institutional contexts.

The comparative study of business systems therefore involves consideration of how 'firms' are constituted as relatively discrete economic actors in different market societies. While all market-based economic systems decentralize control over human and material resources to property rights owners and their agents, the nature of the collective entities that exercise that control, and how they do so, vary considerably, and so what a 'firm' is differs across societal contexts. In particular, it is clearly misleading to rely on purely legal definitions of firms' boundaries and activities if we are concerned to explore their role as economic decision-making units. Not only are French industrial groups often much more important that their constituent firms in making strategic choices (Bauer and Cohen, 1981), but among the expatriate Chinese it is clear that the key decision unit is the family business rather than the often numerous legally defined 'firms' controlled by family heads (Tam, 1990; Wong, 1985). These differences are important features of distinctive business systems which are linked to the institutional environments in which they develop and emphasize the contextual nature of 'firms' as economic agents.

The variability of economic agents between societies and the different roles of legally defined firms mean that comparisons of business systems cannot rely on purely formal means of identifying key units of economic action. Similarly, the importance of business groups and networks of relationships between ostensibly independent firms in many countries, especially East Asian ones (Hamilton et al., 1990), raises questions about how economic agents are to be identified for comparative purposes. If business systems vary in how they constitute firms as units of economic action, in other words, how are we to compare and contrast them in a systematic way? The critical point here, it should be noted, is not so much what 'firms' really are as how we are to conceive of the critical economic agents in market societies so that we can compare them and explain their differences. This obviously depends on our view of how firms and markets function.

Firms are important economic agents in market societies because they, or their controllers, exercise considerable discretion over the acquisition, use and disposition of human and material resources. They function as economic actors by integrating, co-ordinating and controlling resources through an authority system and it is this authoritative direction of economic activities which is their central characteristic. Authority relations provide the basis for continued and systematic co-ordination of activities and so the integrated transformation of resources into productive services (Penrose, 1980: 15–25; Whitley, 1987). It is through this system that firms 'add value' to resources and function as relatively separate units of economic decision making. Although the degree of central direction of economic activities does, of course, vary, as does the primary basis of authority relations, it is this co-ordinated control of a varied set of resources which distinguishes firms as distinct economic agents from co-operative networks and ad hoc alliances. Thus, Taiwanese business groups consisting of informal networks between different family firms based on ad hoc arrangements, joint ventures, financial assistance, etc., do not constitute the primary units of economic action in this view because they are better regarded as informal coalitions of partnerships than authoritatively integrated managerial hierarchies (Hamilton and Kao, 1990; Hamilton et al., 1990; Numazaki, 1987, 1989). Because each family business retains considerable freedom of action and remains the primary locus of authoritative decision making and control in Taiwan, it is the family firm that functions as the dominant economic agent there, rather than the business group.

The importance of the highly personal, particularistic and diffuse ties between family firms in Taiwan, Hong Kong and other Chinese business communities, as well as the long-term alliances between Japanese companies (Futatsugi, 1986; Goto, 1982), demonstrate the variable nature of market relationships and the limited generality of the Anglo-Saxon model of firms and markets. It is particularly important to note here that the nature of inter-firm connections and market organization is closely linked to the nature of firms as economic actors in these societies and to key features of their 'internal' organization and management practices. Distinctive configurations of these interrelated characteristics have become established as separate forms of business organization in the East Asian societies (Whitley, 1990), which will be the subject of later chapters in this book. While not all societies institutionalize such different and integrated business systems, variations in how firms are constituted are usually connected to differences in market organization, and in their authority structures and procedures, to form identifiable and distinct configurations.

The identification of business systems, then, involves consideration of the different ways that firms co-operate and compete as well as their internal structures and how they function as economic agents. Each system consists of institutionalized conventions governing successful ways of organizing economic activities in particular contexts, which include the nature of the activities co-ordinated through authority hierarchies and those variously organized by different kinds of market connection. For instance, the established business systems in Japan, Taiwan and Hong Kong restrict the range of skills and sectors managed by major economic actors more than that in South Korea, let alone the integrated, diversified US corporation (Clark, 1979; Redding, 1990; Silin, 1976; Zeile, 1989). A related aspect of business systems concerns preferences for particular kinds of economic sectors. Contrasting large firms in Britain with those in Germany, for example, reveals many more in heavy, technologically advanced industrial sectors in the latter country than in Britain over most of the twentieth century (Dunning and Pearce, 1985; Hannah, 1976, 1980; Lash and Urry, 1987). Similarly, Taiwanese firms have tended to be more successful in light industrial sectors, while Korean ones have, since the 1970s, become prominent in many capital-intensive industries (Levy, 1988). These differences are linked to variations in institutional arrangements for managing risk as well as prestige hierarchies in elite training systems and political structures.

Business systems also incorporate preferred ways of developing firms and making organizational changes. Where firms are quite specialized and rely on quasi-market relationships to co-ordinate complementary but dissimilar activities, their competitive skills are focused on particular industrial sectors, and so top managers are unlikely to diversify widely, or to see their role as managing a portfolio of separate businesses to be bought or sold as performance dictates. Where, on the other hand, firms combine a variety of skills and activities, and maintain relatively distant contractual relations with each other, they are more likely to manage risks by diversifying into different markets and technologies and to develop the skills for managing diverse businesses. Strategic choices here are likely to be more discontinuous and separate from particular sector specific decisions than in the first case; as Kagono et al. (1985: 83–7) describe it, more deductive and logical strategic planning than an inductive and gradual adjustment approach.

In sum, business systems are distinctive configurations of hierarchy–market relations which become institutionalized as relatively successful ways of organizing economic activities in different institutional environments. Certain kinds of activities are co-ordinated through particular sorts of authority structures and interconnected in different ways through various quasi-contractual arrangements in each business system. Thus, what resources are organized by differently structured hierarchies and markets varies between these systems, as do preferred ways of developing businesses and making choices. They develop and change in relation to dominant social institutions, especially those important during processes of industrialization. The coherence and stability of these institutions, together with their dissimilarity between nation states, determine the extent to which business systems are distinctive, integrated and nationally differentiated.

The Variability of Business Systems and their Institutional Environments

The comparative analysis of business systems presumes that distinctive ways of organizing economic activities become established and effective because of major differences in key social institutions, such as the state, the financial system and the education and training system (Maurice et al., 1980, 1986), as well as more diffuse factors such as cultural preferences and beliefs. However, the distinctiveness and homogeneity of business systems clearly vary between societies, as does their institutional specificity. Those prevalent in East Asian countries, for instance, seem more different from each other and more homogeneous within each society than those apparent in Western European and North American nations where variations between industries are significant (Spender, 1989). Thus, authority relations and structures within firms differ considerably between Japan, Korea and Taiwan, while those in most Western firms share a common reliance on legal-rational norms and bases of legitimacy. Similarly, the prevalence of capital market-based financial systems, and the reliance on 'professional' modes of skill development and organization, in Anglo-Saxon societies means that dominant businesses in Britain and the USA seem to share a preference for financial means of control of operations and subsidiaries, and accord the finance function higher status than many continental

European firms (Granick, 1972; Horovitz, 1980; Lawrence, 1980). As a result, some features of particular recipes, such as financial control techniques, may be readily transferred between particular contexts, such as Anglo-Saxon societies, while others require substantial modification and 'translation'.

The distinctiveness of business systems, then, depends on the integrated and separate nature of the contexts in which they developed. The more that major social institutions, such as the political and financial systems, the organization of labour markets and educational institutions, form distinctive and cohesive configurations, the more business systems in those societies will be different and separate. Where distinctive cultural systems and socialization patterns overlap with national boundaries, and state institutions are also distinctive and closely involved in economic development, we would expect successful firms within nation states to share major characteristics which differ significantly from those of dominant economic actors in different contexts.

Where, on the other hand, major social institutions are more differentiated and plural in a society, business systems are likely to be more varied and not so sharply distinct from those elsewhere. Thus, the strong state commitment to the defence industries in Britain and the USA, in contrast to a more laissez-faire attitude to other ones, can be expected to affect attitudes to long-term investments as well as the composition of the dominant coalitions of firms across industries. Similarly, strong regional variations in the pattern of industrialization coupled with high levels of local political and financial autonomy can generate quite distinct business systems within a country, as in the case of Italy. Here, the industrial districts of north-east and central Italy have developed successful systems of subcontracting and highly decentralized production units which contrast strongly with the predominance of large integrated businesses in north-west Italy (Amin, 1989; Bamford, 1987; Lazerson, 1988).

This contrast highlights the variable nature of the relationship between business systems and national boundaries. Nation states with relatively homogeneous cultures and institutions generate more distinctive business systems than do those characterized by greater heterogeneity. While East Asian societies appear to have business systems that are quite dissimilar, for example, many South-East Asian nations are dominated by the same way of organizing and controlling economic activities, the Chinese family business (Limlingan, 1986; Redding, 1990; Yoshihara, 1988). These latter countries are often based on colonial boundaries that incorporate a variety of quite distinct cultures and different social institutions. Where political elites have tried to develop a business class drawn from the dominant ethnic group, as in Malaysia, they do not seem to have been successful in generating a viable alternative 'national' business system (Jesudason, 1989).

As well as major ethnic and cultural differences encouraging a variety of distinct business systems within nation states, there are of course substantial differences between firm structures and connections across industries, especially in Western Europe and North America. The extent of vertical integration, large firm concentration and diversification differs considerably between industries, and distinctive recipes governing strategic choices have been identified in different industries (Rumelt, 1974; Spender, 1989). These and other variations have been explained in terms of transaction costs (Daems, 1983; Williamson, 1985: 90–8) and by the conditions in which each industry became established (Stinchcombe, 1965).

Just as the national distinctiveness and coherence of business systems depend on the integration and dissimilarity of national institutions, so too the variability of industry-based recipes depends on the differentiation of industrial contexts. However, since many important contextual institutions are common to all industries in each country, such as the financial and political systems, the extent to which industry recipes are sharply distinct and mutually exclusive is limited. While, then, major differences in capital and energy intensity, in market structure and in the organization of transaction costs may well affect the nature of economic actors and their interrelations between different industries, they will not generate highly dissimilar business systems. As Nishida (1990) has shown, different legal and political institutions in Hong Kong encouraged greater vertical integration among Chinese cotton spinners there than in Shanghai. Similarly, Limlingan (1986) has identified distinctive growth patterns and financial strategies in a number of industries dominated by Chinese family businesses in ASEAN (Association of South-East Asian Nations) states, as Abegglen and Stalk (1985) have also suggested is the case for large Japanese firms across different industries. Industry differences here seem less crucial than institutional contexts, especially the significance of family identities and affiliations and of trust relations between business partners (Redding, 1990; Silin, 1976).

The relative importance of industry characteristics, as opposed to more general social institutions in a country, in generating distinctive business systems depends, then, on the extent to which the latter are homogeneous across industries and dissimilar between societies. The more varied and differentiated are major social institutions, the more likely economic actors will differ between industries in certain respects. Thus, societies in which occupational identities are important and distinct, and individual rights and duties are more significant than collective ones, are more likely to have a variety of overlapping business systems than those with more collective and vertical commitments. Anglo-Saxon societies which share a common concern with 'professional' identities, market-based wage systems and commitments to individualism, then, generate greater variations between industries than many continental European and East Asian ones (Child et al., 1983; Dore, 1973; Lodge and Vogel, 1987). These common features, together with similar reliance on capital-market-based financial systems and common law legal systems, also encourage, of course, similarities in dominant business systems in these societies when contrasted with those elsewhere. It should be noted, though, that variations in educational systems, the organization of labour unions and the prestige hierarchy of occupations do limit such cross-national commonalities.

Turning now to consider briefly the major institutions which structure and enable different business systems to develop and become established, we can distinguish between the more immediate and proximate institutions which affect business behaviour currently and in the recent past and those more distant in origin and indirect in impact. In the former category I would place the sorts of phenomena that have been commonly cited as explanations for variations between managerial structures and practices in different countries such as the structure and policies of the state – developmental or regulatory (Johnson, 1982) – the nature of the financial system and its role in economic development (Ingham, 1984; Zysman, 1983) and the education and training system emphasized by the Aix group (Maurice et al., 1980, 1986; cf. Lane, 1987, 1988; Rose, 1985). Also included here are dominant patterns of labour market organization and, in particular, trades union structures and attitudes as well as more general and diffuse attitudes and beliefs about work, material values and authority relations.

The major institutions in the second category are those which developed during industrialization, and, where this was relatively recent, those which were important in pre-industrial periods and influenced the particular patterns of industrialization that occurred. In many countries the dominant political institutions and authority relations reflect those that emerged during or, arguably, shaped the industrial process. Even where earlier political systems have been discredited by the rise of militarism and defeat in war

– as in Germany and Japan – key features of present state structures and policies as well as subordination principles stem from those current in the period of early industrialization and, in some cases, earlier patterns of political and economic relationships. Related significant institutions are family and kinship relations, identities and authority structures. The significance of family membership and prestige, for instance, varies greatly between cultures and has a considerable influence on conceptions of identity and the role of individual rights and duties as opposed to collective ones. Additionally important are historical patterns of trust and co-operation between kinship groups which continue to affect trust relations between exchange partners in recently industrialized societies (Redding, 1990; Silin, 1976). Finally, traditional cosmologies and beliefs about the natural and social world often structure attitudes towards risk, planning horizons and preferences about specialization and formalization within authority structures, as Redding (1980; Redding and Wong, 1986) has suggested in the case of the Chinese family business.

Institutions in both categories affect the sorts of business systems that become established in a society, but the influence of those in the second set is usually more indirect and diffuse than that of more proximate institutions. Especially in societies where major social institutions are highly differentiated, and have been established for some time since industrialization took place – such as Britain and the USA – business systems are not as internally homogeneous and mutually distinct as those in recently industrialized societies which are less institutionally pluralistic. In so far as there are distinct national business systems in these more differentiated countries, they result more from the general characteristics of their market systems which developed since industrialization than from specific features of the industrialization process. In contrast, societies where industrialization was both more recent and more state directed generate more homogeneous business systems which are relatively specific to them. As major agents of industrialization, dominant economic actors here reflect and reproduce the distinctive features of this process in each society, and so are more directly affected by pre-industrial institutions, including, of course, traditional ways of understanding the world and preferred ways of acting in it (cf. Redding, 1980).

The Components of Business Systems

The identification of business systems as distinctive configurations of hierarchy–market relations in which firms function as economic actors through their authoritative co-ordination and direction of human and material resources suggests three broad areas for comparing and contrasting them. First, the nature of the firm as the key economic actor in a particular economy and the dominant ways in which firms develop and compete are distinctive elements of business systems. Second, the connections that firms develop with each other in the same industry or markets, and across industrial sectors, are clearly interrelated with their distinctive capabilities and skills and form particular patterns of market organization. Third, how activities and skills are authoritatively co-ordinated and controlled within firms clearly varies between business systems, as has been shown in numerous studies of organizational processes and structures (for example, Crozier, 1964; Gallie, 1978; d'Iribarne, 1989; Maurice et al., 1980, 1986; Orru, 1991).

These three constituent elements of business systems are closely interconnected, since the ways in which resources are managed reflect differences in their diversity and type, just as market relations are interdependent with strategic preferences and patterns of managerial recruitment and promotion. Each business system can therefore be seen as systematic, interrelated responses to the three fundamental issues of any market-based system. These are: first, what sorts of economic activities are to be authoritatively integrated and co-ordinated towards what competitive priorities? Second, how are market relations of competition and co-operation to be organized and firms' activities connected? Third, how are economic activities to be managed in authority hierarchies?

The first issue is sometimes characterized as the domain of the firm or the nature of the business a firm competes in. While this is certainly an important feature of the nature of firms as economic actors, a rather broader view is meant here. The success of the expatriate Chinese family business in Hong Kong and South-East Asia (Limlingan, 1986; Wu, 1983) as well as Taiwan has emphasized the limited generality of the Anglo-Saxon conception of the firm as an autonomous legal and financial entity facing largely anonymous and impersonal market pressures. Instead, it seems that this is only one kind of economic actor which is competitive in international markets and 'firms' can differ considerably in terms of their mutual independence and membership of networks (Hamilton et al., 1990). The extent to which they are discrete economic actors operating at arm's length from each other, then, varies between business systems, as does their identity with purely legal entities. The example of the Chinese family business in which the key decision-making unit is the family head, not the managers of individual firms, demonstrates the different significance of legal boundaries in different business systems as well as the varied connections between economic actors and kinship structures that are economically viable. Related aspects of economic actors are the nature of their competitive competences, especially the degree to which these are relatively specialized, and the sorts of activities they co-ordinate. In particular, the extent to which they compete in capital-intensive and technologically advanced sectors varies considerably between business systems. These aspects are linked to strategic preferences and ways of making business development choices.

The degree and type of market co-ordination cover both industry networks and economy-wide relationships. As well as incorporating the extent of mutual co-operation and trust between suppliers and customers in relatively long-term relationships, they also refer to the importance of mutual obligation networks across industries and markets which facilitate joint ventures, financial assistance and risk reduction. These networks are sometimes reinforced by mutual shareholdings and kinship connections. A third aspect of market organization is the extent to which firms' strategies are interlinked and co-ordinated by banks or general trading companies, as well as by state agencies. Again, the longevity of such connections and the degree of mutual constraint and commitment in them are important variable features. Although, then, relations between economic actors are fundamentally competitive in market economies, the ways in which competition is organized and risks are shared between firms and other collective actors are quite variable across business systems.

The 'internal' organization and management of economic activities in market economies have, of course, been the focus of a large number of analyses of organization structures and corporate bureaucracies. Here, however, a slightly different conception of the key features of firms' authority structures is being suggested. In particular, the nature of subordination and dependence relations between employers and employees are major features of business systems which vary significantly between societies and cannot simply be subsumed under a broad presumption of bureaucratic regulation. Relatedly, the basis of managerial authority and dominant components of the managerial role also differ between business systems and reflect more general variations in relations of domination and trust between societies. How senior managerial appointments are made and dominant coalitions constituted are also important features of co-ordination and control systems which do not always receive the attention they deserve in comparative analyses of administrative structures. Further important features of co-ordination and control systems are, of course, the division of labour, the organization of different activities and their interdependences and the overall hierarchical structure.

These three broad areas constitute the major headings for analysing differences between business systems. Each, though, contains a number of dimensions and characteristics which require further specification in order to identify distinctive configurations which represent effective forms of business organization in particular social contexts. These characteristics will be abstracted from a comparison of the three major East Asian business systems which are quite dissimilar from each other in major respects and yet quite homogeneous within the national economies of Japan, South Korea, Taiwan and Hong Kong. This comparison reveals significant dimensions on which business systems differ and highlights the critical features which result from the societal contexts in which they developed and are effective.

The significance of these three business systems lies both in their common differences from the Anglo-Saxon corporations which constitute the dominant type found in the research literature and in the considerable differences between them. They thus demonstrate not only the viability of non-American forms of business organization but also the variety of alternatives and therefore the impossibility of dismissing the Japanese example as a deviant type. Although there are a number of important differences between European business systems which also show the limited extent to which the growth and operations of large US corporations should be taken as paradigmatic, these systems tend not to be so distinctive and homogeneous as those in East Asia. It is, then, primarily because East Asian business systems constitute quite distinct configurations of hierarchy–market relations and demonstrate the economic effectiveness of quite different ways of organizing businesses in particular institutional environments that they are the focus of attention here.

In the next chapter I summarize the main characteristics of the distinctive business systems that have become established in post-Second World War Japan, South Korea (henceforth, Korea), Taiwan and Hong Kong as described in the extensive secondary literature in English. These reconstructions form the basis for abstracting the key dimensions on which the three East Asian business systems differ and which are the focus of explanation in this book. These dimensions and their interconnections are the subject of Chapter 3. The explanation of the major differences between East Asian business systems involves both the dominant institutions of pre-industrial Japan, Korea and China and those that developed during industrialization. In Chapter 4 I summarize some of the major features of pre-industrial East Asian societies which affected how industrialization took place and continue to influence family structures and authority patterns. Chapter 5 focuses on the critical features of industrialization in Japan, Korea, Taiwan and Hong Kong, especially the organization and policies of the state and banking systems, and how these differed between these countries. The effects of these differences in pre-industrial societies and patterns of industrialization on the sorts of business systems that have developed in East Asia are explored in Chapter 6, and the key features of the institutional environments which appear to have influenced their distinctive characteristics are identified. The implications of this analysis of East Asian business systems for the study of Western ones are discussed in Chapter 7, and some suggestions are made concerning how this could proceed. Finally, in Chapter 8 I consider how strongly business system characteristics are interrelated in general so as to constitute a limited number of forms of economic organization in market economies and then briefly discuss how institutional and business system changes are connected and the impact of the growing internationalization of firms and markets on business systems.

2
East Asian Business Systems

In identifying particular business systems as characteristic of Japan, South Korea, Taiwan and Hong Kong, I am claiming that these different societal contexts have encouraged and constrained the development of distinctive and effective ways of organizing economic activities which constitute the dominant hierarchy–market configurations there. Deviant patterns are relatively easy to identify and are often the focus of comment and discussion. Thus, while there are some large capital-intensive firms in Taiwan, these are either state owned, controlled or supported, such as Formosa Plastics (Wade, 1990: 80), and do not reflect the dominant pattern of specialized, family businesses interconnected through elaborate personal networks (Gold, 1988b; Hamilton and Kao, 1990; Redding, 1990). Similarly, the existence of some diversified conglomerates in Japan does not invalidate the broad conclusion that large firms there tend to be more functionally and industrially specialized than in Korea or the USA (Clark, 1979: 55–64; Kono, 1984; Okimoto, 1989: 125–9). Most significantly, these dominant characteristics occur across industrial sectors and areas of the economy and are often reproduced in newer industries, thus implying the society-wide importance of key institutions in these contexts (Hamilton and Biggart, 1988).

In all four societies the focus is on forms of business organization that compete effectively in world markets. Thus, state-subsidized or state-protected businesses are not included in the characterization of the Chinese family firm in Taiwan. However, state support and connections are often a crucial aspect of business activities in these societies, particularly in South Korea (Amsden, 1989; Jones and Sakong, 1980), and form a key component of their dominant business systems. This support does not, though, usually extend to the granting of monopoly powers or toleration of sustained inefficiency. Rather, it tends to reward success and punish failure and so 'accelerate market forces' (Abegglen and Stalk, 1985: 136–44). In sum, it is the ways of organizing competitive economic activities which constitute the business systems being analysed here.

The identification of distinctive configurations of hierarchy–market relations as separate business systems in East Asia implies considerable internal cohesion and integration of their components.

Thus, Japanese patterns of long-term employment and internal promotions in relatively specialized sectors encourage incremental strategic changes and limit diversification (Kagono et al., 1985). Similarly, the lack of strong institutional trust mechanisms in Hong Kong and Taiwan inhibits the development of impersonal authority and trust relations within firms and limits the size of Chinese family businesses as well as leading to extensive reliance on personal networks between enterprises (Redding, 1990). The dominant feature of personalism thus pervades both internal and external relations of authority structures in this business system. Effective business systems in East Asia, then, demonstrate particular connections between authority structures, firm type and inter-firm relations which 'fit' together relatively cohesively in these particular institutional contexts.

This mutual consistency and reinforcement are almost an essential aspect of successful business systems because certain combinations are less likely to work effectively than others. For example, high levels of mutual dependence between large employers, their 'core' workers and suppliers/customers in Japan are unlikely to generate effective business systems if they are combined with highly specialized tasks and formalized control systems together with a strong reliance on spot market contracting (Oliver and Wilkinson, 1988: 15–22). However, this need not mean that established configurations of hierarchy–market relations are immune to 'internal' conflicts and pressures for endogenous change. For example, the patriarchal character of authority relations in the Chinese family business is limited by the 'conditional' or 'rational' (Silin, 1976: 127–31) nature of employee commitment and the attractiveness of self-employment as an alternative to continued subservience in Hong Kong and Taiwan (Tam, 1990). Thus, authoritarian and didactic management styles are constrained by other features of this particular business system, especially in economic booms.

Similarly, where Japanese firms have been forced to diversify away from their 'home' industry, because of long-term secular decline in, say, textiles or steel, and have managed this successfully, their managers may extend these new skills to co-ordinate a wider range of economic activities than has been typical (Nishida and Redding, 1992; Okimoto, 1989: 128). Thus, the internal coherence and cohesion of effective business systems do not imply that they are static and conflict free. However, the processes by which they change, and circumstances in which particular pressures become manifest, need to be specified in each instance.

Additionally, the identification of distinctive forms of business organization in East Asia does not imply that they are unchanging products of stable and homogeneous cultures. While particular features of Chinese, Korean and Japanese political, agricultural and cultural systems have been important influences on the sorts of business systems that became successful in the past 40 years, as I will suggest in detail later, much of this influence has been exercised through more proximate institutions which do, of course, themselves change and develop. Changes in these major institutions will clearly affect established business systems in a society, and so it is entirely possible that certain features of, say, the currently dominant Korean conglomerates, or *chaebol*, will alter, but, again, the mechanisms and processes by which this happens need to be carefully spelled out in each case. Since business systems are constrained and directed by the institutional environments in which they develop and become successfully established, then it follows that substantial change in societal contexts will influence effective business structures and practices, as has happened in post-war Japan. However, the examples of Western Europe and North America do suggest that such changes are relatively slow, and, in particular, institutional structures and relations which were established during the process of industrialization remain remarkably influential. The different relations between financial institutions and industrial companies found in nineteenth-century Britain and Germany, for instance, continue to affect large firm structures and actions today (Ingham, 1984; Lane, 1992).

While, then, some aspects of the East Asian business systems described below probably will change as a result of institutional developments, it would be premature to claim they will either become more similar to each other or follow other models. Furthermore, once distinctive business structures become established and successful, they themselves exert some influence on social institutions, such as the political system and financial intermediaries (cf. Kim, 1989a), so that the future developments of these will reflect idiosyncrasies of different business systems.

Bearing these points in mind, I will now describe the major features of dominant business systems in Japan, South Korea, Taiwan and Hong Kong as they have developed in the past 40 or so years. In each case I will summarize the major features of hierarchy–market relations in these societies before describing in more detail how each business system deals with the three major issues identified above. Although Hong Kong and Taiwan are distinct societies, the dominant forms of business organization in both is the Chinese family business (CFB), as it is in many South-East Asian societies (Jesudason, 1989; Limlingan, 1986; Wu and Wu, 1980), and so this will be the business system described for both. Since the main purpose is comparative, I shall not go into great detail about particular variations and differences found in each society but concentrate on presenting an overall synthesis.

Hierarchy–Market Relations in Post-War Japan: the Kaisha or Specialized Clan

One of the most striking features of hierarchy–market relations in Japan, especially when contrasted with those found in the USA (Abegglen and Stalk, 1985; Imai and Itami, 1984), is the pervasiveness of mutual obligation networks and the high level of interdependence between large firms, subcontractors, banks and other financial institutions. Markets are more organized than in Anglo-Saxon societies, and networks of alliances are crucial to the management of risk and uncertainty. This high degree of mutual dependence between firms is linked to the limited variety of economic activities co-ordinated through authority hierarchies in Japan. Related features are the continued importance of small firms in the manufacturing sector and extensive subcontracting. Within large managerial hierarchies, there are high levels of mutual dependence between employers and core employees, long-term employment practices and internal rather than external labour markets (Dore, 1973). Additionally, work groups are able to influence how tasks are carried out and form crucial units of identity and performance assessment (Aoki, 1988: 11–26; Koike, 1984).

The Nature of Economic Actors and their Development

The major locus of authoritative resources control and co-ordination in post-war Japan is the large, industrially specialized corporation, or *kaisha*, run by internally promoted university-educated managers with considerable autonomy from shareholders (Abegglen and Stalk, 1985: 177; Clark, 1979: 55–64). These corporations are enmeshed in extensive networks of mutual obligation and trust which both provide support and constrain strategic choices (Kagono et al., 1985: 26). They are relatively specialized in two ways. First, they tend not to incorporate all the production and allied processes required to manufacture particular products into the managerial hierarchy in the way that large corporations do in North America. Second, they tend to restrict their major fields of economic activity to a single industrial sector and diversify within it. Thus, the degree of unrelated diversification is lower in Japan than in the USA (Kagono et al., 1985: 25–49; Kono, 1984: 79).

Japanese companies concentrate much more on the particular

skills and competences which distinguish them as successful competitors than is common in Anglo-Saxon firms. While the latter typically co-ordinate a considerable variety of activities and functional skills through the authority system, Japanese firms prefer to subcontract many activities which, although essential to produce their products and services, are basically complementary to their main activity. Richardson (1972: 889) defines complementary activities as those representing 'different phases of a process of production [which] require in some way or another to be coordinated', and provides the example of the clutch linings in vehicle manufacturing. These may well be more efficiently manufactured by firms specializing in the production of heat-proof materials than by those whose competitive capabilities lie in car assembly. Similarly, specialized maintenance activities may be better carried out by a separate firm of maintenance engineers than by employees of the assembly firm, as at Toyota (Cusumano, 1985: 312). This separation of dissimilar but complementary economic activities is widespread in Japan, where the rate of subcontracting is high (Okimoto, 1989: 130–2). According to Friedman (1988: 146): 'about 70 per cent of all companies with more than thirty employees subcontract for a proportion of their production needs'. However, as Clark (1979: 63) points out, Japanese firms are unwilling to subcontract management functions such as marketing and design and, in general, rely less on management consultants and outside legal firms than do large companies in North America and Britain. Subcontracting is focused on activities which can be relatively easily measured and assessed, such as the production of standardized parts and services.

This focus on specialized, similar activities relying on the same set of capabilities is echoed by a preference for specializing in a single industry or sector. While diversification into new fields of activity does occur quite often in Japan, this tends to be related to current capabilities, such as Honda moving from motor cycles to cars and Komatsu from construction equipment to fork-lift vehicles. Furthermore, once established as successful growing companies, these subsidiaries are usually hived off as separate, independent companies. Thus Toyota set up a specialized steel factory in 1935 because it could not find a supplier in Japan that could produce steel of the required quality, but then spun it off as an independent firm, Aichi Steel, in 1940 (Cusumano, 1985: 63). Similarly, Fujitsu separated itself from its fast growing numerically-controlled machine tool and robotics division, Fanuc, in 1972 (Abegglen and Stalk, 1985: 180). This separation tends to be more thoroughgoing in Japan than in the West, with former subsidiaries developing their own networks and alliances and establishing their own enterprise union (Clark, 1979: 61).

These two forms of business specialization are connected to three further features of economic actors in Japan: first, their close and stable links with subcontractors, customers and other industry partners; second, their reliance on internally trained and promoted managers with detailed knowledge of, and experience in, one industry; third, their considerable autonomy from property rights holders and the 'market for corporate control' (Lawriwsky, 1984: 165–77). These three features together with high business specialization, encourage an evolutionary approach to strategic choice and a preference for trial-and-error methods of change.

Focusing on a narrowing range of economic activities within authority systems implies a high reliance on market contracting for co-ordinating complementary goods and services. Thus, high levels of specialization are necessarily associated with high levels of subcontracting. However, the ways in which subcontractual relations are organized can vary considerably, particularly in respect of their longevity and specificity. Essentially, economic actors either can buy components and services on an ad hoc, spot market basis from a wide range of suppliers, or can develop long-term relations of mutual dependence and trust with a small number of particular suppliers. Richardson (1972) suggests that the latter are more likely when activities are closely complementary and aggregate demand for particular components is less predictable than that of particular enterprises, but it seems that 'relational contracting' (Dore, 1986: 77; cf. MacNeil, 1978) is widespread throughout Japanese industry, and most firms develop relatively strong and stable connections with suppliers and customers.

Toyota and Nissan, for example, have organized their major suppliers into formal associations and 'discussion groups' to disseminate managerial and technical improvements and help to reduce costs. Membership of the Toyota subcontractors' discussion groups has remained quite stable between the 1950s and the 1980s. Many suppliers sell their entire output to Toyota or Nissan, and some grew out of formerly wholly owned factories, especially those supplying Toyota (Cusumano, 1985: 248–61). Frequently, the leader of the 'group' owns some shares in supplying firms, and sometimes the larger suppliers hold a percentage of the assemblers' shares. Additionally, as in the case of Nissan, executives are sometimes moved between leading firms and their suppliers to improve co-ordination and co-operation. These close links between large customers and the component suppliers mean that vertical integration occurs more within groups of associated firms than in a single company. Thus, while only 26 per cent of the manufacturing and other costs of Nissan and Toyota were incurred for activities organized within these firms in 1983, 78 per cent and 73 per cent of these costs stemmed from outputs of all the firms in each group respectively (Cusumano, 1985: 190). As Clark suggests (1979: 64), while production in North America and Britain is a matter of organizing people within companies, in Japan it is a matter of organizing companies and their interconnections. Large Japanese firms, then, manage their dependence on suppliers by developing long-term, mutually beneficial relations with particular companies which combine flexibility with considerable influence and facilitate rapid growth without incurring high capital costs.

Specialization also results in, and is reinforced by, considerable homogeneity among the workforce and management. Since external recruitment to senior management positions is highly unusual in Japan, and both 'core' workers and managers stay with the same employer until retirement at 55, most employees share extensive experience and knowledge of a single industry and, by comparison with many Western firms, have limited knowledge of other sectors. This facilitates communication and the development of common identities around particular economic activities. The focus on a particular industry also makes it easier to assess a firm's relative performance and standing in the 'society of industry' (Clark, 1979: 50). This in turn enables the workers to understand how successful an enterprise is compared to others in the same field of activity.

A further consequence of business specialization is that purely financial performance criteria and ways of assessing the efficiency of sub-units are not as significant as in diversified Western companies. As Clark (1979: 63–4) points out, the latter have to have some common and standardized means of evaluating the relative performance of dissimilar activities if they are to allocate capital efficiently between different businesses and control them. In contrast, Japanese firms can concentrate on the output of finished goods and services and/or market share as highly visible and straightforward measures of performance (Kagono et al., 1985: 109). Consequently, financial control and financial management skills are not so important within Japanese companies as in North American and British ones.

The extensive reliance of large Japanese kaisha on subcontracting is closely connected to another significant feature of the Japanese business system: the continued importance of small and medium sized firms. In 1982, for example, over 56 per cent of the private sector labour force were working for firms with under 30 employees, and over 39 per cent of those in manufacturing were employed in these small firms. Even the smallest firms with under five people in them accounted for 16,201,000 workers out of a total private sector workforce of 52,691,000 (Patrick and Rohlen, 1987). The significance of small firms in Japan, especially in manufacturing, has often been seen as the key to large firm success there because many are tied to large assembly firms that can squeeze them when demand declines. However, this dual structure appears less widespread in the 1960s and 1970s than it was in the 1950s (Aoki, 1988: 219–23), especially in the machinery industry, and many small firms are less dependent on a single large customer than was once thought (Friedman, 1988: 152–61). Additionally, subcontracting is also common within the small firm sector, in a comparable manner to that found between small firms in Italian industrial districts (Amin, 1989; Bamford, 1987; Lazerson, 1988).

Another important characteristic of large economic actors in Japan is the considerable autonomy their managers have from property rights holders (Aoki, 1987). Although family share-holdings were significant sources of co-ordination and power in the pre-war *zaibatsu*, or financial cliques, which dominated the Japanese economy up to the Second World War, salaried, college-educated managers have been important in most zaibatsu throughout the twentieth century. Since the US occupation, which broke up the zaibatsu and prohibited large holding companies, the owner-controlled business has largely disappeared from the ranks of large Japanese firms, and the separation of ownership from control has become considerable. As Abegglen and Stalk (1985: 184) put it: 'the common stock shareholder in the Japanese company is more in the position of a preferred shareholder in a Western company' and has little, if any, voice in corporate affairs (cf. Aoki, 1988: 120–7; McMillan, 1985: 155; Nishiyama, 1984). This was exemplified in the late 1980s by the failure of Boone Pickens to gain any influence over Koito, a major supplier to Toyota, despite having a 20 per cent shareholding (Holloway, 1990).

These characteristics of large firms in Japan have major implications for the ways in which strategic choices are made and firms develop. First of all, the homogeneity of managerial experience, and the limited use of financial management techniques for co-ordinating different activities, mean that strategic decisions are more concerned with developing the existing business than managing a portfolio of dissimilar business units. Unrelated diversification and radical changes towards new fields of activities are less common than among large diversified US corporations and are less likely to occur through acquisitions (Kagono et al., 1985). Second, the close relationships with suppliers and customers restrict firms' choices and limit their ability to take major breaks from previous activities. This is also restricted by the long-term commitment to the current 'core' workforce and its skills. Kagono et al. (1985: 26) found that top managers in Japanese firms felt much more constrained in seeking new markets and changing direction by their relations with distributors, customers, suppliers and competitors than did those in US firms in the same industries. Third, specialization plus extensive subcontracting plus internal promotions to the board of directors and autonomy from outside shareholders encourage incremental, operational decision making rather than long-term grand designs (McMillan, 1985: 156). Change in large Japanese firms is more a process of continual improvement to current operations and developing internal resources than major shifts in direction involving the acquisition of new and different resources. Pressures for short-term financial results are weaker than in the USA and growth goals dominate (Abegglen and Stalk, 1985).

Market Organization in Japan
The Japanese business system is characterized by high levels of market organization and dominated by strong inter-firm mutual obligation networks, some of which constitute large business groups (Hamilton et al., 1990; Imai and Itami, 1984; Okumura, 1984). The relatively specialized nature of many kaisha means that transactions which would be co-ordinated internally in most Western societies occur across firms' boundaries in Japan. As a result, the volume of wholesale trade in Japan is four times the volume of retail trade compared to a ratio of less than 2:1 in many Western countries (Dore, 1986: 80; cf. Smith, 1991). These transactions are typically organized around relatively long-term commitments between particular firms which range over a variety of exchanges. Networks of such commitments link firms within and across industrial sectors to a much greater extent than is common among Western companies (Clark, 1979: 221–2) and facilitate information exchange, joint technical development and risk sharing. While some of these networks are based on share swaps and joint ownership of other companies' shares, firms are also connected through joint financing of new ventures, joint production agreements and the development of common distribution channels (Orru, 1989).

Because firms tend to trade with a relatively small number of specific partners on a long-term basis, they compete for partnerships covering many transactions with customers rather than for individual, one-off sales (Okumura, 1989). Thus, market exchanges in Japan are more specific to, and reciprocal with, particular economic actors than in many Western countries. They are more organized in the sense that they typically occur repeatedly between specific firms and incorporate a number of transactions. They also tend to be linked to broad obligation and trust relations. In contrast, low levels of market organization are exemplified by spot markets for standardized commodities in which transactions are anonymous and limited to single, specific exchanges.

One consequence of this particularism in market exchanges is that many transactions are quite price inelastic in the short term (Dore, 1986: 74–85). Thus, many firms respond to an offer of lower prices from an 'outside' supplier by asking their current supplier to match the new price. They may also share information and staff to help that supplier to reduce his prices before transferring their business to the new firm. This means that prices change more easily than trading partners, and established networks are difficult to break into, especially for foreign firms who cannot readily offer reciprocal benefits.

A crucial component of these business networks is the general trading company, or *sogo shosha*, which acts as a giant intermediary between suppliers and customers and matches different clients' inputs and outputs (Yoshihara, 1982; Yoshino and Lifson, 1986). These large service companies play a leading role in co-ordinating materials and information flows within and between sectors and thus function as system integrators on a quasi-contractual basis (Yoshino and Lifson, 1986: 60–74). Because their fixed costs of getting to know clients and their business are high relative to their incremental costs of providing additional services for them, the sogo shosha have a strong commitment to maintaining long-term relationships with particular firms and enlarging the scope of those relationships. They therefore invest considerable resources in acquiring large clients and ensuring that these remain committed to using them by constantly seeking new trading opportunities for clients. The sogo shosha have also played a major role in channelling credit and project finance to medium sized enterprises in Japan by borrowing on a large scale from the big 'city' banks and then arranging trade credit and other sorts of loans for firms that are too small to interest the banks directly (Yoshino and Lifson, 1986: 51–3). These trading companies were central elements of the pre-war zaibatsu, or financial conglomerates, which dominated Japan's early industrialization and continue to play a key role in establishing and maintaining business networks in Japan.

A particularly important feature of these quasi-contractual

networks is the emergence of stable business groups which collectively dominate the Japanese economy. These groups consist of quite large numbers of independent firms which are linked by a number of means, such as mutual shareholdings, sharing information, managers and sometimes investments on a long-term basis (Goto, 1982; Hamilton et al., 1990; Kiyonari and Nakamura, 1980; Orru et al., 1989). Two major kinds of business group can be distinguished: vertically organized *keiretsu* and horizontally connected inter-market groups, or *kigyo shudan*. The former co-ordinate flows within a particular sector or industry, while the latter link activities in different sectors, including financial services and international trade. Whereas the former tend to be dominated by a single large prime contractor, the latter groups are less hierarchically organized and there is not usually a central co-ordinating agency.

The 16 largest business groups of both kinds contained 65 of the largest 100 firms in Japan in 1980, controlled 26 per cent of the total paid-up capital of all non-financial enterprises, sold 33 per cent of all manufactured goods by value and employed a fifth of the total manufacturing workforce (Hamilton et al., 1990). Collectively they dominate the financial services and manufacturing sectors, especially in transportation equipment, chemicals, electronics, basic metals and petroleum. While not integrated through formal authority structures, these extensive and cohesive networks of reciprocal shareholdings, joint ventures and information sharing co-ordinate a wide variety of economic activities in Japan.

The largest vertically linked business groups grew out of the networks of subcontractors already described. Thus among the ten largest 'independent' groups are those organized by Toyota, Nissan, Hitachi, Matsushita and Toshiba-IHI. They include their major subcontractors as well as successful subsidiaries that have been set up as separate companies. Additionally, two large groups have formed around the Tokai Bank and the Industrial Bank of Japan which are somewhat more diversified (Orru et al., 1989). These latter groups, and others based upon department stores and railway companies, tend to be less integrated and cohesive than the vertically linked networks dominated by a single large parent company or the six largest inter-market groups.

The six horizontally connected kigyo shudan together accounted for 20 per cent of all manufacturing sales in Japan in 1980 and employed 13 per cent of the labour force. They contained 118 of the largest 250 enterprises in 1980 (Scott, 1986: 177) in a wide variety of sectors, although they all contained banks and most contained life insurance companies, trust companies and general trading companies. They are interconnected through reciprocal shareholdings, weekly or monthly 'presidents' club' meetings, the exchange of senior managerial personnel, joint ventures and mutual support when under external threats (Futatsugi, 1986; Goto, 1982; Scott, 1986: 158–83).

Three of these six groups developed out of the remains of the dissolved zaibatsu, Mitsui, Mitsubishi and Sumitomo. The other three grew around large 'city' banks which funded much of Japan's post-war industrial expansion, Fuyo, Dai-Ichi Kangyo and Sanwa. In contrast to the pre-war zaibatsu, these groups are not centrally controlled through holding companies but share resources and risks on a relatively equal basis (Orru, 1989). The trading companies foster trade between group members and often act as international purchasing and marketing agents (Yoshino and Lifson, 1986: 30–3); the financial institutions provide preferential loans, and industrial firms collaborate in technological development and new ventures (Gerlach, 1987); but members of these groups are able to pursue their own strategies and function as relatively independent actors. Typically, each group competes across all major sectors, including chemicals, iron and steel, textiles, electrical engineering, construction, retailing and property development, although since 1973 some firms have begun to collaborate across group boundaries to a limited extent (Orru, 1989).

These groups, and other forms of inter-sectoral co-operation between firms, enable specialized firms to share risks and concentrate on their own particular field of economic competence without having to diversify as much as firms in many Western economies. They represent a particular kind of economic co-ordination which is neither pure market nor authoritatively integrated organization (Imai, 1988), but networks of reciprocal trust and obligation. Such networks combine the advantages of relatively open and reliable information exchange, resource pooling and risk sharing with flexibility and responsiveness (Orru, 1989). They permit rapid growth and development of new opportunities through bringing together scarce skills and other resources at the same time as enabling highly cohesive and homogeneous hierarchies to focus on their specialist competences. Just as the general trading companies in the nineteenth century facilitated the growth and success of the Japanese textile industry by providing stable and relatively cheap supplies of raw materials and managing export sales, thus allowing cotton spinners to concentrate on technical and production efficiency (Yoshino and Lifson, 1986: 21–3), the post-war business group enables Japanese firms to combine flexibility with specialist capabilities and activities.

*Co-ordination and Control through Authority
Hierarchies*
Turning now to consider how economic activities are co-ordinated
and controlled in the Japanese business system, considerable attention has been paid to the distinctive employment policies of many
large Japanese firms in the post-war period, particularly the so-
called 'permanent' employment system (for example, Cole, 1979;
Dore, 1973; Koike, 1987). While the actual extent of Japanese employers' commitment to long-term employment for most employees
remains a matter of some dispute (cf. Cole, 1979: 60–3), there
seems general agreement that it is a major distinctive characteristic
of Japanese management practices in large firms (Abegglen and
Stalk, 1985: 199–205; Whittaker, 1990). Linked to this commitment, of course, is a reward system based on age and length of
service with the firm and the development of firm-specific skills
through extensive on-the-job training (Aoki, 1988: 13–16; Koike,
1987), as well as a union system which is predominantly enterprise
based. Other distinctive features of co-ordination and control
systems in large Japanese companies are: relatively low levels of
individual specialization and task evaluation; highly differentiated
vertical ranks and statuses; high levels of centralization of formal
decision making but considerable involvement of middle management in initiating decisions; a preference for consensus methods of
decision making; facilitative managerial styles; and considerable
work group autonomy in task performance (for example, Clark,
1979; Cole, 1979; Dore, 1986: 88–119; Kagono et al., 1985: 106–
17; Lincoln et al., 1986; Rohlen, 1974, 1979). Initially I will discuss
the major distinguishing features of the Japanese employment
system as it has developed since the war and then consider the key
characteristics of the 'internal' co-ordination and control systems
of dominant firms in Japan.

The Japanese Employment System   One of the most distinctive
features of Japanese labour markets is their segmentation. Not
only are large firms' employment policies and practices quite
different from those of small firms, but women and young male
workers are more mobile between firms than older males and
women are paid considerably less than men (Clark, 1979: 191–6).
Although the average wage differential between plants employing
5–29 people and those with over 500 people has decreased from 54
per cent in 1960 to 42 per cent in 1980 (Bronfenbrenner and
Yasuba, 1987; cf. Friedman, 1988: 128–61), it is clear that workers
in large firms are still paid considerably more and enjoy better
conditions of employment than those in small ones. Equally, while

women's wages have increased from 37 per cent of men's wages in large plants in 1960 to 48.5 per cent in 1981, their relative position in small plants has actually declined slightly over that period and they remain outside the 'salary man' reward system. While some of this difference is due to many women leaving employment upon marriage or the birth of their children, and so not receiving the higher rewards of seniority and age, the differential income for older men remains greater than that for women of similar education background (Bronfenbrenner and Yasuba, 1987).

According to Clark (1979: 142–56), the dominant pattern of inter-firm mobility is for young and less well educated men to change employers once or twice before they are 30 years old but then to stay with the same firm until retirement, especially if it is a large one (cf. Dore, 1973: 310–11). University graduates, on the other hand, are typically recruited by the larger firms upon graduation and tend to remain there. Women in general are poorly rewarded and not expected to stay beyond marriage. Thus, larger firms in Japan do manifest considerable labour turnover but not among the 'core' employees who are typically male and relatively well educated (Aoki, 1988: 60–9). There is also an important group of 'temporary' employees in many companies who are sometimes employed for as long as 'permanent' ones but do not share the same rewards or commitment to their future (Rohlen, 1974: 17–24). Labour markets and employment practices are, then, highly segmented in Japan.

Focusing on the 'core' or 'permanent' members of the larger firms in Japan, who formed around two-thirds of the workforce at Clark's (1979: 118) Marumaru firm in 1971 and around 90 per cent at Rohlen's (1974: 18–24) Uedagin bank – although this latter figure includes women who constitute a third of all members and who leave upon marriage – the dominant aspect of employer-employee relations in most large firms seems to be a high level of mutual dependence. Because the firm is typically committed to maintaining employment for its members for as long as possible, it cannot react to changing economic conditions simply by hiring and firing people – what Lane (1987, 1988) terms relying on numerical flexibility. It is therefore highly dependent on the skills, flexibility and commitment of employees. Equally, long-term employees are highly dependent on their employer for continued employment, promotion opportunities, bonuses and general social status. They also are often housed in company properties and depend on corporate welfare programmes (Dore, 1973: 202–3). Because movement to other, similar employers is difficult for nearly all members of a firm and would normally result in lower pay, rank and opportunities, 'exit' after the age of, roughly, 25 is not regarded as a feasible response to dissatisfaction with employers in Japan (Cole, 1979: 244).

This high level of dependence upon the 'permanent' core workforce of large Japanese firms means that managers rely on skill flexibility and intra-firm mobility between tasks and roles to deal with economic change and have to generate considerable commitment to corporate objectives among employees (Aoki, 1988: 50– 71). Since enforced redundancy of core employees is often taken as a sign of managerial incompetence among large employers, and sometimes a cause for top managers to resign (Dore, 1986: 88– 119), competitive pressures require extensive on-the-job retraining and skill development together with frequent jobs changes and, sometimes, mobility between work sites (Rohlen, 1974: 104–5). The high rate of successful technological change in Japanese factories reflects, and requires, worker acceptance of the need for role flexibility which, in turn, is based on relatively high levels of mutual trust (Abegglen and Stalk, 1985: 130–2). Because employment for the core workforce is a long-term commitment on both sides of the labour 'contract', high levels of flexibility and willingness to change tasks are easier to develop than in firms where the dominant reaction to reductions in demand is enforced redundancies. Obviously this commitment is easier to maintain in a high-growth economy where political and financial institutions are generally supportive than where long-term growth seems to be a chimera and industry is largely left to its own devices.

Dependence on employees also leads to elaborate and highly selective recruitment procedures as well as extensive socialization and indoctrination programmes (Clark, 1979: 156–64; Dore, 1973: 49–51; Rohlen, 1974: 63–73). First of all, large firms rely on the formal, public educational system to select the most capable secondary school and university graduates. Just as firms are arranged in a strong hierarchy by size and significance, so too are educational institutions, and there is a strong connection between firm status and the educational success of its recruits, both manual and nonmanual. Second, most potential recruits are required to take a formal examination, consisting of a scholastic aptitude test and a personality evaluation test in the case of Rohlen's bank (1974: 66), which is intended to confirm their academic abilities and, more importantly, assess their personal suitability for long-term employment. Third, applicants are then interviewed, sometimes twice, and finally the personnel section undertakes a family investigation and a background investigation to ensure the new recruits have a stable, law-abiding background and are unlikely to prove a bad risk.

While not all of these steps are always taken, especially in very tight labour markets, they indicate the significance of the hiring decision in Japanese firms which, in turn, stems from the long-term commitment being made to employees. As a bank executive expressed it to Rohlen (1974: 63): 'We can replace machines by buying new ones, but when we bring someone into the bank he is with us for a very long time. If he is no good, we must pay him until he retires. If he is uncooperative, the work of others is disrupted and their effectiveness is reduced.' At this bank the president of the firm presided personally at all final interviews for male recruits.

The emphasis in the selection process on personal characteristics and the ability to co-operate with others is continued during the initial induction and training programmes which again are taken extremely seriously by large Japanese firms. Although these do contain some technical and business training, a considerable amount of time is taken up with developing commitment to the firm and a sense of identity with it (Oliver and Wilkinson, 1988: 18–20). Since most technical training is carried out on the job, and employees are expected to develop multiple skills as they move about the company, it is more important to inculcate commitment and a broad understanding of the firm's operations and approach than provide systematic training in a particular skill for particular jobs.

An important characteristic of the post-war Japanese employment system which encourages employee commitment is the organization of unions on an enterprise basis. Although craft-based and industry-based unions have existed during the process of industrialization in Japan (Dore, 1973: 388–403), the dominant pattern in many industries today is one of enterprise unions. Supported by the state and banks, many large firms established these 'second' unions in the early 1950s as a replacement for the more radical industry-wide unions which had developed during the US occupation (Cusumano, 1985: 149–74; Dore, 1973: 327–9), sometimes after a bitter strike such as that at Nissan in 1953.

In general, the level of unionization of the workforce increases with firm size, and unions form an integral part of the managerial system in larger firms. Senior union officials sometimes come from the ranks of middle management, and in some firms taking on such roles is seen as a useful career move. As Cusumano puts it (1985: 171): 'the union's labour affairs department and the company's personnel department [at Nissan] co-ordinated their activities to the point where, to an outside observer, they seemed almost indistinguishable'. Union leaders had considerable influence on managerial promotions, and managers, in turn, ensured that the union was supported by the workforce. However, Koike (1987) points out that not all enterprise unions are simply creatures of top management in Japan, and strikes and disputes are quite common. Overall, although many unions are members of industry federations which negotiate on annual basic wage increases, there seems little doubt that it is the enterprise unions which are the most important representative unit in the regulation of work and the total reward system, and their interests are more tied to the growth and success of the individual firm than are craft- or industry-based unions elsewhere (Aoki, 1987; McMillan, 1985: 175–85).

This focus on the fortunes of particular employers is, of course, reinforced by the seniority-based reward system which ensures continued commitment. Although the extent to which Japanese firms rely on seniority as the basis of wage progression and career progression remains a matter of some debate, there is widespread agreement that the wages of core employees are correlated with age and length of service, as well as education, rank and gender, and that, up to section head positions, promotions are linked to entry year (Abegglen and Stalk, 1985: 203–5; Clark, 1979: 112–25; Whittaker, 1990). As described by Dore (1973: 94–113) and Rohlen (1974: 156–75), Japanese wage payment systems are complicated functions of seniority, merit, job level and, sometimes, piecework, but the main result is that average wages rise with age at the average rate of around 15 percentage points every five years for school-level entrants and over 30 per cent for graduates, although there is some tailing off after 45. Thus incomes of these core employees tend to be greatest when family responsibilities are typically greatest, and this is often enhanced with family allowances; so once established as a company 'member' and married, a worker is unlikely to move.

An important element of these incomes is the twice-yearly bonus which can amount to as much as a third of the total annual wage. This depends upon corporate success to some extent and also, though to varying degrees according to union negotiations, upon superiors' assessments of competence and diligence. A major feature of the wage and grading system in many large Japanese firms is their division into a large number of finely separated ranks. This means that nearly all core workers move up a series of grades over their working lifetime and that the gap between manual and non-manual jobs is less marked than elsewhere. Similarly, managerial status is less sharply distinguished in Japanese firms than in companies where it is reflected in visibly separate reward systems, dress patterns and working conditions.

The importance of seniority and age in the reward system for permanent employees enhances long-term commitment and acceptance of managerial authority. However, the speed at which promotion occurs and, in particular, access to senior managerial roles is obtained, results from more competitive processes. Although most graduate entrants can expect to reach the position of section head by their mid-thirties in large Japanese firms, some will reach that position five or so years before others. These latter 'high-flyers' are also more likely to rise above this level and become department heads and possibly directors. Thus senior managers are not selected by length of service, although, according to Rohlen (1979), it would be most unusual for younger men to be put in charge of older ones. As well as those senior jobs being allocated on a more competitive basis, initiative and competence among middle managers are commonly rewarded by giving them more responsible positions without changing their formal ranks. While formal status is age related, then, actual managerial function is often more flexibly allocated.

Authority and Control Systems Turning now to consider authority and control systems inside large Japanese firms, the most marked contrasts with US corporations concern the division of labour and responsibilities, together with differences in the major unit of performance assessment and management style. Essentially, jobs and responsibilities are less individually specific and separate in Japanese firms and roles often overlap (Kagono et al., 1985: 112–21; Koike, 1984). The dominant unit of work performance and assessment is the work group rather than the individual, and, despite elaborate work manuals, these have considerable latitude in deciding how group tasks are to be carried out (Lincoln and Kalleberg, 1990: 85–9). As a Japanese manager at Mitsubishi Electric USA put it to Kagono et al. (1985: 116): 'Work descriptions in Japan, on the other hand, are merely a framework, with everyone crossing boundaries in performing their work.' Whereas many US firms emphasize the clear allocation of responsibility and resources to individuals who have specialist, externally certified skills, Japanese companies appear to have more 'logically inconsistent' structures which build in role conflict but also facilitate information sharing and collective problem solving. As Kagono et al. (1985: 106) point out, managerial conflicts can be productive when there is clear agreement upon, and commitment to, superordinate goals, which seems to be the case in many large Japanese firms. Obviously, where trust levels are relatively high and common commitments can be assumed, detailed formal co-ordination and control systems are less important than in the reverse situation. Thus Kagono et al. (1985: 111–15) suggest that, whereas US firms are characterized by explicitly well-defined systems for the systematic co-ordination of specialized jobs throughout the organization, Japanese companies rely more on inculcating shared values and disseminating information widely, partly through job rotation and partly through group activities both at work and afterwards (Aoki, 1988: 11–20). This is clearly easier when employees are recruited straight from school or college and stay with the firm for a long time, as well as when they work at related activities in the same industry.

The importance of work groups in carrying out tasks and for assessing performance in Japanese firms means that the management of groups is an important part of managers' jobs (Yoshino and Lifson, 1986: 194–5). Indeed, maintaining morale and group commitment was so crucial for managers at Rohlen's (1974: 112) bank that those whose behaviour led to transfer requests from work group members were likely to be moved sideways or demoted. In general, the managerial role in Japan seems to be regarded more as facilitating group performance rather than directing workers from above (Dore, 1973: 231–42), and foremen often work with group members on tasks. Japanese managers operate more on the assumption of original virtue than original sin in dealing with subordinates and are responsible for developing the skills and achievements of the group.

This close involvement with the work of subordinates and managerial responsibility for group morale are linked to a third feature of managerial authority in large Japanese firms, the bounded nature of managers' superior knowledge and competence. While they are expected to exhibit superior expertise as organizers and directors of work, Japanese managers are not usually supposed to demonstrate omniscience and omnicompetence so that they always know more than their subordinates (Silin, 1976: 131–8). Authority derives more from formal position, seniority and educational attainments than from superiority in all spheres of work, and is exercised through leading group activities and establishing relationships of mutual dependence with all group members rather than through issuing instructions from a distance as an external supervisor (Dore, 1973: 250–1; Yoshino and Lifson, 1986: 192–3).

Responsibilities for making decisions are also shared and collective to a much greater extent in Japan than in many Western firms. The *ringi* system of circulating proposals and suggestions for approval by all interested parties before final approval by top management ensures widespread commitment before decisions are made and diffuses responsibility for it. As Clark (1979: 130) puts it: 'In Japan [decision making] is presented as collective until it is worth someone's while to claim a decision as his own.' In general, individual authority to commit resources is highly constrained and restricted, so that managers usually have to obtain the support of colleagues for any substantial project and cannot make decisions independently. Thus departments and sections are not regarded as 'belonging' to their heads in the way some Western managers consider they have the right to control 'their' organizational unit. Because of overlapping responsibilities and limited individual authority, ownership is shared and collective rather than specific to the individual manager (Clark, 1979: 126–34).

The considerable reliance on 'bottom-up' ways of initiating change in Japanese firms, exemplified by the ringi system, suggests that decision making is less centralized in practice than purely formal measures of the source of ultimate authorization would suggest (Lincoln and Kalleberg, 1990: 206–10). While top management often has to agree proposals, in many cases this is largely a formality once the circulation of the ringi has produced widespread support. Furthermore, where top management suggests changes which are not whole-heartedly supported by middle management groups, they may not be carried through.

The final aspect of the co-ordination and control system to be considered here is the nature of top management, or the 'dominant coalition', and how it is selected in large Japanese firms. First, it is worth emphasizing that nearly all directors are full-time executives with hardly any use of non-executive directors (Kagono et al., 1985: 128–31). Even when firms are part of a large business group where banks, insurance and other companies own substantial shareholdings, these do not usually result in overlapping board membership as they might in Anglo-Saxon countries. Second, because most top managers are internally promoted and have spent their working lives in the same firm in the same industry, their knowledge and skills are highly specific to that industry. As mentioned earlier, this ensures continuity and the accumulation of expertise but equally means that radical changes in direction and resources are unlikely. Third, most have had experience of production and/or sales activities and are very familiar with what Kagono et al. (1985: 136) term 'work site' management. In contrast, finance specialists do not seem very numerous among top managers of large Japanese manufacturing firms, and, in general, finance and control departments are not seen as exercising high levels of influence on strategic choices (Abegglen and Stalk, 1985: 178–9).

This importance of mainstream functional management for top

managers in Japan is linked to their predominantly functional structure and lack of full divisionalization in the same way as US corporations. Even when separate divisions have been formed, as at Hitachi, firms remained largely centred around plants, with engineering and sales departments acting more as staff units than as fully integrated parts of separate divisions (Kagono et al., 1985: 102–6). Partly because of their relatively specialized nature as economic actors, many large Japanese firms have developed quasi-divisional structures in which key activities, such as production, report directly to top management rather than through divisional general managers (cf. Kono, 1984: 106–10). This often means that access to top management jobs lies through successful plant management rather than divisional management. It should, though, be noted that functional expertise tends to be broader in Japanese firms than in US ones, and roles often overlap with multiple information channels being used. Thus plant managers deal with marketing information as well as production and engineering issues.

In summary, the internal organization of large Japanese firms relies on the separation of 'permanent' or 'core' members from temporary workers and develops relatively high levels of mutual commitment and trust between this group and their employer. This trust facilitates considerable work group autonomy in task performance and substantial decentralization to middle management of decision initiation and consideration rights. The low extent of individual specialization and separation of individual responsibilities is allied to an emphasis on group performance and group management as a key skill for Japanese managers. The considerable homogeneity of experience and expertise among workers and managers is reflected in the composition of top management teams which concentrate more on developing existing human and material resources in the same general area of economic activity than on managing a portfolio of separate businesses.

Hierarchy–Market Relations in South Korea: the Chaebol Conglomerate

The most distinctive feature of hierarchy–market relations in Korea is the dominance of large conglomerates controlled by the founder and/or his family (Steers et al., 1989: 33–46). These chaebol, or 'financial cliques', have developed with considerable state backing, especially in respect of preferential access to cheap loans from the state banks, and expanded into heavy industry in the 1970s at the behest of state agencies. Authority hierarchies thus co-ordinate a much broader range of economic activities in Korea than in Japan, and business networks between separate firms are less significant. Within the chaebol, authority is highly centralized around the founding family, and work groups do not have high levels of task autonomy. Labour turnover is greater than in large Japanese firms, and unions, until recently, have been largely state controlled. The dominance of the state is thus an additional key feature of the economic system in post-war Korea.

The Nature of Economic Actors and their Development
There is little doubt that the major agent of economic development in Korea since the military coup in 1961 has been the large, diversified chaebol in co-operation with the state (K.-D. Kim, 1988; E.M. Kim, 1989a). These conglomerates dominate many sectors of the economy, with eight chaebol producing 92 per cent of all sales in the petroleum and coal products industry in 1983 and 13 producing 79 per cent of all sales of transportation equipment in that year (Zeile, 1989). In 1975 the largest 50 chaebol controlled 398 firms throughout the manufacturing, construction and service sectors; by 1986 this had risen to 547 firms. In 1986 they accounted for 32 per cent of the country's total value added in construction, 28 per cent of that in manufacturing and 20 per cent of that in transportation and storage. Almost a half of Korea's exports are handled by the seven largest trading companies, all of which are member firms of the top ten chaebol (Zeile, 1989).

These giant firms are much more diversified than their Japanese counterparts and incorporate many more economic activities within their authority structures. Correspondingly less use is made of subcontractors, and the small firm sector is much less significant in Korea than it is in Japan. Hyundai Motors, for example, only subcontract about 40 per cent of value added in a standard car and a large share of this is manufactured by other firms within the Hyundai group (Amsden, 1989: 184). In particular, the largest chaebol are the most diversified, with subsidiary firms in the financial services sector, construction and trading as well as in heavy industry (Chang and Choi, 1988). For example, of the six largest chaebol in 1986, all had firms in construction and trade, five were represented in financial and insurance institutions, in electrical machinery and real estate, and four had firms in the fibres and textiles, pulp and paper, petroleum, non-electrical machinery and transportation equipment industries (Orru et al., 1988). By the 1980s most of these had largely moved out of light manufacturing, with the largest four having at least a third of their assets in heavy manufacturing industry. Lucky-Goldstar, for example, had 76 per cent of its assets in this sector in 1983. Samsung was the only large chaebol with more than 10 per cent in light manufacturing and it also concentrated on financial services to a greater extent than the others, with 32 per cent of its assets in this sector (E.M. Kim, 1989a). Although not all groups competed against each other in all major markets, the dominant pattern is oligopolistic, with each chaebol competing with at least one other in each of its major markets. According to Zeile (1989), for each of the 78 manufacturing industries in which chaebol are active, there are an average of 3 groups and 3.8 group member firms operating.

This diversification implies, and is facilitated by, a greater variety of managerial backgrounds and experience than most large Japanese firms possess. According to Amsden (1989: 128), new subsidiaries were often established by task forces formed at the group level from member firms, and once experience had been gained about how to manage this process, it obviously encouraged further diversification. The initial experience of managing complex technologies in heavy, capital-intensive industries provided the basis of generalizable managerial skills because they require the effective co-ordination and integration of separate interdependent components. These project and production management skills were more transferable to other manufacturing sectors than those in the textile industry because they were more concerned with co-ordinating interdependent processes and less tied to the operation of particular standardized, stand-alone machines, according to Amsden (1989: 265–8). A related difference from large Japanese firms is the greater willingness of the chaebol to hire senior managers from outside (Chung et al., 1988), especially when they moved into new areas (Amsden, 1989: 229). They also recruit retired civil servants, military officers and financiers to senior posts (Amsden, 1989: 168; Shin and Chin, 1989).

One of the major distinguishing features of Korean chaebol is their domination by the founder and his family (Steers et al., 1989: 37–8). Despite state pressure to sell shares on the stock exchange and dilute family ownership, only 20–30 per cent of chaebol firms were listed in 1986 (Orru et al., 1988). Nearly all the unlisted firms are owned and controlled by the founding family, who often used the group holding company or trading company to control all the firms in the chaebol. This pattern of family ownership despite high growth rates and large size has been maintained by widespread reliance on debt financing, with debt/equity ratios of 3.6 for the top ten chaebol in manufacturing in 1983 and 6.8 in construction (Zeile, 1989). In contrast to Japanese firms, even the pre-war family-owned zaibatsu, family ownership in Korea means strong family control (Hattori, 1984; Steers et al., 1989: 38–41). Nearly all the top management posts in the chaebol are held by close relatives of the founders, and it is a common saying in Korea that founders create subsidiaries for each member of the family to manage. Despite the employment of many salaried engineers and managers in the chaebol, then, these groups are essentially managed by owning families at the top (Shin and Chin, 1989; Yoo and Lee, 1987).

The growth of these chaebol has been extremely rapid. According to Kim (1989a), the average annual growth rate of the total assets of Hyundai, the largest chaebol, between 1970 and 1983 was 20 per cent, of Samsung 11 per cent, of Daewoo 22 per cent and of Lucky-Goldstar 14 per cent. Between 1970 and 1975 the three fastest growing chaebol, Hyundai, Daewoo and Ssangyong, expanded at an annual rate of 33 per cent, 35 per cent and 34 per cent respectively. These three were the most committed to the heavy industry sector, especially cars, heavy machinery and ship-building, which was being promoted by the state at the time. Another feature of these high growth rates was the expansion of the construction industry, both domestically on infrastructural projects and in the Middle East where Korean companies were very successful in obtaining contracts after the first large increase in oil prices. This growth increased the diversity of economic activities controlled by the largest chaebol, most of which were vertically integrated, in a limited number of related sectors in 1970, and was associated with an increase in mergers and take-overs, many with state encouragement (Orru et al., 1988; Zeile, 1989). As Michell (1988: 96) puts it: 'the chaebol became larger by preying on other good-sized companies'.

These very fast rates of growth, and high reliance on debt financing, indicate a strong willingness to take large risks on the part of chaebol owners and competition to become the largest chaebol in Korea, together with a determination to retain personal control. A recent example of these high-risk competitive strategies is the projected expansion of the petrochemical industry in Korea. According to Goldstein (1989), the chaebol are building six big integrated petrochemical complexes which will more than double the output of ethylene at a time when world prices are declining and surplus capacity is widely predicted. While some of this expansion is being undertaken by firms already in the chemicals industry, with the support of state planning agencies, the two largest investments are planned by Samsung and Hyundai, which have so far been kept out of this industry and will still not have access to cheap state loans. As Goldstein suggests (1989: 80): 'the main driving force behind several of the projects is corporate rivalry'. They also, of course, suggest a preference for growth goals over profitability; their primary objective has been to grow, not to maximize short-term profits (Amsden, 1989: 118). Thus, profitability in the key manufacturing sectors has been low in the 1960s and 1970s, with net profit falling to 1.8 per cent in 1971 and remaining at around 3 per cent for the next decade (Michell, 1988: 88–9). This priority has been encouraged, if not directed, by the state, which has offered preferential access to cheap loans and other advantages to firms pursuing growth goals in favoured sectors, especially export markets (Jones and Sakong, 1980; E.M. Kim, 1989a; Steers et al., 1989: 42–5; Zeile, 1989).

Market Organization in South Korea

The size and diversity of the chaebol mean that they are much more self-sufficient than their Japanese counterparts. Complementary and dissimilar activities are co-ordinated through authority hierarchies rather than through networks of relational contracting (Hamilton et al., 1990). Consequently, enterprises are less dependent on each other than in Japan and have less need to organize market connections to reduce risks. The relatively low extent of enterprise interdependence and co-operation in Korea compared to Japan is exemplified by the failure of the chaebol to agree to establish complementary research programmes into computer chip technology in the mid-1980s and their insistence on each developing its own prototype (Wade, 1990: 315–16). Markets are therefore less organized and obligation networks between large firms less significant in Korea. Inter-sector links are relatively short term and not based on mutual, diffuse commitments.

Equally, subcontracting relationships are less reciprocal and long term than in Japan (Amsden, 1989: 183–4). Where they are based on personal connections, such as those between a chaebol firm and an ex-employee who has left to start his own business, these do not appear to have much effect on purchasing behaviour, which is largely determined by short-term market considerations. Thus, overall, inter-firm connections in Korea are less particularistic, less reciprocal and shorter term than in Japan, and the level of market organization is lower, However, considerable co-ordination of firms' policies is undertaken by state agencies.

The dominant role of the state in directing and co-ordinating economic development since the military coup of 1961 has meant that markets are more centrally guided than in most Anglo-Saxon countries. Primarily through credit rationing and control of the banking system, but also through the tax system, control over licences and other administrative devices, state agencies have exercised decisive influence on the strategic choices and investment decisions of the favoured chaebol (Amsden, 1989: 79–93; Jones and Sakong, 1980: 269–85; Kim, 1988; Wade, 1990: 307–9). The oligopolistic pattern of industrial structure in many heavy manufacturing industries is largely the result of state co-ordination of economic activities and encouragement of particular developments. Through cheap loans and other inducements certain chaebol have been pushed into new sectors of activity, while others have been discouraged from entering these areas (Zeile, 1989). Generally, the state ensured that at least two chaebol had firms in each of the new industries it wanted to develop but restricted the total number to ensure significant profits and opportunities for expansion. The importance of the state and political connections has, then, had major consequences for the ways in which the chaebol are managed and strategic decisions made (Hamilton and Biggart, 1988; E.M. Kim, 1989a; K.-D. Kim, 1988).

Co-ordination and Control through Authority Hierarchies

Just as some of the aspects discussed above of Korean chaebol are quite similar to the pre-war Japanese zaibatsu, so too certain features of labour markets and labour strategies in Korea follow earlier Japanese practices. In particular, the segmentation of labour markets and reward systems by firm size, industry and gender is highly significant (Wilkinson, 1988). In 1982 the standard deviation of the average wage distribution across manufacturing industries was higher in Korea than in 13 other countries, and this variation was especially marked for blue-collar workers (Amsden, 1989: 206–8). In general, large capital-intensive firms pay much higher wages than smaller firms in light manufacturing industries like textiles, rubber and wood.

This differential is reinforced by the unrivalled gender-based wage disparities. In 1980 women's wages in manufacturing were, on average, 44.5 per cent of men's (Amsden, 1989: 204). As a result, manufacturing wages as a whole have been lower than wages in any other sector from 1971 to 1984, since women constitute the dominant labour force in labour-intensive industries, especially textiles and garments, where they formed 68 per cent and 77 per cent respectively (Michell, 1988: 115–16). Thus firm size, industry and gender interact to generate large differences in wages and working conditions between heavy industry, light industry and the service sector. Also, as in Japan, women in Korea are still expected to leave employment upon marriage, so that, where wages are linked to the length of work experience, they receive less pay. The relatively high wages paid to manual workers in the heavy manufacturing industries have been explained by Amsden (1989: 208–9) in terms of managers' dependence on their skilled workforce to exploit new technologies efficiently.

Labour turnover rates also differ considerably between industries and large and small firms and by gender. Manufacturing industry in general experienced annual turnover figures of between 52 per cent and 72 per cent of the workforce between 1970 and 1980, and the Ministry of Labour figures suggest that a third of all workers change jobs twice a year (Michell, 1988: 109). Turnover rates in the service sector tend to be lower and wages are higher. Large firms in capital-intensive sectors try to retain their skilled male workers with higher wages and fringe benefits such as company housing, bonus payments and schools. According to Amsden (1989: 209– 12), the Pohang Iron and Steel Company provides its 'regular' workers with a kindergarten-through-university school system, a medical dispensary and free travel on commuter trains as well as wages that are twice as high as the manufacturing average. It is worth noting here that Pohang employs 24 per cent of its workforce on a subcontracted basis which enables it to save about 15 per cent on its wage bill. These less skilled workers undertake the more menial tasks and have much less job security than the regular workforce.

Compared to Japan, employer commitment to workers' welfare and security is low in Korea, even in the capital-intensive sector. In labour-intensive industries, such as textiles and garment manufacturing, low labour costs are a crucial component of competitiveness, and most firms do not invest in long-term commitments, especially in the clothing industry (Deyo, 1989: 173–201; Michell, 1988: 133). Where skills are scarce, critical to firm success and relatively firm specific, large companies do provide much more training and try to elicit longer-term commitments to corporate goals. However, as the example of Hyundai Shipbuilders shows (Amsden, 1989: 275–87), large firms are willing to poach skilled workers from their competitors by offering higher wages and promotion opportunities. Even among managers, mobility between large firms seems greater in Korea than it is in Japan, and, as Biggart (1989) suggests, lifetime employment is not an ideal or practice in most Korean firms (cf. Steers et al., 1989: 123–4). Poor managerial performance can and does lead to dismissal even though the heads of the chaebol claim to develop paternalistic, personal ties of loyalty to the core labour force.

Recruitment practices are similar to those in large Japanese firms in terms of relying largely on the verdicts of the education system to select white-collar staff, undertaking reference checks and setting written exams. Large firms also provide an initial training that focuses more on general induction into company procedures and operations, and commitment to the corporate leader and ideology, rather than on developing specific skills. However, personal and regional connections are additional important influences on selection decisions in the chaebol, and promotion is often dependent upon these characteristics as well as loyalty (Shin and Chin, 1989). As Yoo and Lee (1987: 105–6) put it: 'Employees in Korean companies are promoted largely on seniority, dedication and relationships with top management rather than on contribution and achievement.' Manual workers, however, receive less training than white-collar staff, and it is typically provided on an ad hoc basis tied to specific tasks (Amsden, 1989: 224–9; Steers et al., 1989: 114).

Trade unions are not as important in Korea as they are in Japan. The level of union membership fell considerably after the 1961 coup and state reorganization of the unions on an industrial basis. In 1979 only 21 per cent of workers in mining and manufacturing were members of unions, mostly in plants employing over 20 workers (Michell, 1988: 113). Many employers refuse to employ union members and actively prevent workers joining unions especially in the textile and clothing industries. Although the state has made some attempts to encourage enterprise-based unions in the 1980s, as in Japan, this pattern is by no means common, and workers' response to unsatisfactory conditions is often to leave rather than to attempt to organize collectively in the face of legal, political and employer opposition. Given the extent of state regulation of labour organizations and growth in real wages of manual workers since the 1960s, it is not surprising that union membership is low by European standards and most employers do not need to deal with them seriously (Amsden, 1989: 190–205; Michell, 1988: 111–17). In general, it seems that the level of mutual dependence between large employers and core workers is not as great as in Japan, and the interests of manual employees are not closely tied to the fortunes of their employer in Korea.

Seniority, age and education are major influences on pay and promotion in the chaebol, especially for white-collar workers (Steers et al., 1989: 118–23; Yoo and Lee, 1987). However, while loyalty is rewarded more than in many Anglo-Saxon firms, it is not as systematically built into wage systems as in Japan, and total monthly payments include various kinds of allowances which are often awarded on particularistic criteria by superiors (Park, 1988). Generally, payment systems seem relatively weakly formalized, with considerable scope for personal variation and discretion by business owners and managers (Deyo, 1989: 158–9). The chaebol may attempt to retain skilled male workers by providing higher wages and fringe benefits, then, but their incorporation of manual workers into the corporate family is much less extensive and mutually beneficial than in equivalent Japanese firms.

The reliance on formal educational qualifications for managerial and technical recruits has resulted in much greater wage differentials between this group and manual workers in Korea than in Japan. Between 1975 and 1984 college and university graduates earned around three times the salaries of primary school graduates and about one and a half times as much as secondary school graduates. Similarly, managers received, on average, nearly four times the wages of production workers in 1980, and in general the returns to education are high in Korea, despite an apparent over-supply of college graduates in the 1980s (Amsden, 1989: 230–1; Michell, 1988: 104–5). However, as in Japan, educational institutions are highly stratified in their prestige, and the largest, most desirable employers recruit from the most prestigious universities.

Turning now to consider the organization and control of work in the chaebol, Yoo and Lee (1987) suggest that job assignments are often unclear and overlapping by US standards and that, although the chaebol are quite bureaucratic in terms of their use of formal rules and procedures, the application of control systems is not very standardized (Chung et al., 1988). Job rotation is quite frequent, and senior managers are often transferred between firms in the same group. Through such intra-firm mobility and ad hoc on-the-job training, workers and managers in heavy industry have developed polyvalent, firm-specific skills. This fluidity of roles and responsibilities is also found at top management levels (Shin and Chin, 1989).

The chaebol differ from large Japanese firms in the dominant management style which has been termed militaristic by Liebenberg (1982) in his analysis of Japanese–Korean joint ventures. Compared to typical Japanese managerial practices in large firms, Korean managers are much more directive and authoritarian (Chung et al., 1988). According to Japanese managers interviewed by Liebenberg, the Korean management system is characterized by 'top-down' decision making, enforcement of vertical hierarchical relationships, low levels of consultation with subordinates and low levels of trust, both horizontally and vertically. Middle managers in the chaebol have little autonomy or influence on decisions and are considered as relayers of decisions from top management, in strong contrast to their important integrating and initiating role in Japanese companies. Horizontal communication across organizational units seems relatively difficult in large Korean firms because of the emphasis on vertical relationships. Long-term commitments between companies and employees are rarely expected or encouraged, except for senior managers and skilled workers in new heavy manufacturing firms, although personal loyalty to individual managers can be considerable. Generally, collective loyalties are weak in the chaebol, and obedience is secured through a combination of coercion, bonuses and personal commitments to individuals (Chung et al., 1988; Yoo and Lee, 1987).

The Korean chaebol are organized more similarly to a highly centralized conglomerate than a US multi-divisional company and do not have the elaborate head office staff departments of the latter (Amsden, 1989: 170–3). They do, however, have a strong central 'secretariat' or planning group which is responsible for monitoring performance and allocating investment and managers between member firms. This is staffed by elite recruits and acts as the key implementing agency for the president's decisions (Steers et al., 1989). While, then, individual companies have some autonomy in day-to-day operating decisions, strategic choices and resource allocation decisions are made centrally, often by the president of the chaebol who functions more as a patriarch than as an Anglo-Saxon chief executive. In particular he controls all senior managerial appointments and overall labour management policies. As Amsden puts it (1989: 325): 'The personnel function in general, and the labour relations function in particular, are almost non-existent as a staff responsibility, whether at the group or subsidiary level.' Managerial careers and rewards are thus directly managed by the owner and his family and depend greatly on personal relationships.

This strong central control of personnel policies and decisions means that the chaebol are more integrated than conglomerates controlled through purely financial systems. Managers and engineers are often moved between member companies to transfer expertise and develop loyalty to the group. Thus Hyundai Shipbuilders received managers, engineers and supervisors from Hyundai Construction and other firms in the Hyundai group as well as poaching them from established shipbuilding firms (Amsden, 1989: 274–90). This movement of skilled staff ensures that the overall capability of the chaebol is enhanced at the same time as developing a uniform group culture which is also promoted by the focal role of the chaebol owner.

Top managers of Korean chaebol are usually either from the same family as the founder and owner, or from the same region, or attended the same secondary school (Shin and Chin, 1989). In 1978, 13.5 per cent of the directors of the largest 100 chaebol were members of the owner's family and they held 21 per cent of the total available positions, which implies they were more likely than non-family executives to hold two or more top posts concurrently. Furthermore, although the proportion of family executives declined with increasing size of chaebol, their absolute number rose as corporate size increased. This suggests that, while growth may constrain the ability to fill top positions with family members simply because the supply of competent kinsmen is insufficient for large firms, the preference for ascriptively recruited senior staff does not decline with size. Additionally, it seems that family members are promoted earlier and reach the top management level at a younger age than other executives.

The shortfall in family members for top posts seems to be made up by preferential recruiting from the owner's region of origin and/or his secondary school. Shin and Chin (1989) suggest that common regional backgrounds provide prima facie justification for a social bond and that, if two applicants for a job have equivalent qualifications, the one from the same area or clan as the owner will be appointed because of this presumption. Similarly, those who have been to the same elite school are regarded as more trustworthy and capable than others. For example, 8 out of the top 11 executives at Daewoo attended Kyung-gi school in Seoul (Shin and Chin, 1989). It should be noted that these ascriptive selection criteria are equally in evidence in the more 'modern' high-technology sector and that they tend to function in addition to formal educational success. Thus 85 per cent of all the top managers studied by Shin and Chin had university degrees, and almost 30 per cent had graduated from Seoul National University, which was especially well represented in the larger chaebol. Additionally, many had long military and government careers before joining the chaebol, which is not surprising given the importance of state connections and the dominant role of the military in Korea since the Korean War.

This reliance on close personal ties between top managers emphasizes the importance of personal trust and loyalty in the chaebol and, equally, the widespread distrust of managers and workers who do not share background characteristics. Compared to the Japanese kaisha, then, the owners of Korean enterprises manifestly do not believe in the original virtue of employees and do not expect them to share collective objectives. Rather, they rely on strong leadership and forcefulness because, as one entrepreneur puts it, 'Koreans . . . will not work well together unless there is firm direction. Koreans are like grains of sand; they will not stick together' (Jones and Sakong, 1980: 338). Where such beliefs are widespread, and collective loyalties weaker than individual commitments, trust is limited and personal loyalty a crucial quality for appointment to senior roles.

Hierarchy–Market Relations in Hong Kong and Taiwan: the Chinese Family Business

The dominant feature of the export-oriented sector in Hong Kong and Taiwan, as well as in many South-East Asian countries (Limlingan, 1986; Yoshihara, 1988), is the small size of most firms, coupled with their strong family control and extensive subcontracting (Levy, 1988; Myers, 1986; Tam, 1990). Indeed, the average size of manufacturing firms in Hong Kong has actually declined over the past 20 or so years, during a period of very fast economic growth (Sit and Wong, 1988). In the 1980s, small and medium sized enterprises employing under 200 people constituted 98.9 per cent of all firms in manufacturing in Hong Kong, employed 73.4 per cent of the total manufacturing labour force, and contributed 65.4 per cent of total output and 64.1 per cent of manufacturing value added. Although large firms are more significant in Taiwan, they are predominantly single-unit enterprises and have remained very much smaller than large firms in Japan and Korea (Hamilton and Kao, 1990; Levy, 1988). Furthermore, many of the largest Taiwanese companies are either state owned or largely state supported and not primarily focused on export markets (Gold, 1988b; Orru, 1991), although their outputs do feed into exporting firms and public enterprises are used by the state to support the export-oriented sector (Wade, 1990: 66–70).

A related feature of the small size of each firm in these economies is the critical role of networks of exchange relationships between firms, both for subcontracting parts of the manufacturing process and for mobilizing capital, market information and other resources (Greenhalgh, 1984, 1988a; Numazaki, 1986; Tam, 1990). Small firm size is also strongly tied to the dominant business ideology of 'entrepreneurial familism' (Wong, 1988a) and a patrimonial management style (Redding, 1990; Ward, 1972).

The Nature of Economic Actors and their Development
The primary characteristic of the dominant unit of economic co-ordination and control in Hong Kong and Taiwan is family

ownership and control, to the extent that enterprises are often viewed as part of the family property rather than as separate administrative entities (Wong, 1985, 1988b). This means that the key decision-making unit and locus of resource control is the family business, in particular the head of the household which runs it. Consequently, individual, legally bounded firms are less important as economic units than the family that owns them. This difference between firms and family businesses is reflected in the common distinction between managerial responsibilities which can be delegated to non-family 'professional' managers, and entrepreneurial roles which remain the preserve of the owning family and trusted partners (Redding, 1990: 158–9; Wong, 1988b).

The small size of most Chinese family businesses (CFBs) and their common focus on a single unit mean that they are highly specialized in the economic activities they control directly and their distinctive capabilities. They typically perform intermediate stages of production and rely on trading firms and other businesses to provide material inputs and distribution channels (Stites, 1982), although some Taiwanese electronics firms are now selling complete computers under their own brand names (Levy, 1988). Orders come through intermediaries, who often also provide designs, and most small firms in Hong Kong do little market research or development (Sit and Wong, 1988). In the larger textiles firms more vertical integration has taken place, but many Shanghaiese business owners in Hong Kong remain committed to that industry and its long-term development (Nishida, 1990; Wong, 1988a). Although some have diversified into property development as land prices have soared, they still see their major managerial skills and commitments being specialized in the textile industry (Nishida and Redding, 1992).

This sort of 'opportunistic diversification' has also occurred in Taiwan, sometimes with state encouragement (Hamilton and Kao, 1990). It is often accomplished by establishing a new firm with capital drawn from the retained profits of existing firms under the management of a family member or another highly trusted close associate. Where the investment needed is too great for family resources, and/or where access to different businesses and political networks is required, families enter into alliances with trusted partners to set up the new business and thus develop 'business groups' which operate in a variety of industries (Hamilton et al., 1990; Numazaki, 1986, 1989; Orru et al., 1988).

These groups are not, though, authoritatively co-ordinated and integrated administrative entities like the Korean chaebol. Rather, most of them seem to function more as partnerships united by common investments and mutual trust in which the critical locus of decision making and control remains the individual family business (Numazaki, 1989). Furthermore, they by no means dominate the Taiwan economy. According to Hamilton and Kao (1990), the largest 96 business groups employed only 4.6 per cent of the workforce in 1983, and many of the larger manufacturing firms are not members of them. They are also not as diversified as the Korean chaebol. On a number of diversification indices, they were consistently less diversified across manufacturing sectors in 1983 according to Hamilton (1990), and they do not compete against each other in many different sectors as do the chaebol (cf. Numazaki, 1986).

In sum, individual firms in Chinese family businesses are usually quite specialized in terms of both business functions and sector of activity, but families often do invest in different activities, either on their own or in partnership with others. Large CFBs may, then, span a number of distinct fields, but these activities are rarely integrated through a central administrative hierarchy. Rather, they are interconnected through a network of alliances and particularistic ties between family heads which vary in their performance and cohesion. They can be summarized as combining managerial specialization with entrepreneurial diversification.

According to Limlingan (1986), the typical pattern of business development of the CFB combines cost cutting and competitive pricing to increase volume with expansion into related areas to increase resources. He suggests that a major reason for the success of the expatriate Chinese in South-East Asia has been their willingness to undercut their indigenous competitors by accepting lower gross profits on sales. This lower rate of return is more than compensated for by the higher turnover of assets achieved by Chinese businesses and their much faster recovery of debts coupled with low inventory levels (Limlingan, 1986: 147; Hicks and Redding, 1982). In general, strategic preferences in the CFB focus on the intensive use of resources, short payback periods for new investments, reliance on price and cost competition and a reluctance to share control or responsibility (Redding, 1990: 177–81). Risks are managed largely by restricting commitments and maximizing resource flexibility.

The critical role of family ownership and control of the CFB, together with these strategic preferences, results in a highly personal decision-making style which is very flexible and responsive to environmental change. Technological investments tend to be short term so that they can be written off after a few years and do not seriously constrain resource allocation choices. New ventures can be undertaken quickly by modifying existing facilities and skills if they are in related areas, or else by setting up new firms run by trusted kinsmen or loyal partners. Since most salaried managers are neither trusted nor used in making strategic decisions in the CFB, their experience and expertise neither limit nor direct the allocation of resources (Wong, 1988b). Growth is therefore a matter of seizing market opportunities through the mobilization of networks while retaining personal control. Given the individual entrepreneur's restricted experience in one particular activity in the early stage of firm development, expansion tends to be in related areas initially; but, as his networks and knowledge of other activities grow, the CFB often moves into quite different sectors, usually with experienced partners.

Market Organization in Hong Kong and Taiwan
The small size and highly specialized nature of most CFBs results in high levels of interdependence between firms. Not only are many manufacturing companies dependent on orders from trading firms, large buyers and other manufacturers but they often subcontract work as well (Sit and Wong, 1988). Each firm is connected to a large number of other ones through a complex web of deals, obligations, personal ties and joint activities. Market relations are therefore highly particularistic and are based on personal knowledge or the reputations of exchange partners. Trust generated through personal connections is, thus, a crucial feature of inter-firm exchanges (Silin, 1972; Ward, 1972; Wong, 1988b). As Deglopper (1978: 297) puts it: 'Business relations are always, to some degree, personal relations.'

These connections, however, are more fluid and changeable than those between members of vertically linked keiretsu in Japan. Personal reputations for reliability, speed and low costs are essential for gaining contracts but do not necessarily lead to repeat orders or long-term associations involving risk sharing and reciprocal shareholdings. Since firms are essentially family possessions and most subcontractors are outsiders, commitments between them will always be limited and relatively short term (Redding, 1990). Networks of interdependent firms, then, are based on personal contacts and reputations, and these are crucial to CFB survival, but are not very stable and often change. This 'molecular' system of co-ordination is thus highly flexible and enables rapid changes of products and markets, as is shown by the successful development of the garment, wig making, plastic flower and toy industries in Hong Kong and the plastics and electronics industries in Taiwan (Myers, 1986; Tam, 1990).

Inter-sectoral co-ordination of economic activity in Hong Kong and Taiwan is largely achieved by families establishing subsidiaries or, as mentioned above, by joint ventures and partnerships with personally known and trusted entrepreneurs in business groups. These groups are not usually so cohesive and integrated as the Japanese inter-market groups, and their members do not always work together on new ventures. Thus, partners in one group may set up new alliances and agreements with families in other groups if it is thought that the existing group would not accommodate expansion or diversification. Relative to Japanese business groups, then, Taiwanese ones are more specific to particular activities and ventures, and partners are less mutually committed for long-term development (Hamilton, 1990; Hamilton et al., 1990; Numazaki, 1989). Co-ordination between sectors is therefore more particularistic and restricted than in Japan.

The overriding concern with family control in the CFB leads to a preference for informal sources of finance, such as family members, close friends, revolving credit associations or the unregulated 'curb' market in Taiwan (Deglopper, 1978; Hamilton et al., 1990; Stites, 1982), rather than established financial intermediaries such as banks. Equally the banks, controlled by the state in Taiwan, have been reluctant to finance small and medium sized firms because of their perceptions of the high risks involved and lack of expertise in evaluating lending risks (Myers, 1986; Wade, 1990: 160–5). Because of the Nationalist government's concern for financial stability, even at the cost of economic growth (Amsden, 1985b), the main commercial banks have been very conservative in their corporate lending decisions and preferred to deal with only the largest, established firms. As a result some business groups have set up their own financial intermediaries to generate low-cost funds (Numazaki, 1987). In general, then, the banks do not play a co-ordinating role in the Taiwanese economy and are not closely connected with the strategic choices of family businesses. As Wade (1990: 264) puts it: 'The banks have not been encouraged to take an interest in the well-being of their borrowers . . . Banks have not developed a capacity to analyse company finances, industry structures, or the commercial feasibility of projects.'

The role of the large banks in Hong Kong seems to have been more positive, at least in the development of the textile industry (Jao, 1984; Nishida, 1990), even if long-term loans were less common than in Japan and the banks have not developed large inter-sectoral business groups. Again, though, the predilection for retaining control in the CFB has meant that informal funding sources are preferred, unless the family owned the bank as in the case of the Wing On department store group. Equally, most firms that raise money on the stock market rarely offer more than 20–30 per cent of the total paid-up capital for sale, and/or separate voting from non-voting shares, so that control is firmly retained by the family (Wong, 1989). In both Hong Kong and Taiwan, then, market organization is primarily carried out by inter-family alliances and partnerships rather than through banks, and is more fluid than in Japan.

Similarly, markets are less overtly co-ordinated and managed by state agencies in Taiwan than in Korea. Although state enterprises dominate many industrial sectors, such as heavy machinery, steel, aluminium, shipbuilding, petroleum, synthetics and semiconductors, their overall share of manufacturing production had fallen to 18 per cent in 1980, and, in particular, they play only a minor role in the export sector (Amsden, 1985a; Myers, 1986: 54–6). It is important to note, however, that from the 1950s to the 1970s Taiwan had one of the largest public enterprise sectors outside the Communist bloc and sub-Saharan Africa. Their percentage share in gross fixed capital formation remained over 30 per cent throughout the 1970s, a higher level than Korea's (Wade, 1990: 176–7). The Taiwanese state is 'developmentalist' in the sense that it has systematically encouraged industrialization and export sectors since the 1950s, but is less inclined to intervene in particular firms' decisions than the Korean state (Cumings, 1987; Gold, 1988b; Haggard, 1988). Tax incentives and selective assistance for exporters have directed entrepreneurs' attention to particular sectors, such as plastics and electronics, but the use of administrative discretion to favour individual private firms or push them in particular directions has not been a general feature of state agencies in Taiwan (Amsden, 1985a; Hamilton, 1989; Orru, 1991). Instead, the state has tended to use public enterprises as the preferred instrument for sector development, and Wade (1990: 100–1) suggests that the Taiwanese state has exerted 'big leadership' in the computer, vehicle, shipbuilding, metals, plastics and artificial fibres industries.

The Hong Kong colonial government follows much more regulatory than developmentalist policies and, indeed, claims to be 'positively' non-interventionist. However, the links between the colonial political elite and the leaders of the largest British banks and trading houses have traditionally been close and generally supportive of economic growth, especially in the textile and garment industries after 1945 (Deyo, 1987; Nishida, 1990). Furthermore, through the massive public housing programme of the 1960s and 1970s and investment in public education, the state has both reduced household expenses, and thus wage pressures (Castells et al., 1990: 83–117), and encouraged the development of a literate and relatively educated labour force, albeit with limited technical skills (Fong, 1988). It is also worth pointing out that the state has extensive controls over the main utilities and the food distribution system in Hong Kong and is, in general, more interventionist than its public utterances suggest (Castells et al., 1990; Henderson, 1989). Co-ordination of business strategies is, though, primarily achieved through private deals and alliances in Hong Kong.

Co-ordination and Control through Authority Hierarchies

The high levels of segmentation of labour markets by firm size, industry and gender found in Japan and Korea are echoed by Taiwan and Hong Kong, although most of the large businesses in the capital-intensive sector in Taiwan are state owned and/or controlled (Amsden, 1985a), and Hong Kong has relatively few in this sector. As Deyo (1989: 180–7) points out, the early stages of export-oriented growth in East Asia were characterized by high rates of female employment in light manufacturing firms at low wages and low levels of job security. Although the wage differentials between these industries and heavy industry were not as great in Taiwan as in Korea in 1985, they were still considerable and reflected the greater employment of women in the textiles, garment, plastics and electrical apparatus industries.

Labour turnover rates are also higher among women in light manufacturing industries. In Taiwan in 1983, the monthly separation rate of the labour force in electronic products was 5.28 per cent, whereas it was only 2.04 per cent in chemicals. Higher rates are reported in Hong Kong's garment, textiles, electronics, plastics and toy industries, which employ large numbers of female workers (Deyo, 1989: 191–2). This high level of job change reflects both poor wages and employment conditions for many female workers and highly instrumental attitudes among the mostly young women. In so far as the medium sized firms do offer some career progression and longer-term commitments to non-family members, they are more likely to be available to men and in industries where skilled labour is more critical and relatively scarce, such as machine tools where turnover is relatively low and training is more extensive (Amsden, 1985a). As electronics firms in Taiwan develop from specialized component subcontracting to manufacturing complete units, they invest more in training, welfare schemes and seniority rewards for the higher-skilled male workforce (Deyo, 1989: 198–

201). Similar practices were followed by the larger Shanghaiese textile firms in Hong Kong as they integrated forward (Nishida, 1990; Wong, 1988a).

Loyalty and commitment in the CFB, then, vary according to gender, skill levels, industry and female membership. Neither employers nor employees expect or manifest much mutual commitment for young, female, semi-skilled, non-family workers in light manufacturing industries. Even for older male workers who have scarce skills, the extent of long-term employer commitments is limited by the focus of family loyalties and the common belief that self-employment is to be preferred to working for someone else (Greenhalgh, 1984; Tam, 1990). Thus ambitious skilled manual or white-collar workers in Taiwan and Hong Kong prefer to set up their own business as soon as they can obtain some capital and business experience rather than follow a 'career' in someone else's family business (Wong, 1988b). As Tam (1990: 177) puts it: 'the Chinese are motivated to work in the company but not for the company'. Indeed it is quite common for employers to help certain employees to set up on their own and so develop obligations which, if the new firm is successful, enlarge their networks and trust relations (Deyo, 1989: 160; Numazaki, 1986). While, then, paternalist beliefs and practices in the CFB do resuit in personal commitments to 'permanent' male workers and seniority-based promotion, these are much less institutionalized than in large Japanese firms and more dependent on individual decisions and favours (Redding, 1990).

The importance of personal connections and contacts is also evident in recruitment decisions. Many, if not most, workers in Taiwan and Hong Kong obtain their jobs through relatives and friends rather than through formal channels, and employers prefer to rely on personal recommendations for hiring people, especially skilled male workers. According to Greenhalgh (1984), nearly three-quarters of the migrants to Taiwan's cities find jobs through personal contacts, and those that don't do this feel no compunction about leaving at short notice. Just as personal knowledge is crucial for selecting business partners, so too recruits obtained through trustworthy contacts are considered more reliable than those lacking a personal connection. Formal educational qualifications do not, on the other hand, seem to play as crucial a role in selection decisions as in Japan and Korea.

While higher education had become more widespread in Taiwan over the past two decades, especially in technical subjects (Amsden, 1985b), it does not seem to function as a filtering device for the higher-paying jobs in private business to the same extent as it does elsewhere in East Asia. A college degree often leads to higher wages and preferential hiring in the larger firms, but the returns to higher education are not as large as in Korea. Equally, the match between educational prestige hierarchies and firm attractiveness is less rigid in Taiwan than in Japan or Korea, perhaps because of the tendency of graduates from mainlander families to prefer the state sector (Greenhalgh, 1984; Silin, 1976; Wade, 1990: 219).

Unionization levels are higher in both Taiwan and Hong Kong than in Korea, although lower than in Japan and many Western countries (Deyo, 1989: 68–77). Highly state controlled in Taiwan, unions function more to enforce worker discipline, ensure political support and administer worker services than to represent their demands. Generally they are more significant in the public utilities and transport sectors than in export industries and are actively opposed in most CFBs, not least because they imply the failure of personal control and paternalistic commitments (Deyo, 1989; Wong, 1988b). Any form of intermediating agency between owner-managers and their workforce threatens personal control and the development of personal loyalty to the owner and so is rejected (Silin, 1976).

Given this preference for personal ties and commitments in the CFB it is not surprising that the use of formal co-ordination and control procedures is limited. According to Pugh and Redding (1985) and Redding (1990: 160–1), the CFB exhibits much lower degrees of role specialization and standardization of work procedures than do equivalent firms in Japan and the UK. Similarly, Silin (1976) emphasizes the fluidity of the formal organizational structure in the large Taiwanese firm he studied. Many managers held multiple positions, and their responsibilities were liable to sudden change at the wish of the owner. Tasks and jobs in the CFB, then, appear to be more diffusely delineated and flexibly defined than in the Korean chaebol and Japanese kaisha.

A related feature of many Chinese firms is the comparatively weak position of middle management. Because authority is primarily personal and concentrated in the owner, 'the primary goal of the executive is then to secure and increase the respect of the boss, that is, to increase personal interaction with him' (Silin, 1976: 67), and loyalty to the boss overrides that to immediate superiors. Leaders frequently bypass the managerial hierarchy to find out what is going on and emphasize their personal involvement; thus formal managerial authority is less significant than having a direct personal link to the owner. Formal communication channels and accounting information are often disregarded because of a lack of trust of subordinates and a preference for direct, personal contact (Silin, 1976: 74–85).

Dyadic authority relations between supervisors, managers and the owning patriarch imply high levels of centralization in the CFB. According to Redding (1990: 174–5), this was especially so for financial, marketing and personnel decisions, which were usually made by the owner, who also maintained considerable secrecy over financial transactions. While there was some delegation of operational control over production activities and greater reliance on formal control systems there, planning decisions remained centralized. This central control of decisions in the CFB is reinforced by the common view that leadership is a moral quality of individuals rather than a technical skill which can be modified and taught (Silin, 1976: 57–66). This emphasis on the moral superiority of the leader in Chinese society means that authority cannot be easily delegated or shared since this would suggest a reduction in moral worth. It also encourages considerable distance between the owner and all employees, including managers.

The moral superiority of leaders of Chinese firms is manifested by their economic success which follows from their superior insight into business affairs and ability to control egocentric impulses (Silin, 1976: 127–31). Loyalty to these leaders is therefore conditional on the firm's continuing success and thus the owner's demonstrated superior rationality. When it fails, employees can legitimately withdraw their commitment to the leader and move elsewhere. As a result, employers display relatively little trust and commitment to employees with whom they do not have strong personal 'family-like' connections (Wong, 1988b), and employees display formal subordination to business owners without strong emotional commitments. Essentially, they follow the role performance model of filial piety which specifies appropriate patterns of behaviour rather than personal commitment to the individual leader of the firm (Hamilton, 1984).

This emphasis on the moral superiority and greater rationality of successful business owners is linked to what Silin (1976: 127–8) calls a 'didactic' leadership role in which the leader conveys to subordinates the methods by which he has achieved success. Because of his superiority, social distance and concern for secrecy, however, these methods are rarely spelled out as formal rules. Rather, successful subordinates are those who correctly understand the leader's beliefs and thoughts and can be relied upon to follow them. As moral inferiors they cannot question these beliefs, or even discuss them formally, and are expected to accept the owner's decisions as the product of superior wisdom (Redding and Wong, 1986).

The combination of family ownership with the lack of institutionalized trust relations between non-kin and non-close-friends in the CFB leads to a strong reliance on family members and people with strong personal ties to the owner for filling senior positions. Thus the dominant coalitions of Chinese firms are usually made up of close kin, and economic issues become fused with family ones in what Deyo (1989: 163) calls 'kitchen politics'. Since the firm is typically seen as an instrument for the service of the family, its decisions and activities are essentially family ones, so that salaried managers without close family-type links to the owning group cannot be involved in major choices. This does not mean that nepotism leads to incompetence, since most owners of CFBs invest heavily in the education and training of their successors and take pains to teach them the craft of deal making (Limlingan, 1986; Wong, 1988a: 136–46). Often the patriarch selects the son or son-in-law who displays the most talent as an entrepreneur rather than the best qualified in formal terms, since it is this skill which is regarded as crucial, and does not hesitate to sideline incompetent sons (Redding, 1990: 133–4). Occasionally adopted children are given major responsibilities if they demonstrate the required talents, but Chinese families place greater emphasis on blood ties than Japanese ones (Pelzel, 1970).

The highly personal nature of authority relations in the CFB, the limited separation of the firm from the family and the conditional nature of employee loyalty together restrict the longevity and size of Chinese firms. Succession to the patriarchal role is decided by the founder, but the Chinese principle of equal division of his assets among his inheritors encourages division, conflict and fragmentation. As Wong (1985, 1988b) points out, the typical successful CFB goes through four distinct phases – emergent, centralized, segmented and disintegrative – in three generations. Because each son expects to run his own business, the brothers who do not succeed to the top position are often given a subsidiary to run. If successful this leads to demands for more control and more resources which can result in fission. By the third generation, many inheritors prefer to sell the family business to realize their assets, perhaps to start their own firm independently, and so fragmentation and collapse of the CFB are frequent. Together with the continuing movement of employees away to start their own firms, this pattern leads to the perpetual destruction and creation of Chinese family businesses as a centrifugal process (Tam, 1990). Flexibility and innovation are thus characteristic of market economies dominated by Chinese family businesses.

3
Differences between East Asian Business Systems

These descriptive accounts of the major characteristics of the post-war business systems that have become established in Japan, South Korea, Taiwan and Hong Kong reveal many important differences in their organization of economic activities. These differences stem from the combination of particular features of pre-industrial Japan, Korea and China with processes of industrialization in East Asia which, in turn, partly resulted from these features. In order to consider how distinct business systems have developed in East Asia as the result of differences in dominant institutions, their key characteristics need to be summarized and the dimensions on which they vary identified. This chapter therefore abstracts the significant differences between the hierarchy–market configurations described in Chapter 2 and suggests a number of general dimensions on which they can be compared.

Initially, I shall summarize the major differentiating characteristics of each business system under the three broad headings used earlier: the nature of economic actors and their development; market organization; and the internal co-ordination and control systems of managerial hierarchies. I will then consider how these differences could be further reduced to a smaller set of dimensions which could be used for systematically comparing business systems between societies. Finally, the interconnections between these dimensions within each business system will be briefly discussed to see how they fit together as effective combinations of firm types, market linkages and authority systems and form relatively stable configurations in particular institutional contexts.

The Nature of Economic Actors and their Development

Dominant economic actors in East Asian societies clearly differ considerably in terms of their size, the variety and range of economic activities they co-ordinate and direct, the scope of their competitive competences and managerial experiences and the autonomy of senior managers from property rights holders. These differences are closely related to variations in strategic focus and change, growth patterns and the management of subsidiaries and ways of dealing with risk and uncertainty. The major ways in

Table 3.1 *The nature of economic actors and their development in East Asian business systems*

Characteristics	Kaisha	Chaebol	CFB
Size	Large	Large	Small/medium
Capital intensity	Varied	Varied	Low
Managerial discretion from owners	High	Low	Low
Business specialization and managerial homogeneity	High	Low	High in firms, medium in families
Strategic change	Incremental	Discontinuous	Opportunistic
Growth focus	Sector share	Vertical integration and diversification	Volume expansion and opportunistic diversification
Integration of different activities	Minority shareholding	Authority hierarchy	Personal ties and ownership
Risk management	Extensive mutual dependence	Diversification and state support	Limiting commitment and maximizing flexibility

which they vary are listed in summary form in Table 3.1 and will now be briefly discussed before suggesting three underlying dimensions which incorporate these differences.

Considering first the nature of the firm as the authoritative co-ordination unit of economic activities, the Chinese family business (CFB) in Taiwan and Hong Kong is obviously smaller than the Japanese kaisha and Korean chaebol and tends not to run capital- and energy-intensive enterprises – or at least not without strong state encouragement and support. In contrast, both kaisha and chaebol co-ordinate activities in a variety of industries and are often quite large. A further sharp difference between Japanese, Korean and Chinese firms is the high level of managerial autonomy and independence from shareholders enjoyed by the kaisha compared to the chaebol and CFB. Through mutual interlocking shareholdings between members of business groups and keiretsu, the market for corporate control is considerably weakened in Japan, and financial institutions are more interdependent with large firms than in Anglo-Saxon societies (Orru, 1989). To a very large extent the top management of the large kaisha are able to ignore shareholder pressures and control senior appointments themselves, as well as strategic decisions (Noda, 1979; Zielinski and Holloway, 1991: 6-7). In contrast, of course, both the chaebol and the CFB are tightly controlled by the owning family, through a variety of means (Hattori, 1984).

The other major difference between economic actors in these three business systems is the diversity of economic activities co-ordinated through authority hierarchies. Where senior managers are promoted internally, this is closely related to their homogeneity of experience and skills. The Japanese kaisha is more specialized and homogeneous than the Korean chaebol and is less likely to diversify into unrelated markets. The Chinese family business, on the other hand, demonstrates a strong distinction between managerially co-ordinated activities, which are quite specialized, often subcontracted from a larger enterprise and/or subject to designs provided by a large purchaser, and entrepreneurially linked activities which are often quite diverse. Thus, individual firms usually concentrate on a fairly specific and restricted range of products, but the family business as a whole may be involved in a wide range of industries and sectors through shareholdings, part-nerships and family alliances. However, the critical importance of personal owner control in the CFB does restrict the extent of such diversification, or at least its effective management – as Redding (1990: 212) points out. The experience and expertise of non-family managers within each firm are typically fairly specialized, at least until they leave to start their own business and develop broader entrepreneurial skills; but some members of the family may deve-lop knowledge of, and expertise in, a number of industries, especi-ally the patriarch (Hamilton and Kao, 1990). Thus, the family as a whole may acquire a wide range of expertise through oppor-tunistic diversification, but this is not usually integrated through formal authority hierarchies (Tam, 1990).

These general differences in the nature of economic actors are related to important variations in how they change and develop. First of all, the general pattern of change and growth in the Japanese kaisha is much more incremental and focused on increas-ing its share of a particular market or sector than in the Korean chaebol. In these latter enterprises change is more discontinuous in terms of the activities and resources controlled, and growth has occurred through both vertical integration and diversification into related and unrelated fields. Unlike either the kaisha or the CFB, this growth has partly been achieved through the acquisition of existing firms. Chinese family businesses typically grow through volume expansion into related areas but do also undertake oppor-tunistic diversification if suitable partners and prospects are available. Strategic change can thus be discontinuous and can occur with amazing rapidity, as the succession of important industries in Hong Kong demonstrates (Youngson, 1982: 11–12).

The specialized nature of managerial competences and competitive capabilities in the Japanese kaisha encourages the formal separation of successful new ventures in different fields as soon as they are large enough to be set up as separate enterprises. Although a minority shareholding is often maintained, fast growing subsidiaries develop their own funding arrangements and form their own enterprise union. In contrast, the Korean chaebol integrate new activities through the managerial hierarchy and maintain central control of them. Chinese family businesses diversify through partnerships with trusted associates or through separate firms run by family, or family-like, members. Integration is thus achieved through a combination of financial control and ownership and personal loyalties. In sum, the degree of integration and control of activities and subsidiaries outside the main field of expertise and operation is greatest in the chaebol, considerable in the CFB and least in the kaisha.

These variations reflect different attitudes to risk and the management of uncertainty. By concentrating on a relatively narrow range of activities and competences, the Japanese kaisha avoids the co-ordination costs incurred through integrating many diverse activities and skills but is vulnerable to major changes in product and input markets which render its specialist expertise less valuable. This risk is managed by limiting the firm's commitments to human and material resources through extensive subcontracting, by separating the 'core' workforce from marginal and substitutable employees and by developing strong ties of mutual dependence with banks, suppliers and customers so that adjustments to changing market conditions can be planned jointly for shared interests. Additionally, high levels of investment in employee training and ability to move staff between tasks and plants facilitate flexibility and enable the kaisha to respond quickly to market changes (Abegglen and Stalk, 1985: 131–6).

In contrast, the Korean chaebol internalizes risk through vertical integration and diversifies into relatively unrelated fields with state support. While Korean entrepreneurs, and indeed Koreans in general, are often seen as being willing to take major risks (cf. Pye, 1985: 216–20), the bulk of the uncertainties associated with the high rate of chaebol growth have been managed by the state in partnership with chaebol owners. As Amsden (1989: 85) points out, private firms contributed very little of their own capital to most of the major investment projects in heavy industry, and the initiative to enter new branches of manufacturing industry came primarily from state agencies. The state underwrote and/or arranged for most of the foreign loans for new capital projects and supported the purchase of foreign technology and knowledge for targeted investments. While some chaebol projects have been allowed to fail and/or be taken over by stronger enterprises, most new ventures have in effect been underwritten by the Korean state so that the risks of moving into new fields for the owning family were considerably reduced. Furthermore, by encouraging a limited number of chaebol to enter, say, the vehicle industry or shipbuilding, the state ensured that domestic profits would be considerable for successful producers (Zeile, 1989).

The Chinese family business manages risks by minimizing commitments to a particular product line or technology and relying on high levels of subcontracting. As in Japan, many trading functions are undertaken outside the firm, which typically concentrates on production to externally generated designs. Commitments to key skilled workers are considerable but not to short-term staff without personal ties to the owning family. Thus, flexibility is paramount, and internally controlled resources can be combined with a wide variety of external units controlling different activities and skills to seize new opportunities through networks of personal trust and reputation. Risks are also reduced for the family by establishing new ventures with partners in different fields.

These eight differences between the kaisha, chaebol and CFB can be derived from three underlying characteristics of firms as authoritative economic actors which vary significantly between their institutional contexts. First, the importance of owner control and personal direction of economic enterprises clearly affects their size, growth pattern and capital intensity. Second, the concern with homogeneity and integration of similar activities and competitive capabilities within authority hierarchies is closely related to preferences for business specialization, diversification and acquisition. Third, the ways in which firms manage their risks, and in particular their reliance on strong ties of mutual dependence between firms to share risks, obviously affect how they make strategic changes and their attitudes to major diversification of activities. These three dimensions will now be discussed in a little more detail.

First, the delegation of managerial control over operations and strategic choices to salaried, career managers in the Japanese kaisha forms a strong contrast to the Chinese concern to maintain close family control over all major decisions and direct supervision of middle management activities (Silin, 1976: 127–31). Not only do most owners of CFBs control financial, strategic and personnel matters but they also appear reluctant to trust formal information systems and the formal managerial hierarchy. As a result they are involved in operational issues and establish direct, dyadic relations with employees rather than mediated, indirect ones. This strong identification of ownership with control in the CFB limits the growth of managerial hierarchies in Chinese business communities and is linked to the highly personal nature of business relationships and commitments (Redding, 1990). High levels of owner control in the CFB thus restrict the size of firms as authoritative co-ordination units and their willingness to invest in capital-intensive enterprises, which require operational delegation to managerial hierarchies. Similar levels of strong owner control in the Korean chaebol have been less restrictive because of much greater state support and risk sharing and a greater willingness to rely on formal control systems, probably as a result of the militarization of Korean society and the influence of United States training (Kim, 1988; Lee, 1984). The attractiveness of 'entrepreneurial familism' and personal business ownership as contrasted with employment in large and successful firms also seems less in Korea than in Chinese communities (Wong, 1988b).

Second, the heterogeneity of activities and capabilities co-ordinated through authority hierarchies is linked to their ability to diversify the variety of products and markets that firms are active in and to make discontinuous strategic changes. As we have seen, the relatively specialized Japanese kaisha develops quite a homogeneous managerial and employee culture which focuses attention on market share growth goals and prevents major discontinuities in the human and material resources being co-ordinated or markets served. In contrast, the more heterogeneous chaebol have been pushed by the Korean state into new, diverse fields of activity and have developed a wider range of managerial competences to deal with discontinuous changes. The specialized nature of the Chinese family business limits its ability to diversify managerially and, together with other factors, encourages entrepreneurial diversification rather than co-ordinating varied activities through authority hierarchies. As a result, when enterprises have developed new activities in different markets, the chaebol have co-ordinated these through their managerial hierarchies, the kaisha have usually hived them off as soon as their growth threatens to inhibit the parent firm's access to capital and to increase co-ordination costs and employee commitments, while the CFBs have relied on personal and financial means of integration rather than formal authority relations.

Third, the degree to which market risks are managed through mutual dependence networks with other firms and core employees clearly varies greatly between the kaisha, the CFB and the chaebol. While large Japanese firms share the risks of focusing on one industry or field of competence with their suppliers and other business partners on a relatively long-term basis, and are thus enmeshed in extensive networks of mutual commitment which constrain and direct strategic choices and change, the Chinese family business focuses on flexibility and limiting the extent of their commitments to suppliers, traders and customers. Thus, although the CFB is also highly interdependent with its subcontractors, skilled employers and other partners, these networks are much more personal and restricted than those between the kaisha. Because firms are family controlled, their commitments to non-family, or non-family-like (Hamilton and Kao, 1990), partners are limited and short term. However, where personal trust is high, commitments and obligations are more extensive, and the need to preserve personal relationships restricts radical changes in particular firms' activities. As a result, many CFBs prefer to set up new firms for each new venture in different fields rather than risk creating strains in existing partnerships and relations. Finally, the chaebol have few long-term ties to other firms, and their primary dependence relations are with state agencies and the political executive. Risks are managed through diversification and political networks rather than inter-firm reciprocal obligation networks. These differences are obviously related to variations in market organization, to which I now turn.

Market Organization

The organization of exchange relationships between economic actors in Japan, South Korea, Taiwan and Hong Kong varies considerably in the extent to which they reflect long-term commitments between specific business partners. Relations between suppliers and customers also differ in the scope of transactions that occur and the extent to which dependence is reciprocal and mutual as opposed to one business partner being dominated by the other. The significance of personal knowledge and individual reputations in selecting contractors is a further distinguishing feature of market relations in East Asia. Finally, the extent to which relations between firms within and between industrial sectors are organized through long-term membership of business groups and networks of alliances between formally independent enterprises clearly varies as well, as does the importance of personal trust between business

Table 3.2 *Differences in market organization in East Asia*

	Kaisha	Chaebol	CFB
Interdependence of firms	High	Low	High
Commitment to particular exchange partners	High	Low	Restricted outside family-like connections
Scope of exchange relations with partners	High	Low	Low outside family-like connections
Reciprocity of commitments	High	Low	Mixed
Reliance on personal knowledge and reputation	Low	Limited	High
Vertical integration by quasi-contractual links	High	Low	Low
Horizonal co-ordination between sectors through long-term commitments	High	Low	Limited to personal ties

owners in developing and maintaining such linkages. These differences in patterns of market organization are summarized in Table 3.2.

The high level of specialization in particular activities and capabilities characteristic of the Japanese kaisha and CFB does, of course, mean that they are much more interdependent with suppliers, customers and other business partners than are the chaebol. However, the extent to which they develop relatively long-term commitments to individual firms, and the type of commitment developed, varies between them. Market connections between enterprises in Japan are highly specific to particular firms, reflect long-term commitments and are relatively reciprocal and wide ranging. In contrast, Chinese family businesses limit their commitments to individual exchange partners and usually focus on more specific transactions with subcontractors unless they have strong personal ties to them. Reciprocity is by no means institutionalized, and mutual obligations between firms are limited to those where personal connections are important.

The significance of direct personal knowledge and of particular business partners is, of course, greatest in Chinese business communities. While trust in situations of high uncertainty also tends to be personal in Korea, the extent of subcontracting there is much less and is concerned with relatively standardized and predictable components, so that more formal and standard procedures for ensuring compliance can be relied upon. Personal networks are also important in Japan, more so than in Western countries, but there seems to be greater willingness to rely on collective commitments and organizational representatives. Thus market connections are more between organizations as collective entities in Japan, whereas they tend to be highly personal in Taiwan and Hong Kong.

An important co-ordinating agent of production chains in Japan is the general trading company or sogo shosha (Yoshino and Lifson, 1986: 38–47). These large diversified agencies develop reciprocal links between kaisha and co-ordinate market transactions between formally independent enterprises. By acting as purchasing and distributing agencies they reduce the risks and uncertainties facing firms and enable them to specialize in particular activities. The sogo shosha try to develop close relations with particular kaisha in order to provide a wide range of services on a long-term basis. In so maximizing transactions between their closely allied clients they develop high levels of quasi-contractual market organization within vertical lines of business in particular sectors.

The sogo shosha are most influential in capital-intensive heavy industry where economies of scale in handling raw materials and co-ordinating flows of intermediate products are considerable (Yoshino and Lifson, 1986: 49). In consumer industries where products are more complex, vertical integration in Japan is achieved more through 'relational contracting' between mass assemblers and secondary and tertiary subcontractors (Dore, 1986: 77). Long-term commitments, reciprocal shareholdings and extensive sharing of technical information and skills between suppliers and customers integrate production processes in these industries where the dominant co-ordinating role is fulfilled by the final assembling firm, which also controls distribution and marketing channels directly. Overall, the level of vertical co-ordination through quasi-contractual, long-term relationships is clearly high in both capital-intensive and consumer durable industries in Japan.

A similar reliance on trading houses and purchasing agents for managing input and output markets is found among CFBs, but connections are less focused on long-term commitments to particular businesses than in Japan. While mutual support based on personal ties between CFB owners is greater than in Korea, it is less characteristic a feature of intra-industry relations than in Japanese keiretsu, and information sharing and joint planning are less evident. Mutual dependence between specialized CFBs in the same industry is managed more through networks of personal connections and reliance on the reputations of a number of different subcontractors and customers than through developing stable and long-term commitments with particular firms.

Horizontal relations between business sectors are managed primarily within authority hierarchies in Korean chaebol, as well as by state agencies, and competition between them is strong. There is little evidence of long-term inter-market co-ordination of plans and activities between chaebol. In contrast, the significance of horizontally connected business groups is considerable in Japan, with high levels of co-ordination being achieved through regular meetings between company presidents, common shareholdings and trading agreements in intermediate products (Orru et al., 1989). Future plans and opportunities in new sectors are also co-ordinated by banks and the sogo shosha in the six largest inter-market groups. Thus horizontal co-ordination across sectors by quasi-contractual, long-term reciprocal connections is high in Japan.

Networks of alliances also characterize inter-sector relations between CFBs, but these tend to be more personal and opportunistic. Each substantial family business may develop connections with a number of partners in a variety of fields but these are often specific to particular opportunities and activities. As a result, horizontal co-ordination across sectors in Taiwan and Hong Kong is less systematic and less institutionalized through large, stable business groups than in Japan. The degree of longevity, particularity and scope of business ties between firms in different industries is lower.

These differences in market organization can be summarized under two broad headings: first, the degree to which inter-firm relations in general are organized around long-term, reciprocal and diffuse commitments to particular partners; and, second, the primary means by which such relations develop and are institutionalized. The first refers to the overall level of market organization in the business system, both vertical and horizontal, where market organization is seen as varying between 'pure' market contracting for standardized commodities between anonymous traders and the highly particular, long-term, diffuse and reciprocal connections found between many Japanese kaisha. While this can be further decomposed into sub-dimensions dealing with particular kinds of markets and transactions, this broad summary dimension clearly distinguishes between the Japanese, Korean and Chinese business systems discussed here.

The second broad heading deals with the extent to which these connections are dependent on personal ties and obligations or more general and collective links. Again, the nature of the institutionalized means of co-ordinating firms' activities can be further specified, but for comparing East Asian business systems the general contrast between highly personal alliances and those based on more collective, organizational connections will suffice. In the Korean case, links between chaebol, subcontractors and customers tend to be short term and hierarchical rather than reciprocal. Where, however, inter-firm alliances do develop they are based on personal and particularistic connections.

Systems of Authoritative Co-ordination and Control

The internal systems of authoritative co-ordination and control of economic activities in East Asian business systems vary on a wide range of characteristics, and it is useful to distinguish between two broad aspects. First, employment practices and conditions cover recruitment, training and reward systems as well as the organization of labour markets and structure of labour representation. The major variations are summarized in Table 3.3. Second, the authority structure and control system covers the organization of the managerial hierarchy, authority relations and co-ordination and control procedures.

Employment and Personnel Practices

Labour market segmentation is high in all three systems, as we have seen, but wage and other differentials between men and women, manual and non-manual, and 'temporary' and 'core' workers seem greater in Korea than in the other systems. Similarly, the extent to which employers make long-term commitments to a substantial number of manual and non-manual employees in the Korean chaebol seems less than in the CFBs, which in turn have fewer core workers than the large Japanese kaisha. Correlatively, the willingness of the chaebol to hire experienced workers for jobs at all levels of the hierarchy from outside is greater than in the CFBs and kaisha, and mobility between enterprises is correspondingly greater in Korea.

Among the 'permanent' or core workforce, seniority-based reward systems and promotion practices are found in all three systems but most systematically in the kaisha. In both the chaebol and the CFB a considerable part of the employees' wages is subject to managerial discretion, and promotion is linked to personal loyalty and connections as well as seniority and performance. In general, it seems that reward systems are more institutionalized and systematic in the Japanese kaisha. Similarly, the overall level of trust and dependence on both managerial and non-managerial employees is greater in the kaisha than in the chaebol and CFB.

Table 3.3   *Employment and personnel practices in East Asia*

	Kaisha	Chaebol	CFB
Wage differentials by gender and education	Considerable	High	Considerable
Long-term commitments to core manual workers	High	Limited	Medium
External recruitment of senior managers	No	Yes	Rarely
Importance of seniority-based rewards for core workers	High	Considerable	Considerable
Formalization of reward system	High	Medium	Low
Formalization of recruitment procedures	High	Considerable for white-collar staff	Low
Manual worker training	Frequent	Ad hoc	Ad hoc
Importance and integration of trade unions	High	Low	Low

This high level of trust and dependence upon core employees is linked to considerable investment in recruitment procedures and training. The Japanese kaisha select the most highly qualified employees from the public education system and then use further formal selection procedures before hiring them. The chaebol also rely upon the verdicts of the education system, at least for non-manual workers, but additionally use personal recommendations and contacts. Regional origins are also a common basis of recruitment. In the CFB, personal connections are critical for recruiting reliable and trustworthy employees. While formal educational qualifications are important for white-collar jobs, personal links are at least as important as formal criteria. Thus the importance of formal procedures and standards in selecting employees is greatest in the kaisha and least in the CFB.

The long-term commitment to core employees made by the kaisha is reflected in the frequent retraining they are given and in the development of multiple skills over their working lifetime. Although the chaebol and CFB often provide on-the-job training as well, it is more ad hoc and limited to immediate needs in most cases, especially in the smaller Chinese family businesses. In general the kaisha seem to invest in more systematic training and for a longer period. This training enhances worker flexibility and ability to implement technological changes quickly and effectively.

Finally, the degree of incorporation of trade unions into the management system clearly varies considerably. Enterprise unions in Japan are encouraged by most large firms and often identify with corporate growth goals. Frequently their officers come from junior managerial posts and move on to higher positions in the hierarchy. In contrast, most chaebol and CFBs are antagonistic to unions and seek the support of the state in suppressing their development and rejecting their demands. Recent attempts have been made by the Korean state to encourage enterprise unions in the Japanese manner, but these have not developed very widely and appear to be much more antagonistic to employers than Japanese ones have been since the 1950s.

These differences can be summarized on two broad dimensions. First, the degree of employer commitment to employees and dependence upon the skills and co-operation of core workers is clearly greatest in the Japanese kaisha and much more limited in the CFB and chaebol. This is manifested in long-term employment for men, seniority-based reward systems and extensive training. This commitment is mutual since employees are highly dependent on the particular employer they join because mobility for those over 25 years old is difficult and usually results in a drop in wages; additionally, most skills are firm specific. There is some commitment to highly skilled workers in short supply in the CFB and chaebol but it is much less institutionalized and systematic and more dependent on personal discretion.

Second, the degree of formalization and systemization of personnel policies and practices incorporates recruitment, training, reward and promotion procedures. Again, this is much greater in the kaisha than in the chaebol and CFB, although many chaebol do use formal selection procedures and have formal reward systems as well as relying extensively on personal discretion and recommendation. The most personal and informal personnel practices are found in the CFB.

Authority Structures and Control Systems
The major differences in authority structures and control systems between the kaisha, chaebol and CFB are listed in Table 3.4. Considering first the importance of personal authority relations, it is clear that, although the significance of personal ties in superior–subordinate relations is greater in all three East Asian systems than in many Western countries, they are considerably greater in the chaebol and CFB than in the kaisha. In particular, the importance of the personal authority of the owner/entrepreneur is high in the CFB and the chaebol, whereas the president's authority in the kaisha is much more positional and organizational. Similarly, vertical cliques and factions based on personal loyalty to senior managers are significant phenomena in all three business systems

Table 3.4 *Authority and control systems in East Asia*

	Kaisha	Chaebol	CFB
Importance of personal authority of owners	Low	High	High
Reliance on family top managers	Low	High	High
Centralization of decision making	Medium	High	High
Delegation to middle management	High	Some delegation of operational decisions	Low
Many middle managers	Yes	No	No
Reliance on formal co-ordination and control procedures	High	Medium	Low
Work group task autonomy	High	Low	Limited
Managerial involvement in work group	High	Low	Low
Importance of group morale	High	Low	Low
Omniscience of managers	Low	High	High
Managerial style	Facilitative	Authoritarian	Paternalistic

but are especially so in the chaebol and CFB, despite formal denigration of them.

This emphasis on personal authority relations is linked to top management selection and centralization. The importance of personal loyalty and obligations to the owner and his family in selecting top managers is very high in the chaebol and CFB but low in the kaisha. However, the chaebol are much more willing to recruit externally to senior management roles than are the other two types of firms, especially where personal loyalty is assured and personal contacts with state elites are involved. The importance of personal control is reflected in the centralization of decision making, which here refers to influence and initiating power rather than to formal approval. Thus it is relatively less marked in the kaisha than in the chaebol and CFB where the owner typically takes all strategic and major personnel decisions.

There are, however, important differences between the latter enterprise types in respect of the role of middle management. At least in heavy capital-intensive industry there is some delegation of authority for more operational decisions to middle managers in the Korean chaebol, whereas in general in the CFB middle managers are frequently bypassed and the formal authority hierarchy is much less important in terms of information flow and decision making than in the chaebol and kaisha. As Silin (1976: 80–5) suggests, managerial authority is more dyadic between the individual and the boss than mediated through vertical ranks of managers in the CFB. Middle management is most important in the kaisha, where it can initiate proposals and plays a major role in co-ordinating activities. Relatedly, the kaisha are distinguished by having relatively tall managerial hierarchies and a considerable number of 'indirect' employees. In contrast, the chaebol and CFBs have relatively few vertical ranks and concentrate their personnel on direct workflow activities.

The significance of personal authority relations in the chaebol and CFB also means that they usually rely less on formal procedures and systems to co-ordinate and control activities than the kaisha, although the chaebol do have formal reporting systems. Instead, direct supervision of work and personal reporting relations are more important forms of control, and the formal information system is often ignored and bypassed, particularly in the CFB. Relatedly, worker autonomy in task performance seems lowest in the chaebol, with some limited discretion allowed to skilled workers in the kaisha and, to a lesser extent, in the CFB. Overall, work group autonomy in how tasks are carried out seems greatest in the kaisha, where section chiefs have considerable latitude in how they organize and direct work and the group as a whole is responsible for efficient performance. A limited amount of supervisory discretion over work organization also exists in some Chinese family businesses in a few industries such as machine tools (Amsden, 1985a), subject to direct intervention by top management.

The importance of the work group in task performance and development of loyalty in Japan is reflected in the crucial role its management plays in assessing managerial performance. Managers in the kaisha are expected to maintain high levels of group morale as well as effective task performance. Close personal relations with employees which cover a range of task and non-task aspects are common, and supervisory authority is not usually taken to imply technical superiority in all aspects of the work being undertaken. A major component of the managerial role in the kaisha is to facilitate group performance rather than to direct work as an external supervisor. Thus managers are expected to work with group members and develop their collective capacities and skills.

In contrast, the dominant managerial style in the Korean chaebol is much more authoritarian (Liebenberg, 1982). Supervision here is much more directive and remote from group activities than in the kaisha and concentrates on efficient task performance in the prescribed way. Managers are presumed to be knowledgeable and superior to workers in all aspects of their work. Little group initiative seems to be expected, and the dominant impression is of military-style management, although Amsden (1989: 213) claims that capital-intensive firms such as the Pohang Iron and Steel Corporation do rely on workers' skills and knowledge to some extent and therefore permit more task autonomy. Rewards are firmly based on performance, though, and group morale receives little emphasis in evaluating managerial success.

The dominant managerial style in the CFB is paternalistic, at least for the skilled workers. Supervisors are expected to be benevolent and take an interest in workers' concerns but remain more distant and remote from employees than in Japanese kaisha. Thus, while the scope of authority relations is relatively broad and covers non-task aspects, managers do not develop close personal relationships with members of work groups and are not expected to maintain high group morale as a key aspect of the managerial role. Rather, concern for employees' welfare is more a matter of personal choice and demonstration of moral worth. Superiors are also supposed to be more knowledgeable and competent about tasks and procedures than their subordinates and not to display ignorance or admit difficulties. At the top, of course, the owner is expected to demonstrate his moral superiority through business success and be clearly superior to all employees in his knowledge of the world and ability to control it. Thus, in comparison with managers in the kaisha, those in the CFBs are expected to be omnicompetent, remote and morally superior.

In considering how these differences can be summarized under a few broad headings, it seems clear than many aspects of the authority and control system in East Asian business systems stem from the strong need for personal control and emphasis on personal authority relations in the CFB and the chaebol. This encourages high levels of centralization, limited delegation to middle managers and limited formalization of co-ordination and control procedures. It is also related to the importance of personal cliques and factions in organizing vertical loyalties in those business systems and their preference for family members and others with similar personal ties in key management positions. This feature can be described as the degree of reliance on personal authority and control.

This emphasis on personal control is attenuated in the leading chaebol involved in heavy industry, where middle managers have some discretion over operating matters and formal control procedures are more important in co-ordinating activities and evaluating performance than in the CFB. It is useful, then, to

Table 3.5   *Configurations of hierarchy–market relations in East Asia*

	Kaisha	Chaebol	CFB
Economic actors			
Owner control	Low	High	High
Homogeneity of expertise and similarity of activities	High	Low	High in firms, medium in families
Risk sharing through mutual dependence	High	Low	Low outside personal commitments
Market organization			
Degree of particularism and long-term commitment between firms	High	Low	Low except for family-like partnerships
Reliance on personal networks	Low	Limited	High
Employment and personnel practices			
Employer commitment to, and dependence on, core employees	High	Low	Limited
Institutionalization of procedures	High	Limited to white-collar staff	Low
Authority and control systems			
Importance of personal authority and control in hierarchy	Limited	High	High
Delegation to middle management	Considerable	Limited to operational decisions	Low
Managerial role	Supportive	Directive	Patriarchal

distinguish between these authority structures in terms of the extent of delegation of operational control to middle managers and the willingness of owners to rely on financial information systems in evaluating performance. Finally, there are clear and important differences in how managers are expected to control and direct work groups in the three systems. These can be summarized in terms of dominant conceptions of the managerial role. In the kaisha this is essentially supportive; in the chaebol it is seen more as directive; while the CFB institutionalizes an essentially patri-archal view. These summary dimensions for contrasting the three East Asian business systems are listed in Table 3.5, and their interrelatedness and implications for more general analyses of hier-archy–market relations will now be discussed.

Configurations of Hierarchy–Market Relations in East Asia

Comparing the major differences between the Japanese kaisha, Korean chaebol and Chinese family business, it is clear that many are interconnected and that each combination of features consti-tutes a fairly coherent configuration of hierarchy–market relations that is effective in its particular institutional environment. For example, the specialized kaisha focuses on a limited range of similar activities and relies on extensive quasi-contractual links with suppliers for complementary but dissimilar goods and services. By specializing in a particular sector, managerial co-ordination costs are reduced and managers' and workers' skills and experiences are quite homogeneous. Within the core workforce, mutual commit-ment, trust and dependence are high, so that flexibility and skill improvement are both considerable. Thus the firm is a relatively homogeneous authority system competing on the basis of a con-stantly improving specialized capability and sharing risks with highly interdependent employees, suppliers and customers as well as with members of diversified business groups, including financial institutions. Strategic choices, competitive competences and growth patterns are interconnected with personnel policies, authority struc-tures and inter-firm networks of interdependence and obligation to form a highly successful configuration of hierarchy–market rela-tions.

Similarly, the combination of strong personal owner control in the chaebol with strong state support for diversification into heavy industry and control over market structures, as well as over labour organizations, has produced highly centralized authority structures and highly segmented labour markets with limited employer com-mitment to the workforce. Heterogeneous activities and skills are co-ordinated by a mixture of financial controls and personal authority with little work group autonomy or discretion. Risks are primarily shared with the state, so that managing political and bureaucratic connections is a crucial function of top management in the chaebol, and this in turn further encourages centralization.

The strong emphasis on personal ownership and control in the Chinese family business similarly leads to centralized decision making, but risks are here managed by limiting commitments to core workers and levels of capital investment. Flexibility is the key concern in the CFB, and so firms are highly specialized, with families sometimes diversifying through personal alliances to seize new opportunities and limit dependence on particular industries. Authority relations are of course highly personal in the CFB, and formal control systems and procedures are unimportant. Networks of personal connections between individual owners are crucial for survival and reinforce the tendency to centralize key decision making. Limited trust and family priorities restrict critical management roles to family members, or to those with comparable personal ties of loyalty and commitment, thus reinforcing the tendency of managers to leave and start up their own businesses.

This interrelatedness of many features of these three configurations suggests that they are mutually necessary in the sense that major differences in some features would so change the nature of the business system that it would cease to be effective in that context. Thus, the pursuit of specialized capabilities and homogeneous management in capital-intensive industries in Japan would be difficult without both risk sharing and the development of long-term commitments with business partners as well as highly selective recruitment strategies. Similarly, the flexibility and responsiveness of the CFB are enhanced by centralized decision making and the informality of personal networks and alliances between business owners. While other combinations of these features clearly are feasible, as is shown by many Western business systems, the three configurations described here are formed by particular features that fit together to produce effective systems in their institutional environments.

This can be seen by considering the consequences of radically changing certain features. For instance, the Japanese kaisha could not function in the same way if it began to diversify widely and manage a wide variety of skills and activities through authority hierarchies. Obviously managerial homogeneity would be reduced, common goals and performance criteria would become less straightforward and readily identified, and commitments to particular business partners and sectors would also be reduced. Employer–employee trust would probably decline, and enterprise unions become less easy to incorporate as they began to reflect different interests. In other words, the whole system of risk management and mutual dependence would alter. Given the interdependence of this system with key social institutions, as I shall suggest later, such large-scale changes seem unlikely.

Similarly, none of these three systems could be effective if tasks and roles were allocated to individuals on the basis of fixed, externally certified skills which determined access to particular jobs and standardized work procedures. Flexibility and internal mobility of workers and managers are key features of East Asian business systems, although the precise way they are achieved and practised does, of course, vary. Equally, it seems likely that some labour market segmentation may be an important component of their effectiveness, especially in industries where labour costs are a crucial element of competitiveness. The restriction of long-term commitments to a particular group of highly selected workers in the Japanese kaisha is clearly a major feature of its ability to reduce risks and one which has been maintained by Japanese firms in Europe (Oliver and Wilkinson, 1988: 62–3). Thus, market-based wage systems and highly credentialized and specialized skill development systems are incompatible with these configurations of hierarchy–market relations.

These points emphasize the systemic nature of the connections between the economic actors, market organization and authority systems and suggest that only certain combinations of these features are likely to be effective. As discussed in Chapter 1, it is particularly important to note how 'internal' features of the authority system and labour management practices are connected to competitive strategies and market organization. The three East Asian business systems discussed here manifest different degrees of centralization, formalization and employer–employee commitment which are clearly related to variations in how risk is managed and shared through quasi-contractual market relationships and strategic preferences. Equally, high levels of commitment to particular industries and capabilities are more likely to be effective when organizational flexibility and skill development are at high levels and achieved through mutual dependence and trust between employers and employees.

Considering the interrelationships between market organization, firm type and authority structure at a very general level, the East Asian configurations highlight the contrast between business systems dominated by autarkic, self-sufficient economic actors which deal with each other through largely anonymous, impersonal and remote market transactions and those where economic actors are more specialized and are much more dependent on quasi-contractual particularistic connections with each other. This contrast emphasizes the connection between the degree and type of market organization and the nature of the firm as a particular kind of economic actor in different business systems. Specialization and homogeneity of managerial experience within authority structures require some minimal level of market organization and means of ensuring co-operation and trust between business partners.

The importance of personal and inter-organizational networks of alliances and obligations in East Asian business systems is also related to strategic choices and patterns of firm development. Where commitments to particular business partners are relatively diffuse, mutual and sustained, major discontinuous shifts in activities and goals are clearly more difficult to develop than in business systems where firms are more autonomous as decision-making units. Thus radical diversification and change in core activities are less frequent in Japan and the CFB than in Korea and Anglo-Saxon economies, especially where such changes imply divestment and disposal of previously central activities. Instead, new projects are more likely to develop from current skills and capabilities, and so build on and extend existing networks, or else are established as separate ventures with little formal connection to current authority structures. The Chinese family business, for instance, usually diversifies by setting up new companies and developing new partnerships which only have financial and personal connections to current ones when it does move into new fields, rather than reorganizing existing structures and alliances.

This preference for incremental change within authority hierarchies embedded in networks of mutual obligation is, of course, reinforced by high levels of homogeneity of managerial experience and expertise in specialized firms. Where the bulk of activities and capabilities co-ordinated by managerial hierarchies are focused on a single sector, and often on particular phases of the production or transformation process within that sector, firms will not find it easy to co-ordinate and direct radically different activities, and their dominant coalitions will be reluctant to consider seriously such major changes to firms' identities which would devalue their own competences and experiences. Additionally, where high levels of mutual dependence with a multi-skilled and flexible core workforce have been developed, radical changes in a firm's activities which could threaten commitment are unlikely to occur.

These configurations of characteristics of East Asian business systems are closely linked to particular features of the societies in which they developed and became successfully established. The nature of these features and of their consequences for business systems will now be explored. In the next chapter, I shall discuss the key characteristics of pre-industrial Japan, Korea and China which have had significant influences on the pattern of industrialization in those countries and which continue to affect the institutional environment of firms and economic activities. Subsequently, I shall outline the major features of industrialization processes and state–business relations in the business systems of Japan, South Korea, Taiwan and Hong Kong, which continue to structure their key characteristics.

4
Institutional Influences on East Asian Business Systems I: Pre-Industrial Japan, Korea and China

I suggested in Chapter 1 that effective business structures and practices largely reflected the institutional context in which they developed and are highly interdependent with currently dominant social institutions. Thus, where these institutions are highly integrated within, and sharply distinct between, different societies, dominant ways of organizing and controlling economic activities in those societies will also differ significantly. This is perhaps most obvious in the case of authority relations within firms, which depend on more general patterns of legitimate domination in the wider society, but it also applies to the nature of obligation and trust relations within and between firms and the division of labour in authority hierarchies. Particular ways of structuring work within firms and relations between them – and so the nature of firms as economic actors – are effective only in particular institutional contexts in this view, so that, for instance, reliance on Anglo-Saxon formal planning and control systems for co-ordinating work is unlikely to be very successful in Chinese communities. The establishment and continued effectiveness of different kinds of business systems, then, are explicable in terms of their interdependence with dominant social institutions, including established beliefs and values; and many of their major differentiating characteristics are derived from the process of industrialization and the institutions that developed then.

The East Asian business systems being analysed here have developed remarkably quickly in societies that were homogeneous and stable for a considerable period before industrialization. Although Japan, South Korea and Taiwan have all experienced major discontinuities since 1945 as a result of war and occupation, the speed of their industrialization and the continuity of many primary institutions, such as the family and kinship relationships, mean that certain features of pre-industrial Japan, Korea and China have had a major impact on the sorts of business systems that have developed. Indeed the structure and operation of many key social institutions in the past 40 or so years cannot be adequately understood without considering, for instance, the political systems of these pre-industrial societies, as Jacobs (1985) and Pye (1985) among others have emphasized (cf. Morishima, 1982). Both the major similarities and the differences between the three business systems discussed in Chapters 2 and 3 are the result of particular characteristics of both pre-industrial and industrializing East Asian societies, just as the development of the Anglo-Saxon corporation reflects both the current political and financial systems in which it operates and the particular path of industrialization followed by Britain, which developed a major financial system around foreign trade before the first Industrial Revolution (cf. Ingham, 1984). The significance of primary institutions in pre-industrial Japan, Korea and China is even more marked because of the destruction or discrediting of particular secondary institutions through military defeat and colonialism, as Pye (1985: 324–5) has pointed out.

In considering how the major differences between these societies have affected forms of business organizations there are certain obvious contrasts between East Asian business systems to bear in mind. For instance, the development of highly integrated vertical hierarchies seems much more marked in Japan than elsewhere in East Asia, and in general levels of trust, mutual commitment and interdependence are greater there. Equally, the highly personal nature of business relationships in Chinese cultures and the associated difficulty in establishing long-term managerial hierarchies to control economic activities require analysis. The reluctance of Korean and Chinese business owners to delegate authority and develop trust relations with non-kin is another major difference between the three business systems which can be explained by differences in pre-industrial societies as well as by their contemporary institutional environments, as can their limited involvement in long-term organizational alliances and networks such as those established in Japan. A further major contrast between the three business systems which is related to particular features of pre-industrial Japan, Korea and China concerns the nature of managerial authority and appropriate ways of exercising it. As discussed in the previous chapters, Japanese managers are more closely involved in the work of the groups they are responsible for and are not expected to be technically superior in all aspects of the work undertaken.

These differences focus attention on the organization of authority and subordination relations in different societies, the ways in which trust and co-operation between particular individuals and groups are developed and maintained, and the degree of institutional differentiation and integration which has developed in these industrializing societies. These characteristics in turn are related to the political systems of pre-industrial Japan, Korea and

China, especially the degree of pluralism of political authority and institutions, and the dominant way in which the elite legitimized their position and claimed obedience. They also reflect differences in the organization of authority relations within villages and families as well as patterns of co-operation between families in agricultural and related activities.

I will now outline the major differences between these pre-industrial societies in these respects and then consider their consequences for the major social institutions which impinged upon the process of industrialization in East Asia and the development of effective forms of business organization in different countries. I will discuss initially the major features of their political systems, then the significant differences in the development of their economic systems, the basis on which ruling elites claimed legitimacy and, finally, the organization of village communities, especially their authority structures.

Pre-Industrial Political Systems in East Asia

The common characterization of Tokugawa Japan as 'feudal' (for example, Baechler, 1988) highlights one of the major ways in which pre-industrial Japan differed from Korea and China. To a considerable extent Japan was governed by a class of military aristocrats who did not owe their status and wealth to the grace and favour of the Emperor or Shogun, whereas the central power in Korea and China controlled landowners through state officials and made their rank dependent on access to state offices. However, Japanese feudalism during the Tokugawa period was more centralized than some of its European counterparts, and there were some significant differences between the Korean and Chinese Confucian dynasties. Initially I shall contrast the limited political decentralization and associated features of Japan with the highly centralized political structures of Korea and China and then consider the significant differences between the latter two countries.

After the Taika reform period failed to replicate the Confucian patrimonial political system, and the subsequent relegation of the Emperor to a figurehead role who reigned but did not rule, a distinctive form of Japanese feudalism developed in which the de facto central power was determined by competitive military struggles between clans (Morishima, 1982; Pye, 1985). Formal obeisance to the central authority of the Emperor remained important, but effective political and economic power was, in practice, decentralized to the warring clans and, at times, to religious institutions such as Buddhist monasteries (Jacobs, 1958; 81–3), which controlled land and retainers. Although the establishment of the Tokugawa Shogunate at the beginning of the seventeenth century centralized political authority at Edo (Tokyo) and ensured peace for 250 years, the government did not make the local lords, or *daimyo*, subservient to state officials but instead demanded their personal homage to the Shogun as independent aristocrats and granted them autonomous fiefs on this basis. By requiring the daimyo to reside in Edo every other year, and their replacement by their family as hostages for their continued obeisance when they returned to their fief or *han*, the Shogun ensured his central control over the clans but did not make their status and wealth dependent on holding state offices. The oath of loyalty reflected the imbalance of power between fellow aristocrats, not subservience to the will of the divine Emperor (Craig, 1986).

This limited centralization of political power under the Shogunate is reflected in the development of local administrations in the fiefs run by *samurai* who now had no other obvious function (cf. Smith, 1967). These local 'bureaucracies' often pursued divergent policies, especially in the western provinces which were distant from the capital, and so both facilitated and exemplified administrative pluralism (Hirschmeier and Yui, 1981: 12–17; Mutel, 1988). Thus, although the daimyo administered their estates on behalf of the Shogun, and were responsible for collecting rice taxes from the peasants as loyal vassals of the Shogun, they were able to pursue a variety of political experiments and retain considerable autonomy (Jansen and Rozman, 1986). Even when the Tokugawa government banned foreign commerce in 1636, for instance, some daimyo continued to engage in widespread smuggling and trade and thereby increased their wealth substantially (Jacobs, 1958: 37–8). This administrative decentralization is exemplified by the large number (260) of local government units, each with its own capital, administrative system, army and taxation system. In Craig's words (1986: 63): 'Bakufu [central government] officials administered the controls over the domains but did not administer the domains themselves. Yet, within a domain . . . there was a bureaucracy.'

Aristocratic autonomy in Japan was reinforced and reproduced by the inheritance system. Aristocratic status was itself inherited rather than bestowed by the Shogun, and control over the feudal estates was likewise inherited by the eldest son. The norm of primogeniture resulted in large fiefs being controlled by the same family over generations and remaining intact rather than being broken down into equal parts for distribution to all the sons (Smith, 1967). Consequently, local centres of authority remained relatively autonomous and continuous over two centuries. Central power was therefore limited by the continued existence of independent noble families controlling large concentrations of resources and the need to maintain a balance between them (Baechler, 1988).

In contrast, both China and Korea were dominated by central 'bureaucratic' dynasties of Emperors and Kings who both reigned and ruled. These centralized regimes institutionalized the practice of demoting noble families by one rank each generation and were able in China to demote them to the rank of commoner at any time (Jacobs, 1958: 104; 1985: 31). The ownership of large landed estates in these societies, especially in China, was much more a consequence of holding central state offices than of family position. Access to such posts depended, of course, upon successes in literary examinations which could not be guaranteed by wealthy family membership on its own. This encouraged a circulation of elite members at the national level. While some lineages were able to retain local power and status over generations in Ming and Ch'ing China, they could not ensure continued access to posts in the bureaucratic elite and the wealth that usually accompanied them (Beattie, 1979: 126–31). The maintenance and independence of large landed estates were much more difficult and uncertain in China and Korea, and more dependent on state benevolence, than in Tokugawa Japan.

As well as governmental posts circulating among elite groups in China and Korea, incumbents also circulated geographically. To prevent provincial magistrates and governors from forming local alliances with landowners and establishing local concentrations of power which could threaten the central power, officials were rotated at frequent intervals and rarely served in their native province (Palais, 1975: 55–6). Thus, the central government in these countries did not integrate its authority with local leaders into a vertical hierarchy based on personal allegiances but rather existed as a separate elite culture whose primary aim was to prevent local autonomy developing and challenging its power (Hall, 1988).

The principle of equal male inheritance in China and, to a lesser extent, Korea reinforced centralized control by breaking up large concentrations of land over generations and so making the gentry and nobility more dependent on state offices to repair the family fortunes. As Moore (1966: 170) puts it: 'In the absence of primogeniture, a wealthy family might find itself reduced to penury in a few generations through equal division at inheritance. The main way to prevent this misfortune was to send someone with academic aptitudes into the bureaucracy.' This dependence on the central state for status and wealth limited the development of local political authorities and administrations and focused elite energies on the central 'bureaucracy'. Although countervailing pressures did sometimes result in local centres of power developing in China (Beattie, 1979), usually in periods of disunity and conflict at the centre, these typically succumbed to the next dynasty as the mandarinate reasserted its central authority (Hall, 1988). In Korea under the Confucian Yi dynasty, which ruled from 1392 to 1910, the pressures to obtain central state offices generated what Henderson (1968: 5–8) terms a political vortex that sucked all energies and conflicts towards the central regime (cf. Palais, 1975: 14–16).

An important feature of these centralized, pseudo-bureaucratic Korean and Chinese societies was the combination of influence, power and insecurity among the members of the mandarin elite. Because the allocation of state offices was controlled by the ruler and his closest advisers, who were concerned to prevent any substantial decentralization of power to individual office holders and their families, and because these offices were the dominant means of acquiring high prestige and wealth, they were frequently reallocated and transferred between mandarins as the result of bureaucratic intrigue and factional disputes. Thus, officials were liable to be transferred and/or removed from office altogether at very short notice, which obviously prevented their organizing a stable authority system and encouraged a concentration on short-term gains. This insecurity was especially strong in Korea, where senior officials were sometimes changed daily towards the end of the Yi dynasty. Even in the more stable fifteenth and sixteenth centuries the Chief Censor was changed every few months, and many officials held over 100 or more posts during official careers of 30 or so years, interspersed with retirements, periods of mourning and similar interruptions (Henderson, 1968: 237–8).

This contrast between Japanese feudalism and Confucian centralism affected relations between the peasantry and political elites. In Tokugawa Japan the village headman constituted the key link integrating the village community with the local, and thence national, political system. They, together with the heads of the five family groups in the villages, were responsible to the local daimyo for tax deliveries and maintaining correct social and moral behaviour (Fukutake, 1967a: 96–7; Hirschmeier and Yui, 1981: 14–15). Because the feudal aristocracy was dependent on these tax deliveries for its own sustenance and wealth, as well as for the payment of samurai stipends, it maintained strong links with local villages and ensured that they remained loyal to them (Jansen and Rozman, 1986).

In contrast, Chinese and Korean villages were less integrated into a vertical hierarchy of authority and loyalty because the gentry and officials were more dependent on the central state and changed more frequently. Their basic interest focused on the payment of taxes as state agents, or of rent, and they were less concerned to establish local personal loyalties which could be maintained over generations. Chinese families owed allegiance to the distant Emperor rather than to local noblemen and developed little loyalty to itinerant magistrates or to landlords whose families rose and fell over generations (Moore, 1966: 165–73). While connections between the aristocracy and peasantry in Japan were relatively personal and familial as well as being stable over generations, those between landlords and peasants in China and Korea were more commercial and impersonal after the fifteenth century (Beattie, 1979: 14–17; Fei, 1946).

These major differences in political pluralism between Tokugawa Japan, on the one hand, and Confucian China and Korea, on the other hand, should not obscure some significant differences between the political systems of pre-industrial China and Korea. In particular, it is important to note that a hereditary aristocracy, the *yangban*, existed in Korea but not in China and that the monarch in Korea was much more constrained by his councillors than in China. The significance of the yangban in Korea was not only that aristocratic status was inherited, but also that it was a necessary condition for taking the literary examinations that controlled access to state offices (Palais, 1975: 6–9). Thus, mobility into the bureaucratic elite was more restricted in Korea than in China. However, this restriction began to weaken in the eighteenth and nineteenth centuries as yangban status became widely available, to the extent of constituting 48.6 per cent of the population by 1858 (Henderson, 1968: 41; Jacobs, 1985: 192–202), although this did not apparently lead to a significant broadening of access to elite bureaucratic posts (Palais, 1975: 8). This growth of the yangban class intensified competition for state positions and also generated intense concern with the relative status of each rank within it. Compared to China, the existence of this hereditary class in Korea, although weakening over the course of the Yi dynasty, helped to limit the power of the central authority in the countryside and also generated an obsession with ancestry (Jacobs, 1985: 28–9, 200).

The importance of the Korean aristocracy relative to the land-lord class in China is also manifested in the continued significance of the council system during the Yi dynasty (Henderson, 1968: 245–52). Yangban-controlled councils, initially led by the censorate and subsequently other bodies, restricted executive actions and prevented the monarch from exercising his powers independently.

Because decisions were supposed to be unanimous this oligarchical rule frequently resulted in paralysis, even when faced with foreign invasions and the collapse of the taxation system. The highly centralized nature of Korean politics in Seoul did not mean that the king ruled autocratically but rather that he had less power and independence of action that the Chinese Emperor to whom he paid tribute. This lack of a powerful executive for much of the dynasty, and increased competition for state offices as the number of yangban grew, encouraged intense factionalism and incessant wrangling about decisions (Palais, 1975: 46–50).

Economic Systems

The greater toleration of local power bases in Tokugawa Japan than in China or Korea was echoed by the greater importance of mercantile wealth and activity in Japan. Despite the common Confucian disdain of commercial activities as unproductive and unworthy in all three societies, private concentrations of economic power developed in pre-industrial Japan to a much greater extent than in the other countries, and merchants acquired some political influence through providing loans to the Shogun and leading daimyo. These loans became more and more important as the expenses required for residence at the Shogun's court in Edo mounted and the yield from the land tax remained the same. By the late eighteenth century both the central authority and feudal lords were so dependent on rich merchants for loans that they could not suppress them, and in some cases the aristocracy also undertook commercial activities despite being formally forbidden to do so (Hirschmeier and Yui, 1981: 14–36). Additionally, many merchants invested their profits in land reclamation, so becoming landowners themselves, and began to blur the formal boundaries between the aristocracy and merchants. As the stipends of the samurai declined in the Tokugawa period, some sold their status to merchants or adopted merchants' sons, thus further weakening the formal distinction between classes. An important point to note here about the role of merchants in Tokugawa Japan is that, although they were officially regarded as inferior to the aristocracy and the peasantry because they performed few useful services, the rigid separation of statuses provided greater autonomy and legitimacy for them, as long as they remained merchants, than did the more overtly fluid societies of Korea and China.

Periodic attempts were made by the Shogunate to control the merchants, and the debts of the aristocrats were sometimes repudiated, but the Tokugawa period as a whole witnessed the growing power of merchants within the basically feudal authority system. In contrast to Western Europe, though, they were essentially subservient to this system and did not develop into an independent capitalist class. Their ethical system was derived from the dominant state ideology rather than being separate from it and emphasized honesty and trust to demonstrate their worthy status and socially acceptable role. They did form powerful guilds, which developed intricate systems of inter-urban, inter-family connections and led to the establishment of an effective banking system and a mechanism for trading rice futures as early as the eighteenth century; but these guilds were state regulated and controlled (Hirschmeier and Yui, 1981: 31–41; Jacobs, 1958: 70–4). Thus by the time of the Meiji restoration many concentrations of private, family-controlled economic power, such as the Mitsui retailing and banking enterprise, had become established and dominated the economic system, but these had grown up within the feudal structures rather than separately from them.

In contrast, the Confucian officials of China and Korea resolutely opposed the development of large concentrations of private wealth through strong central control of markets and towns (Jacobs, 1958: 30–2). During the Han dynasty the Chinese rulers established their ethical right to prevent the accumulation of monetary power, except under their control and sponsorship. As a result, any large-scale private accumulation of property, unless it was for religious purposes or public relief measures, was automatically subject to state confiscation. As Mann (1987: 20–1) puts it: 'Although petty traders and peddlers escaped the state's careful scrutiny of commercial profit, businessmen of means were squarely targeted by it.' State control over commercial activity was even stronger in Korea, where foreign trade was forbidden in 1644 and specialist traders were despised as pedlars (Henderson, 1968: 51). These pedlars formed a strong organization under the control of censors or inspectors which was used by the state in the nineteenth century as a source of intelligence and to prevent attempts to develop autonomous political organizations. Also, in contrast to the merchants' guilds in Japan, guilds in China and Korea tended to be highly localized associations of craftsmen with little capital which were controlled by state officials and did not develop high levels of organizational autonomy or influence (Jacobs, 1958: 38–40).

Official restriction of private economic activity and wealth concentration in China and Korea was justified in terms of the ruler's obligation to maintain harmony and frugality. Independent economic power was viewed as extravagant, ethically untenable and punishable (Jacobs, 1958: 62). Thus successful merchants were regarded as potential threats to the official elite by manifesting an alternative basis of prestige and power to the official examinations and by constituting an independent source of economic power. As such they were legitimately subject to official exactions and expropriations with no legal system to provide redress. The movement of goods between towns, especially along the Grand Canal, was taxed and often subject to arbitrary official interference which usually required bribery to ensure continued passage (Mann, 1987: 39–49). In Godley's terms (1981: 34): 'Relations between officials and merchants were characterized by the near absolute dominance of the former group over the latter. Those engaged in commercial activities paid dearly for the privilege of pursuing their chosen social roles not only in the abstract sense of moral condemnation, but also in kind.' Together with the frequent debasing of the currency and issue of new paper currency which was often non-convertible, the frequent official interventions in mercantile activities and periodic 'squeezing' of profits encouraged a widespread distrust and wariness of public officials and state currencies on the part of merchants, as well as a preference for landownership once wealth had been acquired (Beattie, 1979: 11–12; Hall, 1988; Jacobs, 1958: 66–70). As Redding (1990: 120–7) suggests, this heritage of official hostility to private wealth, which was echoed in some South-East Asian countries where the Chinese began to dominate economic activities (Wu, 1983), generated high levels of defensiveness and a preference for personal connections and trust among Chinese business owners. Even when the Chinese state actively sought expatriate investment for new projects in the 1900s, 'it was still extremely difficult to convince overseas Chinese merchants to invest large sums of money in their homeland . . . the fear of mandarin squeeze remained deeply ingrained' (Godley, 1981: 118). In contrast, Tokugawa merchants had a distinct and recognized, if subservient, status which they accepted, and this encouraged them to demonstrate their social worth by their honesty and probity in business dealings. As a separate estate they developed relations of interdependence with the central government and claimed a legitimate role in contributing to national goals (Hirschmeier and Yui, 1981).

Legitimacy and the Basis of Authority

These differences in political and economic pluralism between pre-industrial Japan, Korean and China were linked to major differences in the ways that domination was justified and the processes by which it was achieved. Whereas Japanese feudalism was organized around the competitive struggle for military domination by clans, Chinese and, later, Korean rulers adopted Confucian ideologies which asserted their superior moral worth and relied on the Confucian mandarinate to legitimate their virtue and hence right to rule. Thus, Japanese leaders claimed authority on the basis of their ability to maintain political and social order through mobilizing military resources and retainers loyal to them, while, on the other hand, Confucian monarchs asserted their moral superiority as attested by the literary elite (Jacobs, 1958: 77–96).

This difference meant that power in pre-industrial Japan was dependent on the active demonstration of military superiority and ability to attract the loyalty of samurai and peasants rather than the passive exemplification of superior virtue (Pye, 1985: 57–8). Feudal lords were able to entice peasants away from Imperial estates during the Taika reform period, for instance, by protecting them against forced labour service for the Imperial authority, and so domination was linked to some notion of reciprocal services, albeit to a lesser extent than in some variants of European feudalism (Jacobs, 1958: 29; Moore, 1966: 233–4). However unequal such reciprocity in relations of subordination was, and remains in modern Japan (Hirschmeier and Yui, 1981: 51), the critical point here is that it existed, and superiors had to maintain the loyalty of subordinates through competitive success.

This emphasis on military success in Japan became less important during the two and a half centuries of peace under the Tokugawa Shogunate. The large numbers of samurai were reduced to the status of dependent retainers with no obvious economic or social function. Removed from direct links with the land, unable to play a military role and prevented from undertaking commercial activities by the rigid Tokugawa separation of classes, some became administrators of the daimyo and *bakufu* (central government) estates and developed into a de facto class of salaried officials (Bendix, 1967). The combination of declining samurai incomes, as the rice stipends received from the daimyo fell in real terms over this period, lack of an apparently useful role and the opportunities for a few to rise through bureaucratic service generated what Smith (1967) terms the ideology of 'merit' during the eighteenth and nineteenth centuries.

According to Smith, the importance of inherited rank and fief income for access to official positions in both central and local government grew after 1700 and became the focus of a number of public attacks and satirical diatribes about the stupidity of the daimyo. As the relevance of earlier military success for daimyo superiority and claims to samurai loyalty faded, and their near monopolization of official posts seemed to depend solely on inherited rank, the ties of personal fealty between daimyo and samurai declined in intensity and became more distant and impersonal. 'Merit', however understood, became the favoured means of allocating positions among many samurai, and competence came to be seen as the crucial feature of superior status and rank rather than inheritance (Pye, 1985: 161; Smith, 1988a: 138–40). The growing importance of competence as the preferred criterion for access to official posts was reflected in the common practice of adopting clever children if existing male heirs were judged incapable. Thus, the Tokugawa peace radically changed the warrior class in Japan from a feudal group directly controlling their own fiefs, and owing personal fealty to their military chiefs, to an urban set of retainers seeking essentially bureaucratic office in the service of the daimyo as titular heads of large estates. Power and domination could no longer be justified by previous military success but rather, for many samurai, became increasingly linked to claims of relatively impersonal competence.

In contrast to this focus on military competitive success, and later development of administrative competence as important justifications for superiority in Japan, the Confucian dynasties in China and Korea formed 'virtuocracies' (Pye, 1985: 22–4) in which rule was justified in terms of the moral superiority of the ruler and his advisers. This superiority was demonstrated by success in competitive literary examinations which controlled access to state office and authority. Once in office, the mandarins did not need to demonstrate their competence or justify their rank by performing useful services for the uneducated, and hence morally unworthy, because they had already shown their virtue by mastering the Confucian classics. By controlling the interpretation of these classics and the examination system, the Confucian elite effectively controlled the definition of virtue, hence authority, and therefore who was virtuous. They were thus able to prevent the establishment of independent power bases and economic centres by mobilizing resources against evil, unworthy and disruptive accumulations of land or goods. Because virtue and moral superiority were the basis of the regime's legitimacy, the political order was a moral order, and any attack on the competence of the ruler and his advisers became an attack on virtue itself. Challenges to the dominant group were then viewed as accusations of moral failure and, as such, subject to severe sanctions.

The importance of virtue and personal moral worth for justifying domination in Confucian China and Korea can be seen in the minimal role of the legal system. As Jacobs (1958: 97) puts it: 'Law was regarded as a poor substitute for virtue and ethics, and reliance on law as a sign of moral delinquency.' Formal law consisted of the elite's conception of what was ethically correct and was enforced through 'rectification' of names, that is, the co-ordination of the reality of the social situation with its legal definition. Since the Confucian elite controlled the definition and enforcement of rectification, they effectively controlled the legal system and prevented the law from being codified. Non-Confucians, such as merchants, could not use the law since they were not qualified scholars and so were morally inferior. Consequently the law never became a relatively autonomous, impersonal system to obtain redress but was rather a means by which the Confucian elite displayed their moral superiority and ensured harmony (Godley, 1981: 35).

In contrast, a system of law courts developed in Tokugawa Japan with a body of relatively clear and consistent rules, statutes and binding precedents. The Tokugawa Shogunate trained judges who were expected to apply the formal criminal and civil codes rather than their own personal interpretation of diffuse principles (Jacobs, 1958: 100). Law remained a primarily administrative system for the ruling elite, but individuals gained some protection in the code of 1721, and the foundations of law as an impersonal tool of individual justice were laid during the Tokugawa period. While not exactly approximating to Western ideas of an independent, impersonal formal legal system for settling disputes and seeking justice against arbitrary and overweening power (Upham, 1987: 67–70), these developments are clearly quite different from Confucian conceptions of law in Korea and China.

A final important aspect of claims to obedience and subordination to the Emperor and his mandarins in China was their basis in the norms of filial piety to fathers as heads of families. Essentially, loyalty to the central political authority was demanded as an extension of family loyalty. This commitment was more a matter of fulfilling role expectations and role performance than deep personal loyalty to individual leaders and so less intense than feudal ties of emotional commitment (Hamilton, 1984). Thus if the leader ceased to manifest his moral superiority by, for instance, failing to prevent natural disasters or behaving in a flagrantly illegitimate manner, loyalty could be transferred to a new ruler (Jacobs, 1958: 77). Commitment of subordinates to collective authority was therefore dutiful and restricted rather than intense and overriding.

The combination of these differences in political centralization, economic pluralism and claims to legitimate domination in pre-industrial Japan, Korea and China affected the degree of vertical integration of commitments and loyalties in each country and the capacity to institutionalize collective commitments to relatively large units of social organizations. Because the feudal landlords in Japan had to mobilize retainers and peasantry in order to compete effectively, they were more involved with local production systems and social structures than were the Korean aristocracy or the Chinese gentry-scholars who concentrated on the rewards of central favour and preferment in essentially patrimonial systems (Jacobs, 1985: 28–35). They thus developed relatively integrated hierarchies of control of the peasantry through their samurai administrators and village headmen (Smith, 1959: 54–64). Finely graded ranks and statuses in Tokugawa Japan constituted a strong, continuous vertical hierarchy linking peasants with the central political authority in a way which did not exist in Korea and China. As Pye (1985: 57) suggests: 'In Japan family loyalty did not end with the boundaries of the family or clan but included loyalty to whatever superior authority the family acknowledged.' In patrimonial Korea and China, on the other hand, the central power did not directly administer the villages but relied upon the local gentry, in informal collaboration with itinerant officials, to ensure control and tax payments. Loyalties were not mediated through personal commitments to local notables but rather were claimed on behalf of a distant and unknown Emperor or King. Thus, 'though higher echelons of Chinese government seldom came into contact with the household, throughout most of Japanese history, manorial, fief or national government impinged bureaucratically – through village headmen and neighbourhood association leaders – on the smallest residential unit' (Pelzel, 1970: 243).

The Organization of Village Communities

The final feature of pre–industrial Japan, Korea and China which has had major consequences for patterns of industrialization, and the development of authority hierarchies controlling economic activities, concerns the organization of authority relations within villages and families and patterns of co-operation between families. Differences between countries in taxation systems, landownership and modes of political control in the countryside were related to differences in village cohesion and solidarity which, in turn, affected inter-family relations and the structure of authority relations within and beyond kinship groups.

The outstanding characteristics of Japanese villages in the

Tokugawa period were their cohesion and relative political autonomy. As T.C. Smith (1959: 60) puts it: 'the most important social characteristics of the Japanese village, its fierce and pervasive sense of solidarity . . . was manifest in the legal personality that history had given the village: its competence to make contracts, borrow money, sue and be sued, and its collective responsibility in matters of taxation and criminal law.' This solidarity was so strong that individual deviance from group norms was severely sanctioned and private affairs were often conducted through public channels such as the village headmen. The greatest sanction was to be excluded from village life, and the mere threat of ostracism prevented overt expressions of deviant views or conflicts of opinion. During industrialization the collective cohesion of some villages was so great that sometimes entire villages moved together to the new urban centres and industrial employment.

This strong desire for collective consensus and conformity obviously helped the village headmen to maintain their authority and obtain acquiescence. However, they had to guide the villages to the desired view on any particular issue rather than impose their own wishes. If they relied on public displays of their authority and made threats, they ran the risk of mobilizing opinion against them, according to Smith (1959: 62–3). The political virtues of tact and discretion were critical to the effective exercise of authority in Tokugawa villages, and decisions had to emerge as the collective wish of the community, or at least the senior members of it, rather than as the individual choice of the leader. Thus whether the headman inherited his role or acquired it through rotation among the leading families, his authority was essentially communal rather than personal or familial. The importance of gaining village support and acting in villagers' interests sometimes led headmen to side with the village in opposition to the lord, even when that resulted in their own death (Smith, 1959: 59–60; Upham, 1987: 68).

An important aspect of village solidarity in Tokugawa Japan, especially in the seventeenth and early eighteenth centuries, was the high level of co-operation between families in carrying out agricultural tasks (Fukutake, 1967a: 82–7). This was particularly important during the spring planting of rice seedlings, which required a single large labour force and the flooding of fields in rotation (Smith, 1959: 50–2). These groups of families shared labour, tools and material for common and individual tasks (Johnson, 1967). While the growing commercialization of agriculture in the later Tokugawa period – coupled with greater intensity of cultivation as technologies improved and an increasing shortage of labour occurred – encouraged tenant farming and led to some decline in importance of these large multi-family co-operative groups, inter-family co-operation remained important for the maintenance of the irrigation system, the allocation of water and the upkeep of roads and other communal property (Smith, 1959: 140–52). Collective interests and activities still overrode familial ones (Fukutake, 1967b).

This cohesion and solidarity were linked to considerable village autonomy during the Tokugawa period. With the removal of the samurai from the land to the castle towns, direct aristocratic control of agriculture and, in particular, of individual taxation ceased. Although some samurai returned to the villages as officials of the feudal han, or fief, they were far too few in number to maintain direct rule, and had no military force to support them. Each district magistrate was responsible for thousands of peasant families with 'no immediate source of support more substantial than his insignia of office' (Smith, 1959: 202). Thus, each village collectively performed a wide variety of administrative functions within the overall political framework of Tokugawa Japan. They maintained their own roads and irrigation works, policed their territories, administered common land, mediated disputes, enforced the lord's laws and their own and allocated the collective village taxes to individual families and households. In Smith's terms (1959: 203), the Tokugawa gave 'the village an extraordinary degree of autonomy after removing the warriors from it' and so created a remarkably stable system of local government depending on the continuing loyalty and discipline of the peasants.

An indication of the limitations of feudal power in dealing with the villages is the inability of the daimyo to increase the tax yield greatly over the Tokugawa period (Smith, 1988b). The land tax was based on the assessed yield which all the land in a village was expected to produce and was levied on the community as a whole. Each year the daimyo sent a document called a *manjo* to every village, recording both the assessed yield and the rate of tax to be paid. For the 11 villages studied by Smith, land ceased to be surveyed for tax purposes around 1700 despite increases in agricultural productivity. Furthermore, the tax rates applied to these yields were also not increased annually, although greater fluctuation did occur than for the anticipated yields themselves. Thus, despite increasing daimyo expenses and samurai concern over decreasing stipends, the real rate of agricultural taxation declined during the Tokugawa period. The rewards for improving agricultural productivity accrued largely to the peasants as a result, as did the results of their involvement in non-agricultural occupations such as rural industries (Smith, 1988a: 78–100). This inability to realize increasing tax revenues in line with agricultural outputs implies considerable limitations on the power of the Japanese aristocracy in dealing with the powerful force of the cohesive villages.

In contrast, pre-industrial Chinese and Korean villages were much less cohesive and more subject to the exactions of land-owners and officials. As Moore (1966: 208) summarizes the situation:

> The Chinese villages . . . evidently lacked cohesiveness . . . There were far fewer [than in Japan or Europe] occasions on which numerous members of the village co-operated in a common task in a way that creates the habits and sentiments of solidarity. It was closer to a residential agglomeration of numerous peasant households than to a live and functioning community . . . the primary unit of economic production (and consumption as well) was the household.

Typically, Chinese villages owned very little property as a unit, in strong contrast to Japanese ones (Fukutake, 1967b). This lack of sustained co-operation and interdependence between households was encouraged by the general surplus of labour in southern China in the eighteenth century which enabled families to use landless members of the same class or migrant workers to help at critical times such as the spring planting of rice seedlings. Thus the need to share collective labour resources was not so strong as in Japan.

Similarly, Chinese households from different kinship groups do not seem to have worked together developing and maintaining irrigation systems and other collective resources. In Fukutake's words (1967b: 21): 'different kinship clans in the same village rarely cooperate and often come into open conflict . . . repair of roads or construction of irrigation systems is hardly a village-wide task'. Even though land was held in strips scattered through the territory of the village, the rarity of animals and intense pressure on the land seem to have prevented collective decision making and sharing of resources (Moore, 1966: 210–11).

This contrast between China and Japan is exemplified by the different results of introducing the *pao-chia* system of mutual surveillance in which ten household heads were made responsible for one another's conduct in the two countries. According to Moore (1966: 206, 211, 260), the system became entangled with the tax collection system in China and thus discredited and ineffective (cf. Baker, 1979: 118). When the Tokugawa rulers revived and extended it in Japan, albeit reduced to five household heads, it proved highly successful in maintaining order and social cohesion as a mutual aid system (Fukutake, 1967a: 96–7). In Korea it seems to have had the same effect as in China, operating much as an instrument of government surveillance and so avoided by the peasants as far as possible (Jacobs, 1985: 40).

In general, the Korean village seems to have been more similar to the Chinese in its relatively low degree of solidarity, although families did work together at rice planting and harvesting times and also helped each other out on other occasions (Brandt, 1971: 154–61; Jacobs, 1985: 37). Similarly, the more fortunate villagers were expected to share food with indigent members of the village community when times were hard (Henderson, 1968: 232). Such inter-family co-operation seems to have been greater in the poorer villages which were not dominated by yangban families (Brandt, 1971: 238); and, overall, while the traditional Korean village appears to have been considerably less cohesive than many Japanese ones, some undoubtedly exhibited greater co-operation than Chinese ones. An important form of communal organization in the pre-colonial Korean village was the *kye*, a volunteer organization of individuals from different families who came together and pooled resources for specific goals which could not be achieved by individuals. These kye have developed into capital-raising groups for small-scale businesses in the twentieth century and remain a persistent and widespread form of Korean communal organization (Jacobs, 1985: 37).

In addition to Chinese and Korean villages being less cohesive than Japanese ones, they were also more susceptible to varying, usually increasing, taxation and rent demands. As a patrimonial system, the central government could vary its share of agricultural output when it wished and could also require additional tribute and forced labour service as required (Jacobs, 1985: 86). Village autonomy in pre-industrial Korea and China was thus low, with leaders typically being appointed by state officials and primarily interested in private power and wealth. As Fukutake (1967b: 22) puts it: 'village administrators [in China] depend on the support of the upper classes and are subject to their influence. Power is monopolized by individuals and bribery is common.' Often, the right to collect taxes and other forms of tribute was sold to agents, who naturally ensured their own services to the state were well rewarded, as did officials who increased their salaries several times over. Furthermore, landlords increasingly rented their land to the peasants on a sharecropping basis which limited the incentives to improve agricultural productivity. Since peasants competed for access to productive land, the landlords had a basic interest in a large population which could be squeezed for higher rents. Thus, competition between households in areas where land was relatively scarce reinforced the fragmented nature of Chinese villages and restricted the ability of peasants to increase their share of agricultural output arising from increased productivity (Moore, 1966: 179–80).

This limited ability to prevent official and landlord exactions increasing in China and Korea is manifested by the failure of the villages to control irrigation schemes and retain substantial proportions of the extra surplus they produced. Many, if not most, of these schemes were carried out by drafted peasant labour under the control of local officials and centrally provided experts at the instigation of landlord families who often seized the opportunity to appropriate communal land (Jacobs, 1985: 90; Moore, 1966: 169). Because rents and taxes usually rose with increased access to water, the peasants were not able to reap the benefits of such schemes and did not develop strong communal forms of organization to develop and maintain them. Thus Chinese and Korean villages were more open to official and landlord control and extractions of the agricultural surplus than Japanese ones, and were less able to organize collectively to resist increased demands and improve productivity.

In summary, the Japanese village developed much stronger feelings of solidarity and cohesion than Chinese and Korean ones, was characterized by greater inter-family co-operation and willingness to accept collective goals rather than focus on purely familial interests and seemed able to resist taxation increases over a long period, thus encouraging agricultural improvements and rural industries on a much larger scale than in China and Korea. Because household loyalties were integrated around the village community in Japan, the headman could represent both the village to the feudal fief, or han, and the daimyo to the village, thus serving to integrate the village authority system with the feudal estates and thence to the Shogunate in Edo. Chinese and Korean villages were less cohesive, and village administrators rarely had the support of villagers. Appointed on a rotating basis for official purposes, they did not usually consider the welfare and improvement of the village to be a crucial part of their role. They did not therefore help to integrate the peasantry with the national political system; and, since landlord–peasant relations were predominately commercial by the nineteenth century, little vertical integration of loyalties developed in China and Korea.

Turning now to consider family authority relations, it is first important to note that families have been, and remain, the primary focus of individual loyalty and identity in East Asian societies, and authority patterns between family members are often taken as the model for those between ruler and ruled (Pye, 1985: 61–75). As a result, variations in these have had significant consequences for the organization of larger-scale collectivities in market economies. In her discussion of the family firm in Taiwan, Greenhalgh (1988a: 227) suggests that

> A close look at traditional Chinese social structure reveals remarkably strong familial institutions that dominated nearly every feature of social, economic, political and cultural life in the centuries before large scale contacts with the West . . . it is inconceivable that this family system did not play a central role in determining the manner in which capitalism was absorbed and the character of the resulting patterns of development.

In all three societies, family authority was, and remains, concentrated in the father, but the scope of his authority and its nature varied significantly between Japan, Korea and China. According to Lucian Pye's (1985: 72–9) reconstruction of the three models of family authority, patriarchal domination is most complete in the Chinese family, less so in the Korean and least in the Japanese. In the latter two societies, authority roles are more separated, with the mother taking responsibility for household matters and the children's upbringing. As a result, children in Korea and Japan become more accustomed to dual authority sources and the more independent existence of maternal authority.

This difference in scope is reinforced by contrasts in how paternal authority is exercised. Chinese and, to a lesser extent, Korean fathers develop a rather distant and aloof attitude to their sons when the 'age of reason' is reached at about six years old (Wolf, 1970), so that emotional ties become less intense. Japanese fathers, however, remain emotionally interdependent with their children and feel more able to express their feelings to them. Similarly, Chinese and Korean patriarchs are supposed to be totally responsible for the fate of the family and rarely show any weakness; ideally they should be omnicompetent and omnipotent. In contrast, Japanese family heads can admit their weaknesses and call upon other members of the family for support and to share burdens (Pelzel, 1970). Thus paternal authority in Japan is less monolithic and remote than it is in Korea and China, although Pye (1985: 67) does suggest that Korean fathers are also supposed to display nurturing and sympathetic attitudes to their children.

A further point about East Asian families concerns relations between brothers. Because inheritance in Chinese families is equal between the sons, considerable rivalry and competition are common between married brothers, especially near the time of estate partition, and are often exacerbated by their wives (Cohen, 1976: 194–206; Freedman, 1966: 46–7). As a result, the cohesion

Table 4.1   *Institutional differences between pre-industrial Japan, Korea and China*

	Japan	Korea	China
Political system			
Centralization	Low	High	High
Autocracy	Low	Limited	High
Significance of aristocracy	High	Considerable	Low
Inheritance principle	Primogeniture	Mixed	Equal
Stability of officials and local leaders	High	Very low	Low
Growth of formal procedures	Considerable	Low	Low
Economic system			
Economic pluralism	Considerable	Low	Low
Security of merchants	Considerable	Low	Low
Legitimacy			
Basis of elite legitimacy	Maintaining order and competitive success	Moral worth	Moral worth
Reciprocity of vertical relations	Weak but institutionalized	None	None
Village and family organization			
Village solidarity and loyalty to leaders	High	Low	Low
Inter-family co-operation	High	Mixed	Low
Village autonomy	Medium	Low	Low
Family authority	Differentiated	Differentiated	Monopolized by father
Father's closeness to sons	Considerable	Low	Low
Father's willingness to share responsibility and admit anxiety	High	Low	Low

and unity of the Chinese family become considerably weakened once the sons marry and have children. In contrast, the primogeniture inheritance system in Japan ensures that younger sons are encouraged to compete outside the family for material success and prestige, perhaps to establish their own family line (Pye, 1985: 68–9). In Korea, inheritance principles seem to have been more mixed, with equal male inheritance being practised largely by the aristocracy and the elder brother being the primary recipient of family property in the poorer villages (Brandt, 1971: 113). Fratricidal conflict seems to have been less marked in rural Korean families than in Chinese ones as a result.

These differences between pre-industrial Japan, Korea and China are summarized in Table 4.1. Autocracy here refers to the extent to which the monarch combined reigning with ruling and was able to exercise personal power without being subject to moralistic constraints. The importance of the council system in Korea clearly demonstrates the significance of the elite aristocracy in that country, although of course it was less secure and independent than in Japan. Inheritance principles in Korea were less clear cut than in China or Japan, and the role of the elder brother seems to have been more economically important than in China. The emphasis on moral worth to justify elite domination in Korea and China meant that leaders in those countries felt no need to perform reciprocal services in return for deference and obedience, whereas Japanese daimyo and Shogun were obligated to maintain social stability to the extent that peasant protests, although unauthorized, were recurrent and often successful in achieving redress (Upham, 1987: 67–9).

The Legacies of Pre-Industrial Japan, Korea and China

The differences summarized in Table 4.1 highlight the distinctiveness of Tokugawa Japan when contrasted with patrimonial Korea and China. In particular, pre-industrial Japan was much more politically and economically decentralized, and manifested greater merchant security and higher levels of solidarity and trust between kinship groups than pre-industrial Korea and China. These features were important influences on how and when industrialization took place in East Asia and the considerable degree of institutional continuity over the course of Japanese industrialization (Pye, 1985: 158–66). Although the United States occupation of Japan after the Second World War did result in some significant institutional changes, as will be discussed in the next chapter, there were significant continuities with pre-industrial society in the post-war social order. In contrast, industrialization in Korea and the Chinese diaspora was characterized by radical changes in some institutions as a result of colonization and civil war. These considerably altered the institutional context in which effective forms of business organization became established. Without such changes it seems unlikely that economic development would have been so rapid and successful in Korea and Taiwan. The considerable continuities in dominant institutions observable in the People's Republic of China (PRC), and their effects on economic development there, illustrate this point (Pye, 1985: 183–213; Redding, 1990: 231–6).

The institutional legacy of pre-industrial China in Taiwan and Hong Kong has been less direct than in Japan, and mostly reproduced through the Chinese family and patterns of village organization which appear to be quite strong agencies of social reproduction (Bond and Hwang, 1986; Ho, 1986; Redding, 1990: 183–7). In particular, the overwhelming importance attached to family ownership and control and unwillingness to trust business partners outside the family, or those who have not developed family-like relationships, appear continuous with pre-industrial mercantile practices (Greenhalgh, 1984, 1988a). A further continuity in Chinese business practices is the generally low level of trust of state officials and strong desire to keep business success secret from them which was reinforced in many South-East Asian countries by the discriminatory practices of newly independent states (Wu, 1983; Yoshihara, 1988: 40–62).

In the case of Taiwan, the political authority is, of course, Chinese, and so there are clear continuities with earlier political structures and ideologies (Wade, 1990: 257–61), as was reflected in the debates over the liberalization of the economy in the late 1950s. As Gold (1986: 77) puts it: 'Many officials still disliked businessmen, and these [liberalizing] policies would further the state's retrenchment from the economy and grant even greater rein to private capital. This would entail concentration of capital, something Sun Yat-sen opposed.' However, the particular circumstances in which the Kuomintang (KMT) took control of Taiwan clearly affected their claim to legitimacy and the development of the political system, so that their attitudes to economic development were more positive than those of traditional Chinese regimes (Haggard, 1988). The traditional dislike of private concentrations of economic power, though, remains an important feature of state policies in Taiwan.

As in China, an important legacy of pre-industrial Korea was the low level of trust between non-kin, together with the predominance of the central power which was reinforced by Japanese colonialism. However, the significance of the aristocracy and overt battles for power between factions institutionalized competition between leading families in a way that was not acceptable in China because of the strong ideological priority given to harmony there (Pye, 1985: 63–5). Competition outside the family was thus more developed among Korean elites than Chinese ones, and the relative ranking of different families more a focus of public struggle. These and other consequences of pre-industrial Japan, Korea and China will now be discussed in a little more detail under the same headings as those in Table 4.1, although many do, of course, reflect combinations of pre-industrial institutions.

The Political System

Perhaps the most significant result of the differences in the political systems of these three countries was the development of vertical ties of loyalty and attachment to local political leaders to a much greater extent in Japan. Because the daimyo had continuous control over their fiefs over many generations, and their castle towns constituted relatively strong local centres of power, rural villages were much more integrated into the political system than they were in Korea and China. Furthermore, through the daimyo's administration of their fiefs on a continuing basis, relatively stable relations of subordination to particular families and their agents developed in Japan in a way that did not happen elsewhere in East Asia. Especially in Korea, the turnover of officials was so great as to prevent any stable patterns of loyalty developing, and the attractions of the political centre in both Korea and China limited the interest of the landlords in developing long-term involvements in particular areas. Vertical loyalties were instead directed towards the unseen and distant Emperor, whose officials appeared capricious and frequently changing. Thus the importance of stable and local centres of power in Japan facilitated the institutionalization of vertical loyalties beyond the family and the village; their weakness in Korea and China inhibited it.

The second major consequence of the greater differentiation and pluralism of political institutions in Japan was the relative diffusion and fragmentation of power at the centre. For most of the past 100 years, power in Tokyo has not been centralized around a single political leader or ruling group, as it has been in Korea and Taiwan, but rather shared between factions, clans and, later, political groupings and ministries. Indeed some have suggested that the lack of a strong central source of political authority in the 1930s encouraged the military's colonization of Manchuria and later seizure of power (Pye, 1985: 180; Wolferen, 1989: 39–40). This fragmentation of central power has been maintained throughout the post-war period, so that the Liberal Democratic Party (LDP) is more a collection of factions than a cohesive political party in the European mode, and the central bureaucracy is riven with territorial and patronage conflicts (Johnson, 1982). Just as the Shogun maintained control through balancing the demands of the daimyo and preventing them combining to overthrow him, so too contemporary Japanese Prime Ministers maintain their position by balancing LDP factions and keeping control of their own – or that of their patron. The degree of central political authority and control over the bureaucracy and other major social organizations remains, then, much lower in Japan than in Korea or Taiwan.

A related feature of Japan's political system which continues to differentiate it from Korea or Taiwan is the separation of the reigning political authority, that is, the Emperor, from the current ruler, that is, the Shogun and then Prime Minister. This separation, which enabled the Emperor to survive over many changes of regime, has facilitated the peaceful change of ruler in Japan because this does not threaten the national focus of political loyalty. Contrarily, where the central symbol of power and authority is also the secular rule of a society, and power is personal and patrimonial rather than positional, it is clear that changes of ruler can threaten the entire political system and the legitimacy of its institutions. Succession problems are therefore much more acute in China and Korea than in Japan, where leaders in the Western sense are not politically significant in any case (Pye, 1985: 178–81, 331–2). Similarly, the much more personal and centralized locus of power in Korean and Chinese organizations renders changes of leadership more infrequent and difficult in firms than in large Japanese corporations.

A further important inheritance from the Tokugawa political system was the creeping bureaucratization of many central and han administrative functions (Craig, 1986), together with the beginnings of a formal legal system for regulating administrative actions and settling disputes. While scarcely a fully fledged Weberian bureaucracy, and certainly not a modern centralized state, the transformation of the samurai into officials following rules and procedures which began in the late eighteenth and nineteenth centuries was a crucial factor in the success of the Meiji reforms and the development of the central state bureaucracy after 1868. Particularly important was the institutionalization of formal rule-following behaviour on the part of officials in contrast to the much more personal and individual decisions of patrimonial officials in Korea and China.

Whereas magistrates and their officials in pre-industrial Korea and China held office by virtue of their examination success and central patronage, and only had very broad and diffuse interpretations of the Confucian classics to rely on when making decisions, Tokugawa administrators were beginning to develop norms of specialist expertise and to apply standard rules and procedures. As Henderson (1968: 235–44) emphasizes, the value of specialized competence was denigrated by the Confucian educated generalist, especially in Korea, and this prejudice remains important today (Jacobs, 1985: 20–1). Thus, the development of formal rule-governed organizations during Japan's industrialization was considerably easier than in Korea or China.

Two additional legacies of the pre-industrial political systems of Japan, Korea and China are: first, the much greater willingness to tolerate open competition between interest groups and corporate bodies in Japan, and between factions in Korea, than in China, where overt factionalism was illegitimate (Pye, 1985: 190–1); and, second, the greater significance of formal hierarchical status in Japan and Korea than in China. This last can be partly attributed to the aristocratic heritage of the former two centuries.

Economic Systems
A major feature of Tokugawa political decentralization was its toleration of independent, private concentrations of economic power. This acceptance of the differentiation of economic ownership from political control facilitated the growth of the zaibatsu during the Meiji period and, in particular, the private ownership of banks and other financial institutions. The long experience of the merchant-controlled credit system during the Tokugawa period enabled privately owned joint stock banks to develop at the end of the nineteenth century, after a few false starts, without a great deal of state support or direction (Clark, 1979: 32–5; Hirschmeier and Yui, 1981: 85–100), although many of the Tokugawa merchant houses failed to adapt to the new environment and disappeared. Thus, although industrialization was initially led by the Meiji government, which established model state enterprises with the help of foreign experts in the 1870s, it sold off most of these at low prices to private owners within a few years, and subsequent industrialization was largely a privately owned, but state-supported, process in Japan.

In contrast, the suspicion of the Confucian elite of independent economic power inhibited the development of the textile industry in China (Nishida, 1990), and agrarian interests continued to oppose the development of commercial and industrial enterprises into the 1930s (Moore, 1966: 195–6). Although the foreign control of China's overseas trade and commerce probably did hamper the ability of the central state to channel funds into new industries (Moulder, 1977: 189–97), there seems little doubt that the stifling effect of Western imperialism on industrialization in China could 'not have happened without prior stifling by purely domestic forces' (Moore, 1966: 177). The weakness of the central government compared to that of Meiji Japan was not such as to prevent the mandarinate from blocking the development of an independent commercial and industrial class in nineteenth-century China. As Hall (1988: 23) suggests: 'Although the bureaucracy was not able to penetrate far into society, it could and did prevent other forces from gaining much autonomy . . . this capstone government blocked the fully fledged emergence of intensive capitalist relationships.' The lack of trust between merchants and the Chinese state is exemplified by the preference of many coastal merchants for trading under foreign names with foreign protection in the nineteenth century (Hao, 1986: 263–4). The considerable amount of Chinese investment in joint enterprises with foreign firms 'unmistakably showed that Chinese businessmen were afraid of the exactions of officials of their government . . . they tried their best to prevent their wealth from being exposed to the attention of the officials' (Hao, 1986: 258).

Similarly, in Korea the development of a commercial economy was seen as a threat to the Confucian patrimonial order based on landownership and cultivation. At the same time, though, the opportunities for increased taxes and other forms of state income presented a dilemma to the political elite and led to central direction and control over commercial and, later, industrial enterprises through the sale of monopoly rights and manipulation of markets. In Jacob's (1985: 134) terms: 'By manipulating the supply of commodities made available to the monopolists and by threatening to rotate the graceful privileges it bestowed, the polity tried to assure that commercialists would be both politically inactive and economically co-operative in accepting official demands for formalized levies and capricious exactions.' Additionally, the monetization of the economy was limited by the purist elite's focus on agriculture and periodic curbs on the minting of coins. This concern with direct political control over commerce and industry, which included the state regulation of what could be produced and to whom it could be sold, as well as the use of the police to discipline workers, and the expropriation of the economy's surplus, prevented sustained economic development; and so the commercial economy was unable to resist the invasion of Japanese commercial enterprises at the end of the nineteenth century.

In sum, the essentially patrimonial attitude to the economy in pre-industrial Korea ensured its subservience to the centralized political elite, and this emphasis on central direction and planning has continued into the post-war period despite the growth of privately owned chaebol. Whether the contemporary political system is as fully patrimonial as Jacobs claims, it is clear that the highly centralized nature of Korean society remains a major distinguishing characteristic, and the low degree of economic differentiation found in the Yi dynasty continues to distinguish Korea from contemporary Japan.

A further consequence of the contrasting treatment of merchants and private concentrations of economic power in East Asia was the development of different attitudes and conventions among the commercial elites. In China and Korea, the insecurity of commercial activities and wealth encouraged secrecy and distrust of public officials, as well as a preference for landownership instead of continued investment and development of the business. In Tokugawa Japan, on the other hand, the mercantile elite had a distinct and stable social status which, although low, provided some protection against official depredations and enabled them to build up family enterprises over generations. Since they were not officially supposed to control land or become aristocrats, they focused on commercial activities and constituted a separate, continuing mercantile class. This relative security of position and continuity encouraged them to follow dominant norms and conceptions of appropriate behaviour by emphasizing their public honesty and probity. As good citizens of Tokugawa society, merchants sought to demonstrate their correctness and obedience to official dictates by co-operating with public officials rather than remaining isolated from them. The growing interdependence of the Shogunate aristocracy and mercantile elite over the Tokugawa period meant that merchants could publicly display their wealth and confidently claim their legitimate function in society (Hirschmeier and Yui, 1981: 20–44). Secrecy and reliance on purely personal bases of trust were therefore less critical to survival than in China or Korea.

Furthermore, trust extended beyond the immediate family to long-serving and loyal clerks as well as to adopted sons who sometimes had no direct family connection with the owners. This willingness to trust loyal servants of the merchant 'house' developed into the widespread employment of salaried managers at senior levels of the zaibatsu after 1868, although families retained ultimate control through holding companies (Hirschmeier and Yui, 1981: 127–37). They reigned but did not rule. This early separation of ownership from operational control in the zaibatsu was probably facilitated by the Japanese experience of differentiated authority structures from the long-established distinction between the Emperor who reigned and the Shogun who ruled, as well as the traditions of vertical loyalties to collective entities beyond the family.

Legitimacy

The most important consequences of the differences in claims to legitimacy by ruling elites in Japan, Korea and China were the general identification of leadership with moral superiority in the latter countries and the development of competence and technical 'merit' in collective undertakings as crucial components of Japanese elites' justifications of their positions. The virtuocracies of Korea and China ruled because of their superior moral worth, demonstrated by their mastery of the Confucian classics. This meant that they did not need to justify their status further by performing some useful function on behalf of society as a whole, except perhaps maintaining 'harmony', or to continue to demonstrate their worthiness by excelling in some competitive arena. Thus, governing elites were not committed to economic development as the primary means of demonstrating their superiority and crucial function. As a result, their interest in the economic system was more predatory than developmental.

Another consequence of this emphasis on the moral superiority of the ruling elite was the infusion of political debates with discussions of personal morality and worthiness. The emphasis on moral worth rather than technical efficacy meant that conflicts were highly personal and were concerned more with general qualities of individuals than the merits of their particular actions. As a result, debates over political choices were as much concerned with the personal standing and worth of decision makers as with their achievement of desired objectives. Thus criticism of decisions and suggestions of alternatives were seen as personal attacks on the integrity of leaders rather than as relatively technical discussions of the advantages of different choices. The conflation of elite membership with moral worthiness in Korea and China in effect meant that debate and discussion of leaders' actions became impossible, except as personal attacks on their moral status.

In contrast, the Meiji revolutionaries in Japan emphasized their merit in leading Japanese industrialization and development and performing collectively useful functions. In Pye's (1985: 161) terms: 'Merit meant to them achievement in terms of competence in doing things not in pretending to superior wisdom or virtue.' Contrasting the administrative competence of junior samurai with the indolence and stupidity of the daimyo, their spokesmen sought to bolster the position of meritorious retainers in terms of their ability and loyalty to higher authority (Smith, 1967). Merit became demonstrated initially through success in the formal educational system and then through success in bureaucratic offices in the public and private sectors. Although legitimacy was claimed through examination successes, as in Korea and China, it did not imply moral superiority and worth but simply competitive superiority. This technical superiority was further demonstrated by performing better than others in a variety of settings and so was more pragmatic and activist than moral and passive. Elite legitimacy during Japan's industrialization was thus much more performance focused than in Korea and China and, in particular, based on national economic development and success. Elite involvement in business became justified because of its contribution to national development, and its status was legitimized by business success.

A further important aspect of these differences in claims to legitimacy and obedience was their link with reciprocity. However limited it may have been in traditional Japanese society, subordination did imply some reciprocal services on the part of superiors, either for individuals or for the common collective entity. In contrast, the emphasis on the moral worthiness of the elite in Confucian Korea and China meant that subordination entailed no such reciprocity, since it simply reflected different moral statuses. Consequently, while the patrimonial elite might dispense some favours to its faithful followers, this was purely a matter of personal grace and benevolence rather than following from legitimate expectations about how superiors should behave. As a result, vertical ties of subordination in Japan involve the expectation that leaders provide reciprocal benefits to a greater extent than they do in Korea and China and tend to be more intense. As mentioned earlier, subordinates in Chinese society were expected to obey the authorities more as a matter of role performance, in a manner comparable to filial piety within the family, than as personally linked dependents who had a legitimate claim on superiors' attention and support. According to Silin (1976), this expectation remains institutionalized in Taiwanese society and its firms. Whereas, then, subservience in Japan implies certain reciprocal duties of superiors, this is not institutionalized in Chinese and Korean communities.

Village and Family Organization
The major differences in the organization of families and village communities between Japan, Korea and China have had four important interrelated consequences for authority relations and patterns of co-operation and trust. First, the greater cohesion and interdependence between families in Japanese villages facilitated the development of horizontal relations of co-operation and trust between non-family members during industrialization there. Second, the higher levels of loyalty to village headmen and the village authority hierarchy in Tokugawa Japan enabled managerial hierarchies to develop similar loyalty and commitment more easily than in Korea and China. Third, the strong preference for group consensus and leadership from behind in traditional Japanese

communities has encouraged a more consensual and group-focused form of managerial behaviour in Japan than elsewhere, particularly in heavy industry. Fourth, differences in family authority patterns have institutionalized much more supportive conceptions of authority in Japan than in Korean and Chinese societies where authority is seen as remote and omnipotent.

The relatively high levels of inter-family co-operation and mutual dependence in Japanese villages during the Tokugawa period weakened the power of family ties and identities in comparison with those in China and Korea and facilitated the growth of commitments to broader collective entities. Because the village as a whole was a much more important unit of collective organization, identity and loyalty in Japan than it was in China and Korea, co-operation and trust between families was more institutionalized, and the family was by no means the only focus of attachment and commitment as it appears to be in Chinese communities (Pelzel, 1970; Redding and Wong, 1986; Silin, 1976).

A further aspect of this different emphasis on the family was the much greater importance of blood ties in China than in Japan, as is shown by differences in adoption principles and practices. While the Chinese rarely adopt outside the directly related kinship group, the Japanese are much more willing to adopt competent relatives by marriage and family outsiders (Hirschmeier and Yui, 1981: 159). Thus the family is more sharply defined and bounded in Chinese society and forms the basic unit of trust. As Pye (1985: 70) puts it: 'The Chinese were taught to recognize a vivid distinction between family members, who could be relied upon, and non-family people, who were not to be trusted except in qualified ways.' In Korea, the family appears to be less firmly bounded than in China but more narrowly defined than in Japan. Ties between brothers are less strong and households are more likely to be based on the nuclear family (Pye, 1985: 68). According to Jacobs (1985: 208–9), the clan is the crucial unit of kinship structure which commands loyalties across parochial, geographic and provincial boundaries and forms the key intermediary unit between the nuclear family and the state. However, the intensity of such loyalty is obviously limited, given the size of these clans, and kinship networks appear less constitutive of trust relations than in Chinese communities.

The considerable cohesion and autonomy of the Tokugawa village facilitated the development of cohesive work groups in factories, and loyalty to the village headmen was transferred to supervisors and foremen relatively easily (Smith, 1988a: 11). The ability of village leaders to command the respect and commitment of villagers was an important factor in easing the transition to industrial society in Japan which both Korea and China lacked because they were seen more as government agents and tax officials than as village leaders. Also, their frequent rotation prevented long-term ties of loyalty developing which could be transferred to industrial undertakings. A further important factor in Japanese industrialization was the greater stability of the countryside and continuity of village structures during it. Unlike many industrialization processes, economic development in Japan did not lead to wholesale uprooting of rural communities and destruction of traditional communities but rather to the growth of many rural industries, some already established before the Meiji restoration, and the continuation of migration patterns to the cities which did not greatly disrupt village patterns (Dore, 1967). Thus traditional patterns of authority and commitment to hierarchies were relatively easily transferred to the new industries in Japan, and claims for redress in industrial conflicts were often expressed in terms of traditional status obligations rather than as employee 'rights' (Smith, 1988a, 238–65).

This relative continuity of authority patterns and village organization during Japanese industrialization can also be seen in the importance of group consensus and close managerial involvement in group tasks and morale in Japanese organizations. In particular, the high level of interdependence between the headman and the leading families, the norm of following the group consensus rather than leading it and the traditional emphasis on representing the village to the superior authority, as well as acting as the agent of the daimyo, all seem to have been transferred to managerial roles in Japanese firms and, indeed, to the general conception of leadership as a warm, non-aggressive skill and activity (Pye, 1985: 166–81). The traditional importance of group solidarity and cohesion has enhanced managerial control but also required that managers are closely involved with work groups and maintain their morale. As Pye (1985: 171) puts it: 'In the hierarchically ordered society superiors could expect deference, but in return they were not expected to push their views but rather to work for consensus.'

In contrast, Korean and Chinese villages did not have a settled system of authority relations which integrated loyalties and commitments. Rather, authority was imposed from outside, and stable local leadership which could represent villages to the patrimonial bureaucracy was discouraged. Thus, there was little or no institutionalized authority hierarchy which could rely on the common loyalties of a number of families and lineages and so serve as the

Table 4.2 *Legacies of institutional differences in
pre-industrial East Asia*

	Japan	Korea	China
Political systems			
Integration of vertical loyalties	High	Low	Low
Diffusion and differentiation of power at the centre	High	Low	Low
Leadership change	Institutionalized	Difficult	Difficult
Acceptance of formal rules and procedures	Considerable	Low	Low
Level of overt intra-elite competition	High	Considerable	Low
Economic system			
Independence of centres of economic power from state	Considerable	Low	Low
Trust between state and enterprises	High	Low	Low
Trust of non-family	Considerable	Low	Low
Legitimacy			
Importance of technical competence to elite authority	Considerable	Low	Low
Importance of economic development to elite authority	Considerable	Low before 1961	Limited
Leader's obligations to subordinates	Strong	Limited	Weak
Village and family organization			
Inter-family co-operation and trust	High	Mixed	Low
Loyalty to local leaders	High	Low	Low
Importance of group consensus and morale	High	Low	Low
Dominant authority type	Supportive, nurturing	Omnipotent, sympathetic	Omnipotent, remote

basis of integrated organizations. Instead, family authority patterns
formed the basic model for hierarchical relationships in face-to-
face groups, and many features of the traditional patrimonial
organizations were carried over to larger hierarchical structures.
Additionally, of course, both Korea and China have had a much
more disruptive history in the past 100 years than has Japan, and
secondary institutional continuities are fewer in number and
strength. Family relations and norms are therefore even more
important.

The characteristics of family authority relations summarized in Table 4.1 suggest a much more supportive conception of authority in Japan than in Korea and China. Here, fathers are expected to share authority with mothers, and to display emotion and dependence, and are not supposed to be totally responsible for the family's fate. Korean and Chinese fathers, on the other hand, appear to be much more remote and are expected to cope single-handedly with all their problems. Total obedience to the patriarch's wishes is expected in these families. However, the greater differentiation of authority roles in Korean families means that children become more accustomed to divisions of authority than do Chinese ones. Additionally, according to Pye (1985: 67): 'like the Japanese leader-father, he [the Korean father] is expected to be sympathetic, nurturing, and sensitive to the wishes of his followers-family.' Thus omnipotence and strength are somewhat more tempered with emotional obligations, at least ideologically, in Korean views of authority than in Chinese ones.

These different legacies of pre-industrial Japan, Korea and China are summarized in Table 4.2. They highlight the greater levels of trust and security among merchants in Japan and the greater willingness to co-operate between families there. Additionally, reliance on formal rules and procedures seems to have developed much more in Japan, and authority was less personal and less threatened by subordinate success. Finally, collective loyalties beyond the family were stronger and more integrated with superordinate collective entities. These legacies had important effects on both industrialization patterns and the sorts of business systems that became established in East Asia, as will be shown in the next two chapters.

5
Institutional Influences on East Asian Business Systems II: Industrialization and Institutional Development

The previous discussion of institutional differences between pre-industrial Japan, Korea and China and their consequences has emphasized the contrast between Tokugawa feudalism and patrimonial Korea and China. This contrast, together with differences in the actions of Western states at the end of the nineteenth century and during the first half of the twentieth century, had important effects on how industrialization developed in East Asian societies and on the dominant political and economic institutions that became established during this process. Indeed it may be wondered how the patrimonial societies have managed to become industrialized, given the characterization summarized in Tables 4.1 and 4.2, especially the nature and beliefs of ruling elites. Certainly the ways in which Korea and Taiwan have developed economically in the twentieth century differ quite markedly from Japan and, to a lesser extent, from each other; and these differences are closely interconnected with variations in the institutional environments in which distinctive business systems have become established.

In considering the major differences in industrialization processes between East Asian countries and the interdependent development of major social institutions, the organization and role of the state are crucial features. As in many 'late' industrializing societies, the state has played a critical part in the economic development of Japan, Korea, Taiwan and Hong Kong, and the development of their distinctive business systems cannot be adequately understood without an appreciation of its role (Amsden, 1985b; Haggard, 1988; Henderson, 1989; Wade, 1988). Equally, the nature of the state and of its development during industrialization in each country varies in ways that have had important consequences for economic development. The major emphasis in this chapter, then, will be on the role of the state in the economic development of these four societies, how state institutions developed in the course of industrialization and how particular state–business relations became established.

Another key institutional arena for business development, the financial system, varies rather less between these countries in that it is 'credit based', in Zysman's (1983: 55–75) terms, in all of them

(Wade, 1988), although the significance of capital markets has become greater in Japan recently (Zielinski and Holloway, 1991). Furthermore, financial institutions have been heavily controlled by the state in post-war Japan, Korea and Taiwan, so that they are best considered as part of the overall system of state–business relations rather than as a separate institutional system. Similarly, except for Hong Kong, the legal system and other major social institutions are more controlled by the state than is typically the case in Western Europe and North America, and the overall level of institutional pluralism is lower in East Asian societies.

Initially, I shall outline the major features of East Asian political systems that developed during industrialization, focusing particularly on those which affected economic institutions and the role of the state in economic development. Japan, Korea, Taiwan and Hong Kong will be considered separately and their major differences will then be summarized. Next, the more specific details of state–business relations in each country will be discussed and contrasts in these identified. Finally, the major consequences of differences in political institutions and state policies for business systems will be summarized. I should perhaps emphasize that the focus here is on how dominant institutions in these societies have developed differently during industrialization and so helped to generate different forms of business organizations in them. Thus, neither general processes of economic development nor how particular institutions in individual countries developed will be considered in detail here.

Industrialization and the Development of East Asian Political Systems

In considering the development of political institutions and their role in economic change and industrialization in East Asia, one of the most crucial features is the extent to which state agencies and controllers are able and willing to develop policies independently of powerful economic and social groups and then have the capacity to implement them. This is commonly discussed in terms of the 'autonomy' of the state to pursue objectives that do not simply reflect the demands or interests of social groups, classes or society and has been evaluated in terms of the backgrounds of bureaucratic elites and their ties to the dominant landed, commercial and industrial classes (cf. Skocpol, 1985; Wade, 1990: 337–42). An important aspect of state autonomy here is its capacity to implement its policies, either through direct control of economic institutions and resources or through indirect manipulation and guidance.

A related significant feature of political systems is the overall commitment of political and bureaucratic elites to state-led industrialization (cf. Samuels, 1987: 19–21) and their perception that state legitimacy rests significantly upon rapid economic development.

Political systems also differ in the cohesion of their components and the extent to which the executive is dominant. While the strong separation of powers between the executive, legislature and judiciary institutionalized in the USA is not echoed in any East Asian society, there are none the less important variations in their degree of integration and in the level of executive domination. These are partly due to differences in the origins of political elites and the processes by which they come to power, especially the role of military support and the extent of ethnic differences between the dominant group and the bulk of the population.

The Japanese Political System during Industrialization

The autonomy of the Japanese state and its capacity to direct the path of economic development have conventionally been considered high and comparable to those of the French state. Zysman (1983: 91), for example, cites both countries' development as instances of the 'state-led model of development' in which 'the government bureaucracy attempts to orient the adjustment of the economy by explicitly influencing the position of particular sectors, even of individual companies, and by imposing the solutions on the weakest groups in the polity. The state seeks to select the terms on which sectors and companies confront the market.' Recent studies of energy markets (Samuels, 1987; cf. Wade, 1990: 326–7) and the machine tool industry (Friedman, 1988) in Japan have, however, thrown some doubt on this 'strong state' view, and most historical accounts of early industrialization in Japan emphasize the strength of the zaibatsu and limitations of state control over the economy (for example, Allen, 1981: 135–40; Hirschmeier and Yui, 1981).

In fact, after the sale of the state pilot plants to what became the zaibatsu in the 1880s, the Japanese state adopted a relatively distant stance towards industrial development until the 1930s (Johnson, 1982: 84–90). In this period 'large capital cliques more or less independently ran the financial, extractive and common commodity markets, whereas very small firms produced final goods for actual sale on the market' (Friedman, 1988: 39). It is worth noting that this functional differentiation of large and small firms before the 1930s was reversed in many of the new consumer industries that have developed since the 1950s, where the large firms have tended to be the assemblers of final goods. Although the zaibatsu were in a sense created by the Meiji oligarchy through preferential and cheap sales of state assets and various forms of state subsidies, contracts, access to licences, etc., they rapidly grew to constitute quite powerful independent centres of economic activity and by the 1920s dominated political parties and substantial parts of the economic system. In Allen's (1981: 138) words: 'whereas in early Meiji days they could be regarded as agents of the Government, though probably never as passive agents, by the later twenties they had reached a position in which they could, to an increasing extent, impose their wishes on the Government'.

This limited autonomy and independence of the Japanese state during early industrialization reflected the relatively non-revolutionary nature of the Meiji restoration and the continuity of many aspects of Japanese society throughout the Meiji period, as well as the high degree of commonality between private business interests and official objectives. As Jansen and Rozman (1986) emphasize, compared to the major European revolutions the transition from Tokugawa to Meiji Japan was relatively smooth and did not involve radical social upheavals and intense class conflicts. The process of reform was more groping and pragmatic than derived from a radical programme for a new society, and reordered existing hierarchies rather than demolishing them and constructing new social orders (Jansen, 1986). The Meiji leaders followed rather cautious and flexible policies in consolidating their power and were at pains not to antagonize powerful interests, or at least not until they had been able to mobilize sufficient military force to overcome rebellions (Craig, 1986). Thus, administrative centralization, abolition of the Tokugawa status system and samurai stipends and the restructuring of the feudal domains were combined with the elevation of the Emperor to the national symbol and focus of institutional legitimation, the resurrection of the Court and the House of Peers as a check upon radicalism, and the absorption of the Tokugawa house and branch families into the new aristocratic system. Although, then, military force was used to suppress rebellions and impose reform upon old elites, the establishment of the Meiji state involved considerable accommodation and compromise and it was interdependent with, rather than totally independent from, existing dominant groups.

Overall, then, while the modern Japanese state dominated the social system during most of its first half-century, and established a much greater degree of administrative centralization than existed during the Tokugawa period, it did not pursue economic developmentalist policies independently of other major groups and institutions. Its commitment to economic development did not imply a directive, planning role for state agencies but rather a more informal and ad hoc supportive one for private groups. Thus, substantial assistance was provided for the shipping and shipbuilding industries, partly for military reasons, but not much for the largest industry, cotton spinning (Blumenthal, 1976; Saxonhouse, 1976; Teretani, 1980). The state helped 'private entrepreneurs to accumulate capital and to invest it in ways that seemed to promote Japan's need for military security and economic development' (Johnson, 1982: 85). This help was largely organized through informal and personal relations between the Meiji oligarchs, later the leaders of the political parties, and private investors which were often cemented by common clan origins and strategic marriages.

This limited extent of state autonomy and commitment to state-led industrialization before 1930 both reflected and reinforced the highly differentiated nature of the Japanese state. Although the Emperor was elevated to be the supreme symbol of national identity and unity, he did not rule and could not provide the unifying force for integrating the key components of the political system. The junior aristocrats who led the Meiji restoration succeeded in creating a national bureaucracy which organized large sectors of Japanese society around national developmental goals, particularly through the centrally controlled education system and police force, but did not establish a central political focus for the state comparable to the political executives of many Western states. Thus, power and responsibility in the Japanese state were, and are, diffused between competing groups, factions and ministries with no clear central direction and leader (Pye, 1985: 159–76). In prewar Japan this segmentation and differentiation of power groups were exemplified by the rivalry between the military services and their right of access to the Emperor rather than being under the control of the Prime Minister (Black et al., 1975: 153–4).

This lack of strong political leadership in Japan has been connected to the dominant role of the bureaucracy throughout the industrialization process. Because both the bureaucracy and the cabinet of oligarchs preceded the establishment of the Diet, or Parliament, and political parties by over a decade, they were able to control the terms on which the parties operated and also restricted their actions by recreating and dominating the House of Peers (Jansen, 1986). Appointed directly by the Emperor, selected by fiercely competitive examinations and overtly dedicated to achieving national development goals, the Japanese bureaucratic elite dominated the political system and prevented strong parties and leaders emerging (Black et al., 1975: 150–2; Johnson, 1982: 36–40).

This elite regarded themselves as officials of the Emperor rather than as servants of the public and so not subject to the formal legal system or accountable to the general public. Indeed the legal system was viewed more as a means for administering society than as a separate social institution for dealing with conflicts and allowing redress against the executive. Through bureaucratic control of the number of practising lawyers and judges, the state still limits the independence of the legal system today and maintains much of this pre-war attitude. In particular, formal litigation is systematically discouraged by the state, and informal mediation preferred as the basic means of resolving disputes (Upham, 1987: 14–25). An important feature of Japanese industrialization, then, has been the subservience of the legal system to bureaucratic rule and interests (cf. Wolferen, 1989: 203–25).

The general prestige hierarchy of the Japanese bureaucracy was dominated by the Ministries of Home Affairs, Finance and Foreign Affairs, so that ambitious recruits to the civil service would only rarely consider joining the Ministry of Agriculture and Commerce (MAC) or the later Ministry of Commerce and Industry (Johnson, 1982: 87–9). Thus, the strength of the bureaucratic elite in pre-war Japan did not lead to a strong interest in state-led industrial development by the state or to close links between bureaucrats in MAC and industrial leaders. Indeed the largest industrial firms at that time, the cotton-spinning firms in Osaka, maintained a considerable distance from the national government. Furthermore, the importance of agriculture, both in the domestic economy and in the export trade, meant that commerce and industry concerns were in a subordinate position within MAC, and so industrial policy received little attention until the late 1920s.

These general features of the Japanese political system during early industrialization were modified in a number of ways by the post-war occupation of Japan and the reforms imposed by the Supreme Commander for the Allied Powers (SCAP). In particular, the power of the civilian bureaucracy, especially the economic ministries, was greatly enhanced (Johnson, 1982: 41–5). By purging the military and breaking up the zaibatsu, the occupying powers effectively removed the bureaucracy's major rivals from political life. Equally, by redistributing the powers of the Ministry of Home Affairs among new ministries, and so destroying its prestige and pre-eminent position in the pre-war bureaucratic hierarchy, they offered the largely unpurged economic ministries the opportunity to expand their jurisdictions and improve their status. This opportunity was enhanced by the key role played by the bureaucracy in the post-war economic reconstruction and recovery which took over many of the functions formerly performed by the zaibatsu. As a result the size of the civil service grew by 84 per cent over its wartime employment, and the Ministry of Commerce and Industry controlled the third largest share of the general account budget in 1948 and 1949 (Johnson, 1982: 44, 176). Together with the weaknesses of the political parties and their leaders after the purges, these developments led to increased bureaucratic domination of the political system, both in terms of the legislative process and bureaucrats' privileged access to leading positions in the LDP and cabinet.

This increased domination of the economic ministries can be seen in the common practice of retired senior civil servants moving into politics as LDP members of the Diet, and relatively quickly reaching cabinet rank, and the tendency of most Prime Ministers to have headed one of the economic departments. In the 1960s, for instance, 'at least 50 per cent of the main cabinet positions were held by former bureaucrats' (Pye, 1985: 173; cf. Okimoto, 1989: 216–22); and in 1977 ex-bureaucrats reached the cabinet after winning seven elections on average, as distinct from the nine or ten elections needed by politicians from different backgrounds (Johnson, 1982: 45–6). The three Prime Ministers who dominated Japanese politics from 1957 to 1972, Kishi, Ikeda and Sato, had earlier been vice-ministers – that is, top civil servants – of the Ministries of Commerce and Industry, Finance and Transportation respectively. Considering the ten Prime Ministers between 1956 and 1984, no less than nine had previously been Minister of either Finance (six) or of International Trade and Industry (MITI) (eight), which demonstrates the much greater significance of the economic ministries after the Second World War, particularly MITI (Kosai, 1987). Whereas before the war previous experience in diplomatic and military service, as well as in the Ministry of Home Affairs, was common among Prime Ministers, familiarity with the issues involved in economic management has now clearly become an implicit requirement for successful political leaders in Japan.

This circulation of the economic bureaucratic elite to senior political roles is matched by the practice of *amakudari* or 'descent from heaven' of early retirees to lucrative posts in private industry. Because of the rigid post-war convention that formal positions in the bureaucracy must match one's seniority, the promotion of one member of an entering class to a senior post – of which there are of course a limited number – usually leads to the resignation of his colleagues in that class, and it is the responsibility of the top officials in each ministry to find suitable jobs for them. Typically, these posts are in firms and other organizations that depend on the ministry for support, licences and similar benefits, so that it is in the interest of each unit of the bureaucracy to maintain a wide range of 'clients' or interest groups dependent on it. This encourages intense rivalries between ministries over jurisdictions and responsibilities, with the result that, whenever a new area of state activity or responsibility develops, there is fierce competition to control it (Johnson, 1982: 63–73). These rivalries are further intensified by the lack of mobility between ministries, so that careers and retirement opportunities are closely tied to the fortunes of one department. This, in turn, reinforces the diffusion of power and responsibility in the central Japanese state.

This twofold circulation of the bureaucratic elite in post-war Japan highlights the considerable interdependence and integration of bureaucratic, political and business elites that developed after the occupation. As Johnson (1982: 50–2) suggests, the LDP's role is to legitimate the bureaucracy and ensure its policies do not stray too far from what the public will tolerate, while the bureaucratic elite provides highly skilled cadres for Parliament and policies that encourage economic growth, which increases opportunities for political patronage and demonstrable success. The business elite funds the LDP and provides jobs for top civil servants in return for political and bureaucratic favours as well as a generally 'developmentalist' state that supports business expansion. This support is less directive than it was in the 1930s and 1940s but more co-ordinated and systematically focused than in most of the Meiji and Taisho periods. As a broad strategic approach to economic development it involves setting substantive social and economic goals which promote particular industries and implementing policies to achieve them.

Another significant reform of the SCAP destroyed the political and economic power of the landlord class in Japan. The removal of restrictions over the sale of land by the Meiji government had increased the proportion of arable land farmed by tenants from around 20 per cent to 45 per cent in 1910 (Allen, 1981: 66), and the agricultural depressions of the 1930s had further increased pressures on small peasant proprietors. These pressures were seen as partly responsible for the growth of militarism in Japan. In 1946 the Owner-Farmer Establishment Law provided for the enforced sale of all landholdings in excess of a small area to the state and the redistribution of this land to the former tenants. Since inflation rapidly reduced the value of the compensation paid to landowners considerably, this reform effectively expropriated them (Allen, 1981: 222). It also encouraged democratization of rural villages and investment in mechanization, thus improving agricultural productivity

(Johnson, 1967). The success of this imposed land reform not only was significant in Japan but additionally encouraged the United States government to press for similar reforms in Korea and Taiwan.

A further major set of reforms initiated by the SCAP have also had long-lasting consequences: the legalization and encouragement of trade unions and collective bargaining (Allen, 1981: 219–22). In a series of laws passed in 1946 and 1947 workers were given the right to organize and to strike, while employers were penalized for refusing to recognize unions. As a result, the number of union members rose from none to nearly 6.75 million by 1948, and by the late 1970s about a third of the total non-agricultural labour force were members of unions. While the Dodge deflation of 1949 and later legal changes inhibited further fast growth in union membership in the 1950s, and it has now declined to 26 per cent of the total workforce in 1989 (Rosario, 1990), unions have become a firmly established institution in Japanese society, a fact which has undoubtedly influenced large firms' policies. This represents a major change from pre-war Japan and has helped to maintain greater political pluralism.

The Korean Political System during Industrialization

If Japanese industrialization displays considerable continuities with pre-industrial institutions and patterns of societal organization, then Korean industrialization represents a strong contrast. From the account of pre-industrial Korean society presented in Chapter 4 it is clear that it lacked many of the components that enabled Meiji Japan to undertake economic development relatively successfully. In particular, Korea lacked a modernizing elite that justified its dominant position in terms of national economic development as well as a bureaucracy that used standard rules and procedures to organize its activities and provide a fairly stable and predictable framework for economic development. It also lacked: (a) a tradition of economic pluralism; (b) an agricultural system which could continue to produce a surplus for urban workers; and (c) a rural artisanal tradition that could serve as the basis for rural industries and the development of a skilled workforce. In many important respects, then, the industrialization of Korea reflects major discontinuities with pre-industrial Korean society, although both Henderson (1968) and Jacobs (1985) emphasize the continued significance of some pre-industrial institutions.

The Japanese annexation of Korea from 1910 to 1945 followed a brief protectorate from 1906 to 1910 in which basic Japanese administrative and legal forms were introduced (Jacobs, 1985: 68–72). This period of forced incorporation into the Japanese economy effectively destroyed the decaying political institutions of the Yi dynasty but without generating new ones which could survive the Japanese defeat and liberation of Korea. Because Koreans were excluded from almost all middle- and senior-ranked posts in both the bureaucracy and private Japanese-owned and -managed enterprises, a distinctly Korean group of technically competent administrators did not develop. Most of those that did work with the Japanese were considered collaborators and discredited after the liberation. Although a few Korean entrepreneurs established businesses that survived into the post-colonial era, they were very small in number and were highly dependent on the colonial state for capital (McNamara, 1990: 9–12). The forced industrialization of Korea in the 1930s and 1940s was directed almost entirely towards supporting Japanese expansion in mainland Asia and dominated by Japanese capital and personnel (Cumings, 1984).

The Japanese owned 90 per cent of the total paid-up capital of all corporations in 'Chosen' (the official name for Japanese Korea) in 1938 and 85 per cent of all manufacturing and industrial facilities in 1945 (Henderson, 1968: 97–8; Ho, 1984). Such Korean enterprises as did become established during this period were concentrated in textiles and food processing and were heavily dependent on the toleration of the Japanese administration. As Jacobs (1985: 165) puts it:

> although the Governor General proliferated formal, very modern commercial and industrial codes and regulations, he did nothing to shake the conviction of those Korean entrepreneurs who were emerging on the scene that the way to protect one's economic interests and survive . . . was still to be opportunistically self-serving and somehow come to terms with a dangerously capricious and heartless bureaucracy.

In his terms, the Japanese began to modernize the Korean economy while reinforcing the essentially patrimonial nature of Korean society (Jacobs, 1985: 162–70). Similarly, McNamara (1990: 127–37) has emphasized the insecurity and instability of indigenous enterprises during Japanese colonialism which encouraged a reliance on close family ties among top managers and the intensive cultivation of state connections, characteristics which he sees continuing into the post-war period.

The Japanese-directed early industrialization of Korea generated widespread urbanization and population mobility. By 1945, fully 20 per cent of all Koreans were living abroad or in provinces other than their native ones (Cumings, 1984). Between 1935 and 1940 the population of the 11 largest cities in Korea rose by 91 per cent and a number of new cities mushroomed during this period, so that by

1940 over 13 per cent of the population was located in cities of over 15,000 people (Henderson, 1968: 99–100). Seoul alone had a population of almost one million in 1940, a figure which represented a growth of over 100 per cent in ten years. Colonialism also led to a significant labour surplus. As Amsden (1989: 191) puts its: 'minimal investment in health and sanitation by the colonial authorities enabled the population to grow, minimal investments in industry and agriculture dampened demands for labour's services'.

Later industrialization intensified this urbanization, so that by 1985 over a fifth (23.8 per cent) of the population lived in Seoul, and in 1982, 61 per cent lived in cities of over 50,000 people (Steinberg, 1989: 15). This tremendous movement of people fragmented rural commitments and identities so that traditional political loyalties were broken and competition for access to central power became more intense. Colonialism, then, succeeded in destroying the pre-industrial framework and mobilizing a large proportion of the population for political participation without providing the stable institutions for channelling and developing such participation which could survive its demise.

This failure to develop new forms of political organization and allegiance meant that, when the US occupation of Korea ended in 1948, traditional patterns recurred, fuelled by the growing urban and unemployed population as well as the even greater concentration of power at the centre as a result of the occupation (Henderson, 1968: 126–47). The combination of widespread economic upheaval, inflation, unemployment and high population growth with US indecision and uncertainty about the role of the US Army military government led to considerable disorder and insecurity. Dependence on the central government increased dramatically at the same time as its apparent competence decreased, and ambitious Koreans competed intensely to gain access to the military government and the resources it controlled.

When Syngman Rhee took over in 1948, the attractive power of the central government was stronger than in the nineteenth century because of the dislocations of colonialism and occupation and the much greater involvement of the state in agricultural and industrial affairs. Land reform, begun by the US authorities in 1946, weakened the landlord class and reduced the proportion of agricultural land farmed by tenants from 75 per cent in 1945 to 33 per cent in 1948 (Henderson, 1968: 156); but it also increased peasants' dependence on the central state and the patrimonial powers of the bureaucracy. The Japanese had developed an administrative system that integrated village communities with the central state for the first time in Korea; this was now used by the Korean elite to control rural development centrally and prevent local centres of power emerging.

The increased competition for access to central positions of power in the post-colonial era was accompanied by a return to earlier patterns of official mobility. Within six months of taking office Rhee changed half his ministers, and on average he changed more than ten of them each year between 1948 and 1960 (Henderson, 1968: 238–9). These changes often involved vice-ministers and bureau heads as well, so that the bureaucratic elite was highly unstable and could not develop a coherent administrative system. This overall pattern of frequent personnel changes continued through the short-lived government of Chang Myon and the early days of the subsequent military regime of Park Chong-hui, reflecting the desire 'to prevent the consolidation of groups, bonds, personal powers and vested interests in any province, ministry or board' (Henderson, 1968: 239–40) which is such a striking feature of Korean patrimonialism (cf. Steinberg, 1989: 96).

A related feature of pre-industrial Korea which recurred after 1945 was factionalism. The intense competition for central power between leading yangban families characteristic of the late Yi dynasty (Palais, 1975: 15–16) was encouraged by the Japanese and was generalized more widely after the liberation as numerous cliques and small groups based on kinship, locality and academic training formed 300 political 'parties' in 1945–6 to gain access to the military government (Cumings, 1984). Since these groupings were essentially collectivities of individuals who joined together to enable their leaders to attain and maintain power rather than to represent interest groups or pursue specific policies, they were highly opportunistic and co-operated only for their own short-term advantage (Jacobs, 1985: 26–7). Thus, when the Democratic Party took office in 1960 it fragmented into the various factions that constituted it as they fought over the spoils of government, confirming, in Henderson's words (1968: 304–5), 'an ancient Korean political rule . . . that the unity and cohesion of groups must yield to the demands of individuals or subgroups for access to power; there is a deep cultural aversion to firm bonds lest they impede equal mobility'. This factionalism continued during the military regime and remains a significant feature of Korean society today, inhibiting the development of stable political organizations (cf. Pye, 1985: 84–6).

The Korean War destroyed most of the industrial infrastructure developed by the Japanese, generated further massive movements of the population, expanded the military and entrenched intense factionalism and corruption in it (Henderson, 1968: 346–50), and largely completed the process of land reform. It also, though, focused US political attention on Korea in a way that had not been apparent during the occupation and led to the establishment of new training establishments and an Americanization of the army which had major consequences. In particular, the reopened Korea Military Academy, modelled on West Point, systematically set out to produce an officer class that had high cohesion, group loyalty and a strict code of conduct. It became, in Henderson's (1968: 353) words, 'a kind of island off Korea's moral coast, governed by standards quite different from those of the society around it'. Gradually the Korean military standardized recruitment and training procedures, developed some career specialization and reduced the importance of personal favouritism in promotions (Henderson, 1968: 352–4).

This formalization and systematic organization of the Korean armed forces not only 'converted an inept glorified constabulary into one of the most efficient professional fighting machines in the world' (Jacobs, 1985: 178), but also produced a powerful and cohesive social institution committed to economic development for the first time in Korea's history. The courses of the National Defence College and other training for the military elite developed skills in administration, control and decision making as well as emphasizing development goals and the backward state of the Korean economy. Thus senior officers 'acquired strong impressions of the possibilities of the nation and the limitations of the existing political system' (Henderson, 1968: 345). These perceptions were sharpened by the decline in promotion opportunities as the rapidly expanded army, which grew from 50,000 in 1950 to 655,000 in 1953, stopped growing, and the more recently trained officers saw their access to higher rank blocked by men only a few years older who were often less well trained, less rigorously selected and frequently with no more experience. Despite some purging of the higher command in 1959, not all of the old-style faction leaders and others suspected of corruption were removed; and their retention formed one focus, among others, for the military coup in 1961 which led to the dismissal of 2,000 senior officers (Henderson, 1968: 355–7; Steinberg, 1989: 109–12).

The relative ease with which the coup took place reflected the lack of strong intermediary organizations in Korean society which could have served as the focus for opposition. As with previous changes of regime, the ambitious quickly seized the opportunity to join the key agency of central power, in this case the Korean CIA, and developed new factions there (Henderson, 1968: 264–8). However, the traditionally low prestige of the military in Korean society, and the need to legitimate its rule, led to a much stronger commitment to economic development goals than in many military dictatorships (Steinberg, 1989: 129), as well as its formal 'civilianization' in 1963 (Cumings, 1988). While the coup and the subsequent domination by the military may reflect patrimonial goals of monopolizing prebends and the spoils of office to some extent (Jacobs, 1985: 178), they have also ensured that Korea is ruled by a relatively cohesive elite which has been trained in administrative and technical skills and legitimizes itself in terms of developmental goals.

This situation is a considerable contrast to pre-industrial Korea and bears some similarities to the political structures of Japanese colonialism. As Henderson (1968: 190–1) puts it:

> Economic rewards and values have started to take the place of political ones, much as the old colonial administration intended. Inflation and corruption, by outrunning official salaries and placing the bureaucracy at the mercy of business bribing, have increased the trend toward business and the enthusiasm of young men for entering it in place of government.

Thus the militarization of Korean society led to some significant changes in the operation of the political system, its overt goals and the skills it rewards. While scarcely transforming it into a 'rational' and efficient machine for economic development, it has altered key features and institutions (Cumings, 1988). In particular, it reinforced and intensified the acceptance of authoritarian discipline which was deliberately institutionalized by the Japanese through the elementary schools. As Kim (1988) has emphasized, this high level of militaristic discipline throughout Korean society has been an important factor in the economic development of Korea and has reinforced traditional Confucian acceptance of hierarchical authority.

The Korean developmental state established by the 1961 coup is a much more centralized and autocratic one than was the Meiji state in Japan. The civilian bureaucracy is subservient to the political–military leadership and the Presidential 'Blue House' administrative apparatus dominates both the central government machine and society at large. As Jacobs (1985: 19) points out, the President rather than the formal legal system defines and maintains the civil service code, and the executive controls the high civil servants by making their security dependent on ministerial patronage. Each President tends to enact his own constitution which reflects his singular vision of the presidency and his distinctive ruling style. Executive authority, then, has become highly centralized and remarkably free from either· bureaucratic or legislative constraint. This, together with the military command structure (Steinberg, 1989: 113), has enabled developmental goals to be implemented extremely quickly but also, of course, has intensified traditional Korean dependence on the central state and inhibited the development of semi-autonomous political institutions. The extent of central administrative control of local affairs has also grown, building on the inheritance of Japanese colonialism. As Jacobs suggests (1985: 34): 'Korean administration has profited . . . from the Japanese modernizing improvements . . . and from advanced American techniques of public administration, both of which have streamlined the system and made it possible to exercise jurisdiction at local levels far beyond the reach of the older apparatus'.

The Political System in Taiwan during Industrialization
The Japanese colonization of Taiwan from 1895 to 1945 developed both the physical and social infrastructure of Taiwanese society through expanding the transport system, introducing the legal protection of private property, improving agricultural productivity and expanding the educational system (Gold, 1986: 34–54; 1988a; Ho, 1984). Initially concentrating on agricultural development to provide food for Japan, the colonial government later developed the food processing and some other industries as the Japanese economy became more industrialized and militarized. As in Korea, the Japanese controlled nearly all industrial activities, and the few favoured Taiwanese in business were restricted to commercial, textiles and food-related activities. Thus the development of technical and managerial skills among the indigenous population was limited. However, the infrastructure and factories built by the Japanese were dispersed throughout Taiwan, and so the 'modern' sector of society was not restricted to a small area. Additionally, Taiwanese peasants retained their private holdings, and in general landownership patterns were marked by considerable continuity, so that rural development and learning took place throughout most of this period without great disruption and dislocation (Wade, 1990: 73–5). Politically, the Japanese seem to have allowed rather more indigenous activity and organization in Taiwan than they did in Korea, at least up to 1935 (McNamara, 1986); but overall, of course, control was firmly retained by the colonial power, and a strong policy of assimilating the Taiwanese into Japanese culture was followed (Wade, 1990: 232).

Taiwan was returned to China's control in 1945 and was then plundered by the Nationalists over the next few years, leading to a spontaneous uprising in 1947 which was brutally suppressed by the occupying power at the cost of between 10,000 and 20,000 deaths (Gold, 1986: 49–55). At the end of 1949 Chiang Kai-shek moved the Kuomintang (KMT) government to Taiwan, together with over one million civilian and military refugees, at a time when the native population was only six million. According to Gold (1986: 59), most of these were personally loyal to the Generalissimo and willing to make sacrifices, whereas the more obviously corrupt leaders of the KMT scattered to Hong Kong, South-East Asia and the USA. This facilitated the reform of the KMT and destruction of many of the previously important factions, as well as providing 'an abundance of well-trained, extremely talented and committed men who found their way to the top, especially in the bureaucracies charged with management of the economy' (Gold, 1986: 62; cf. Wade, 1990: 247–8; Winckler, 1988). It also, however, meant that a large number of mainlanders had to be rewarded for their loyalty with posts in the state bureaucracy and state-owned industries, thus excluding Taiwanese from careers in the civil service, the military and, subsequently, large-scale industry.

The military force controlled by the KMT was crucial in its gaining control over Taiwan and establishing hegemony over Taiwanese society. However, the military was not superior to the party and was closely supervised through a system of political commissars administered by Chiang Ching-kuo, the Generalissimo's son (Winckler, 1988). Thus the KMT regime was not just a civilianized military one, as in Korea after 1961. As an external occupying force, though, it had few ties to existing elites; indeed it had largely destroyed the old intellectual and political elites and had no capitalist or financial class to contend with, and so could act autonomously with respect to native dominant groups (Wade, 1990: 231–4). This domination was further increased by extensive land reforms carried out with US advice and supported between 1949 and 1953 (Simon, 1988). All landholdings of over 3 hectares were compulsorily purchased by the state for resale to the current cultivators, and landowners were compensated 70 per cent with land bonds in kind and 30 per cent with shares in four state enterprises (Gold, 1986: 65–6). Most of the smaller-scale landlords quickly resold their shares to a few mainlander financier-bureaucrats and so failed to develop as a business class (Simon, 1988). By 1953 the amount of land cultivated by tenants had fallen to 16.3 per cent and owner-farmers constituted 57 per cent of all farmers. The small landowning family became the dominant force in rural Taiwan, and the landlord class ceased to exist as a distinct economic force.

This reform of land tenure was accompanied by an extension of state control over the peasantry. Through 340 KMT-controlled farmers' associations, the government increased productivity, introduced new techniques and crops and ensured central domination of the agricultural economy. As in Korea, the state squeezed the rural sector to feed the growing urban population and to provide funds for industrialization, primarily through a land tax, the compulsory sale of rice at fixed prices and the inequitable rice–fertilizer barter system (Gold, 1986: 66–7). However, because of the role of the peasants in the Nationalists' defeat in the Chinese civil war, the KMT was careful not to risk alienating the peasantry in Taiwan and pursued less authoritarian and discriminatory policies than its Korean counterpart. In general, rural–urban disparities in Taiwan have been less marked than in Korea, and the disruption to rural communities caused by industrialization has been less. Rural industries have been more important in Taiwan, and the rate of urbanization lower (Cumings, 1987; Haggard, 1988; Stites, 1982).

Politically Taiwan has been a one-party state since the KMT took over. Operating under martial law from 1947 to 1987, the regime has proscribed and repressed attempts at establishing alternative or 'non-party' political organizations, although opposition parties have developed in the past few years. A highly centralized political executive has dominated both the bureaucracy and the legislature and monopolized power. However, the early exclusion of Taiwanese from the upper reaches of the KMT has now been reversed, to the extent that the current President, Lee Teng-hui, is a native. As the KMT stabilized its rule and began to reap the rewards of economic development, it co-opted and incorporated Taiwanese technocrats and other elite groups, so that it is no longer a cohesive vanguard elite but has become more open and pluralist (Gold, 1986: 118–20; Wade, 1990: 248–53; Winckler, 1988). By developing a local government system under KMT control and ensuring party control of rural associations and the labour movement, the Taiwan state has succeeded in integrating Taiwanese society to a greater extent than its equivalent in Korea and ensured greater political continuity and stability. Local political activity has formed a channel for some grievances to be aired and skilful co-option of potential dissidents has enabled the KMT to neutralize a considerable amount of potential opposition (Haggard, 1988).

This relative stability was, of course, greatly facilitated by the high rates of economic growth achieved by Taiwan since 1950 and the restricted inequalities of income that have developed during this growth (Greenhalgh, 1988a). Given the traditional disdain of

Chinese mandarins and political elites for private business, and their reluctance to tolerate private concentrations of wealth, this expansion of the market economy may seem surprising. Indeed there were considerable disputes in the KMT about the desirability of opening up the Taiwanese economy and promoting exports in the 1960s, and it is not clear that this path would have been followed in the absence of US pressure (Barrett, 1988; Gold, 1986: 75–8; Haggard, 1990: 90–3; cf. Wade, 1990: appendix B). However, the declining credibility of the initial legitimation of KMT domination – that control over Taiwan was the basis for retaking the mainland – together with the increasingly apparent pay-off from economic expansion based on the private sector encouraged the KMT to concentrate on promoting economic development as the primary means of justifying its role (Cumings, 1987), and as a way of providing opportunities for the ambitious Taiwanese outside politics and state employment. Thus, a distinctive division of labour developed between the mainlanders who controlled the political system, the bureaucracy, military and state firms and the native Taiwanese who concentrated on business success in the private sector (Gold, 1988b). This division of labour and political subordination of the Taiwanese made business careers more attractive to the educated Taiwanese than in traditional Chinese society and encouraged them to invest in vocational education and training as well as more traditionally prestigious subjects. Together with state expansion of engineering education, this helped Taiwan to train 50 per cent more engineers per 1,000 population in the 1970s than did the USA (Amsden, 1985a; Wade, 1990: 190).

In sum, then, the particular conditions of KMT rule in Taiwan led the highly autonomous and centralized political executive to pursue economic development goals through a decentralized private sector guided by a powerful economic bureaucracy. The combination of defeat in the civil war, dependence on United States aid, domination of Taiwan as an external elite controlling the military and the need to demonstrate the success of a non-communist regime enabled the KMT to neutralize or destroy rival elites and also encouraged it to seek economic growth through competition between privately controlled enterprises. This commitment was implemented by 'an extraordinarily able cohort of economic technocrats' (Gold, 1988b: 203) who followed 'Japanese-style' developmentalist policies, rather than the pure market models advocated by many US advisers, and exercised considerable control over private firms' opportunity sets through state enterprises, investment incentives, import restrictions, the banking system and foreign exchange control (Wade, 1990: 217–27).

The Political System in Hong Kong during Industrialization

Hong Kong's political system is, of course, quite different from the other East Asian economies considered in this book, and its pattern of industrialization has also varied in significant ways. As a British colony throughout the industrialization period, the political structure has been much more simple and stable, if not indeed frozen, than that of Japan, Korea and Taiwan. Its small size and origins as a centre for trade with China have meant that it has always been highly trade dependent and could not pursue thoroughgoing import substitution policies or depend on the home market for industrial development. As a highly urbanized society, the need to increase agricultural productivity and the possibility of shifting surpluses from the primary sector to manufacturing were clearly not significant, and relations between urban and rural communities have not been a significant feature of Hong Kong's development. Finally, its close connections with, and dependence on, China have restricted its political autonomy and the development of indigenous institutions.

These differences have meant that the institutional environment in which successful businesses have been developed in Hong Kong over the past 40 years varied significantly from that in Japan, Korea and Taiwan. In particular, the structure and role of the state during industrialization have been quite distinct, together with the official ideology justifying its role. Additionally, the colonial nature of Hong Kong has resulted in the development of an Anglo-Saxon legal system and liberal professions such as accountancy, as well as a British-based education system. Consequently state–business relations have taken a rather different form from those elsewhere in East Asia, although the free market rhetoric of some administrators should not obscure the very considerable role played by the state in Hong Kong's success, especially since the mid-1960s (Schiffer, 1991). As a result the Hong Kong economy has been much more open to external influences and changes, and long-term, large-scale state co-ordination of economic resources has not received particular support or encouragement.

As in Korea and Taiwan, industrialization in Hong Kong took place in a remarkably short period. Until the 1950s the Hong Kong economy was largely based on entrepôt trade between China and the rest of the world. As late as 1951, two-thirds of Hong Kong's exports went to China, and most exports to the USA and Britain were re-exports of Chinese goods (Henderson, 1989; Youngson, 1982: 1–3). Although some manufacturing of commodities such as furniture and cotton garments had developed by the 1930s, this was

largely artisanal in character and formed only a very small proportion of the colony's exports. The 1951 United Nations embargo on
trade with China destroyed the bulk of this entrepôt trade and
threatened to destroy the entire economy. However, the combination of the Korean War, expansion of demand for textile products
and immigration of Shanghaiese cotton spinners, together with
some of their workers, machinery and cotton, led to the development of the Hong Kong textile and garment industry, which still
dominates its manufacturing economy (Nishida, 1990; Wong,
1988a). By 1959 the number of registered factories had risen to
5,023 from 1,426 in 1949, and factory employment stood at
217,367. In the same year, 70 per cent of Hong Kong's exports
were of local origin and only 30 per cent were re-exports, a reversal
of the proportions obtaining in 1953 (Scott, 1989: 70–1). In 1961
the manufacturing sector accounted for 43 per cent of the total
labour force and contributed 23.6 per cent of gross domestic
product.

The growth of tourism and the financial services industry in the
1970s has boosted service sector employment, to the extent that by
1987 manufacturing employment had fallen to 33.3 per cent, but
manufacturing still provides more jobs in Hong Kong than elsewhere in East Asia (Henderson, 1989). While new industries, such
as plastics and electronics, have developed since the 1950s, manufactured exports are still dominated by textiles and apparel; and
overall the industrial structure of Hong Kong is highly focused, to
the extent that textiles, garments and electronics contributed nearly
two-thirds of all manufactured exports in the 1980s. This concentration has meant that economic development in Hong Kong has
been based on light industry and services rather than capital-
intensive industry and has not required large-scale co-ordination of
human, financial and material resources. Thus, small firms
continue to dominate Hong Kong's economy especially the export
sector, and indeed establishments employing less than 50 people
increased their share of manufacturing employment from 26.2 per
cent in 1951 to 36.4 per cent in 1978 and 40.5 per cent in 1981
(Castells et al., 1990: 66). According to Sit and Wong (1988), this
tendency for the small firm sector to increase in importance in
Hong Kong continued through the 1980s. In 1986 firms employing
under 200 people accounted for 73.4 per cent of the total manufacturing labour force and contributed 65.4 per cent of total output,
an increase on equivalent figures for 1973.

This industrialization of Hong Kong took place in a colonial
state whose leaders refused to invest in technical training or
provide a basic infrastructure for the cotton industry, let alone

arrange an international loan for capital investment to resuscitate the Hong Kong economy after the Communist take-over in China (Scott, 1989: 67–9). Essentially the bureaucratic elite maintained its commitment to the minimal colonial state whose basic function was to maintain law and order and protect the interests of British merchants. This conception of the state, common to a number of British colonies in the nineteenth century which were expected to be financially self-supporting, had remained substantially the same since the early period of the colony, although some commitment to support voluntary agencies providing health, education and welfare functions did develop. As Scott (1989: 73) puts it: 'fiscal conservatism, and the ever-present threat of criticism from vigilant and entrenched business elites, meant that government expenditure was pared to a minimum'.

As a colony Hong Kong's political system is clearly subservient to that of the colonial power, and there is no independent political executive. Thus, the 'state' is essentially the public bureaucracy, since there are no political parties, the military has little involvement in local politics, and there is little decentralization of political control. This administrative state has incorporated major economic elites into its decision-making processes since the end of the nineteenth century and, although vulnerable to sustained and cohesive attack from dominant business interests, retains a certain autonomy from them. Despite the old cliché that power in colonial Hong Kong resides more in the hands of the Jockey Club, Jardine Matheson and the Hong Kong and Shanghai Bank than the government and the civil service, Scott (1989: 65; cf. Haggard, 1990: 123) claims that

> The reality was that power still lay with the bureaucratic elite in the civil service. Their actions might be modified by other elites and they were careful to follow cautious and elite-approved policies towards the Chinese community. But they still retained relative autonomy in decision making, and they could manipulate opinion through judicious appointments to committees . . . and through appeals to the over-riding authority of the Secretary of State who increasingly acted as the Hong Kong government wanted him to act.

While the rise of a new Chinese business elite with international assets and activities may have reduced the patronage control of the bureaucratic elite (Wong, 1989), the superior position of this elite still seems widely agreed (Castells et al., 1990: 91). As Schiffer (1991: note 3) puts it: 'It is agreed by both orthodox and radical writers that the person who *really* runs Hong Kong is the Financial Secretary.'

The power and autonomy of the bureaucratic-political elite,

however, are clearly much less than those of the political executive in Korea and Taiwan during industrialization. Their titular position as subordinates to the British Colonial and Foreign Secretaries and need to accommodate the demands of both British and Chinese business elites have both restricted their freedom of action and inhibited the development and implementation of long-term economic development policies. Their ability to coerce business leaders in a comparable manner to the post-1961 Korean state is limited by the existence of a relatively independent legal system and a much more pluralistic institutional framework. Equally, their lack of control over foreign exchange and capital movements, highlighted in various financial crises, obviously restricts their capacity to direct investment plans or promote particular strategies. While, then, the bureaucracy may constitute the state and thus dominate the political system, its autonomy from business elites seems much less than in Korea or Taiwan, and its ability to co-ordinate industrial policies seems less than that of its Japanese counterpart. Furthermore, its organization into separate departments, which had little interaction with each other and considerable autonomy to pursue their own goals, inhibited co-ordinated planning and development (Scott, 1989: 117–18).

These brief accounts of East Asian political systems during industrialization have highlighted a number of important differences between them which can be summarized in terms of the four features listed in Table 5.1. Considering first the degree of state autonomy and its ability to implement development plans regardless of pressures from other elite groups, it seems clear that the Japanese state for most of the industrialization period has only displayed a moderate degree of autonomy, albeit greater after the SCAP reforms in the 1940s than in the earlier pre-1930 phase, if Johnson's (1982) account is accepted. In contrast, the Korean and Taiwanese states have exercised high levels of autonomy and been able to implement their economic policies as 'hard states', in Jones and Sakong's (1980: 133) terms. In the case of Hong Kong, the colonial state may have functioned as the dominant component of the political system in the twentieth century, but its need to accommodate business elite interests and, after 1949, Chinese pressures implies much less autonomy than elsewhere in East Asia.

State autonomy needs to be combined with a political commitment to economic development led by state institutions, of course, if it is to play a major role in the industrialization process and structure the sorts of successful forms of business organization that develop. For the reasons discussed earlier in this chapter, this

Table 5.1 *Differences in East Asian political systems during industrialization*

	Japan	Korea	Taiwan	Hong Kong
State autonomy and implementation capacity	Limited before 1930, medium after 1945	High after 1961	High after 1950	Limited
Commitment to state-directed industrialization	Limited before 1930, high afterwards	High after 1961	High after 1950	Low
State cohesion and domination by executive	Low	High	High	n.a.
Domination by external elite	No	No	Yes	Yes

commitment was quite high in Japan, Korea and Taiwan for much of the post-war period, although less tied to direct state control of resources and enterprises in Japan than in Korea and Taiwan. In Hong Kong, however, it was much more muted and expressed in relatively indirect ways. Broad elite support for industrialization and economic growth here did not imply a leading role for the state.

The degree of differentiation between, and relative power of, the bureaucracy and the political executive, as well as the degree of cohesion of each, has also varied significantly between East Asian countries. In Japan, state institutions have been more differentiated, and the executive has been much less powerful and unified than in post-1961 Korea or post-1950 Taiwan, where the central political authority has clearly dominated the bureaucracy and integrated state institutions more cohesively. The lack of a separate political executive in Hong Kong has meant that the bureaucratic elite has developed a political role, so the bureaucracy can be said to dominate, or even constitute, the state; but this is clearly different from the Japanese situation where power and responsibility are fragmented and diffused between the LDP factions, business elites and important ministries. Focusing on the degree to which the executive is cohesive and dominates the state highlights the important differences between Japan and Korea and Taiwan but is not really applicable to Hong Kong.

The final important differences between East Asian political systems to be considered here is their domination by ethnic outsiders. In both Taiwan and Hong Kong industrialization took place in political systems where the indigenous population, and ethnically related immigrants in the case of Hong Kong, were excluded from the political system and most state-owned institutions by the ethnically distinct dominant group. Elite status was therefore predominantly accessible only through private business success. Most Koreans, of course, were similarly excluded from political activity after the 1961 coup, but they were not excluded from senior posts in the bureaucracy, and the divide between the state and private business activities was not reinforced by ethnic differences there. Partly as a result, connections between state agencies and leading businesses have been much closer in Korea and Japan than in Taiwan and Hong Kong.

State–Business Relations in East Asia during Industrialization

Japan

State–business relations in Japan have changed significantly during industrialization, just as the political system has. In particular, the extent of state steering and encouragement of industrial development grew considerably in the 1930s and during the occupation. As mentioned above, the ability of the economic bureaucracy to intervene in firms' strategic choices was greatly enhanced by the dismantling of the zaibatsu and the reform of the financial system. Thus, both the balance of power between big business and the state, and the commitment of bureaucratic and political elites to state-coordinated development, have altered since the reforms of the early Meiji period.

An indication of the limited economic role of the Japanese state before the 1930s was its limited ownership and control of enterprises. Except in the early years of the Meiji restoration, when the state established a number of model enterprises in mining, shipbuilding, railways, machinery and armaments manufacturing, the extent of state ownership has been quite small in Japan. As Samuels (1987) shows, ownership of coal mines, electric power producers and oil companies by the Japanese state has been among the lowest in the industrial world. Similarly, ownership of what other countries, particularly developing ones, often consider to be strategic industries has tended to be private in Japan, with the exception of the iron and steel industry, which was dominated by the state-owned Yawata Ironworks for many years (Allen, 1981: 82). Thus state co-ordination and guidance in Japan has not been exercised through public ownership of economic enterprises and assets. Rather it has been a matter of personal networks and mutual obligations, together with state control of foreign exchange and access to foreign technology in the post-war period, as well as considerable influence on the banking system in the 'high-growth' 1950s and 1960s.

The banking system itself is an important example of the relatively low degree of state ownership in Japan during industrialization, and the concomitant high level of economic decentralization and pluralism compared to many developing nations. Although the Meiji state established a number of specialized banks for long-term industrial and agricultural development, such as the Industrial Bank of Japan in 1900 and the Hypothec Bank of Japan in 1896, as well as the Yokohama Specie Bank to control foreign exchange and finance foreign trade, a considerable number of privately owned banks were established in the years before the First World War and the largest of them formed the core companies of the zaibatsu (Allen, 1981: 52–62). The large private banks were quite independent of the Bank of Japan because of the relatively weak position of the central bank. As Allen (1981: 59–60) puts it:

> the central bank's functions were more narrowly restricted than those of the central banks in most European countries . . . it could not be said that the banking reserves of the country were centralized through the medium of that institution . . . its slender connection with them [the commercial banks] in normal times meant that it was unable to exercise control over their policy.

Thus the Japanese banking system during the early stages of industrialization was dominated by large commercial banks which were members of conglomerate industrial groups to which they channelled funds raised from fixed deposits. The weakness of the Tokyo Stock Exchange and other capital market institutions (Clark, 1979: 33–4) meant that the private banks became the main intermediaries between savers and corporate borrowers and substantial owners of shares in the growing industrial sector in Japan. In addition, the zaibatsu established insurance and trust companies to raise funds for their subsidiaries and so developed very powerful privately controlled financial groups which were quite autonomous from the state until the 1930s.

As well as encouraging the development of joint stock banks, which became the core institutions of the politically supported zaibatsu, the Meiji oligarchy also stimulated the formation of general trading companies (GTC), or sogo shosha, to concentrate scarce skills and other resources in the management of foreign trade and to compete effectively with Western trading firms. These companies were initially set up to control coal exports and imports of foreign technology, often on the basis of official monopolies, particularly Mitsui Bussan and Mitsubishi Shoji (Yoshihara, 1982:

15–23). Later they expanded to become the dominant agencies controlling Japan's imports and exports of a wide range of raw materials and manufactured goods. In 1907, for instance, Mitsui Bussan alone was responsible for 18 per cent of Japan's total exports and nearly 21 per cent of its imports (Yoshino and Lifson, 1986: 13), and dominated the development of the cotton textile industry by controlling the importing of raw cotton and machinery and the exporting of finished goods. It took the initiative in organizing Japanese spinners and weavers into export guilds and became the sole agent representing them abroad. As key components of the zaibatsu, the sogo shosha played a critical role in Japan's industrialization and in the institutionalization of organized markets that are such a distinctive feature of the modern Japanese business system.

It is important to note here that, despite the growth of the electric power and machinery industries in the 1920s, the dominant manufacturing industries in terms of employment remained textiles and garments well into the 1930s, and 46.8 per cent of the occupied population remained employed in agriculture in 1930 (Allen, 1981: 251–3). In terms of value added, the textiles industry contributed 36.5 per cent of the total of all industrial groups in 1930, with food and drink constituting the next largest category at 16 per cent (Allen, 1981: 259). This dominance of the textile industry was even more marked in the export trade. In 1929 it accounted for 65 per cent of total exports, with raw silk alone contributing 37 per cent (Allen, 1981: 114). Thus 60 years after the Meiji restoration, the Japanese economy was still dominated by light manufacturing industry using largely female labour from the countryside, and exports remained highly dependent on the semi-finished commodity of raw silk produced by farmers and small-scale reeling establishments. Industrialization did not, then, lead to a sharp break with the agricultural sector but developed symbiotically with it. The success of the Japanese silk industry, incidentally, depended closely on the co-operation of the peasant producers, reeling firms, banks and exporters which was organized by the state through a system of licensing and regulation. In contrast, the Chinese silk industry failed to develop because of the indifference of the state and the inability of the foreign firms to develop close links with silk raisers (Allen, 1981: 71–2). The co-ordinating role of the state clearly made a crucial difference in developing this fragmented and geographically dispersed industry.

The increasing militarization of the Japanese economy in the 1930s, and the collapse of the export market for raw silk in the slump, encouraged a sharper shift into heavy industry and led to the rise of the 'new' zaibatsu, which were more closely associated with the military and industrial development in Manchuria. The most significant of these was Nissan, which had a more dispersed shareholding structure than the older zaibatsu and was more focused on heavy industry. Between 1930 and 1937 the output of ferrous metals and chemicals nearly tripled, and the export trade became far more diversified, with machinery and metal manufacturers taking a greater percentage. However, these developments had not gone far enough to support an extended war with fully industrialized societies such as the USA, and the military's attempt to control the zaibatsu through establishing control boards to regulate each industrial sector failed to take account of the predominantly horizontal links between their constituent firms. It did, though, lead to the expansion and formalization of middle and lower management, according to Hirschmeier and Yui (1981: 238–53).

The post-war reforms provided a variety of both formal and informal instruments for state agencies to pursue economic development policies. Among the legislative acts that were passed during and after the occupation, for example, the Foreign Exchange and Foreign Trade Control Law (1949) and the Enterprises Rationalization Promotion Law (1952) enabled the MITI to control the terms and conditions on which foreign technology was imported and to exclude foreign entrants to Japan until the mid-1970s (Johnson, 1982: 194–220; Murakami, 1987; Okimoto, 1989: 27–8), as well as to restrict the entry of Japanese companies to new industries and so reduce corporate risks. More informal methods were used to guide investment plans, co-ordinate developments in new industries and organize recession cartels.

These methods have become famous under the term 'administrative guidance', and developed greater significance in the 1960s as a result of external pressure to liberalize the Japanese economy which restricted MITI's ability to use more formal powers (Okimoto, 1989: 93–5). Their effectiveness is due to the generally high prestige of the bureaucracy, its ability to retaliate in a variety of ways if firms do not follow the proffered guidance, its claim to represent the national interest and the overall pattern of state–business relations established in the 1930s (Johnson, 1982: 266). It should be noted, however, that the capacity of MITI and other agencies to compel firms to follow their policies is bounded, and their ability to implement proposals sometimes appears inadequate, as in the attempts to restructure the machine tool industry (Friedman, 1988). Consent is more often negotiated and reciprocal than imposed by the bureaucracy (Wakiyama, 1987), although the positive role of the economic ministries in co-ordinating firms' strategies, and organizing competition in new industries and restructuring declining ones, is clearly more significant in the post-war period than it was in the early twentieth century (Boyd, 1987). MITI, for example, played a major role in co-ordinating investment strategies through organizing 'discussion groups' in the petrochemicals, synthetic textiles, paper pulp and ferroalloys industries in the 1960s. It also helped to reamalgamate the component firms of the pre-war Mitsubishi Heavy Industries and was heavily involved in the restructuring of the Japanese steel industry (Johnson, 1982: 267–72, 282–4).

With regard to the financial system, the occupying authorities undertook a major reform which was intended to separate the larger banks from industrial and commercial firms as part of the break-up of the zaibatsu and encouragement of the more Anglo-Saxon separation of finance from industry (Allen, 1981: 204; Zysman, 1983: 234–51). Some of the specialist banks established by the Meiji government were closed down and others transformed into commercial banks. However, this process of restructuring and 'liberalizing' the financial system did not fundamentally change its nature, as became clear when Japan regained its sovereignty in 1952. In that year the Industrial Bank of Japan was re-established as the leading long-term credit bank, and several new state-owned or state-controlled specialist banks were set up around the same time, such as the Export–Import Bank and the Japan Development Bank. The segmentation of financial institutions and markets was carefully maintained and enhanced by the Ministry of Finance to facilitate its control of the financial system and help reduce instability. Thus the national 'city' commercial banks are restricted to particular localities; long-term credit and trust banks are separated from general commercial banks; and small businesses and agricultural loans are the preserve of specialist institutions (Lincoln, 1988: 134–5).

This segmentation and its regulation by the state highlight one of the important differences between the post-war financial system and that existing before the militarization of the economy – the more influential role of the state and its more systematic pursuit of economic growth. As mentioned earlier, the post-war purge and reforms greatly increased the relative power of the economic ministries in Japan, and this was particularly true of their control over the banking system. This power was used to promote industrial growth, especially in heavy industry, at the expense of household incomes and social infrastructure. Essentially, the state channelled both private savings in the Post Office Savings Banks and those deposited with the commercial banks into industrial investment and improving the physical infrastructure at artificially low interest rates. Together with other economic policies, such as the income doubling plan of the 1960s, this encouraged high corporate demand for bank loans and enabled policy makers to direct investment funds to favoured industries and sectors through administrative regulation (Lincoln, 1988: 131–7). As Zysman (1983: 75–80) has pointed out, such state direction of capital is much easier in credit-based financial systems, like the Japanese one, than in capital-market-based ones (cf. Cox, 1986).

As well as controlling the boundaries of financial markets and institutions, and their ability to raise funds through opening new branches, the state also controlled banks' behaviour by the 'window guidance' of the Bank of Japan and informal co-ordination of lending policies with the needs of corporate borrowers through various committees such as the Financial Institutions' Funds Council and the Industrial Finance Committee of MITI (Hamada and Horiuchi, 1987). The window guidance system of monetary control enabled the central bank to restrict credit growth by allocating loans preferentially to banks that followed its wishes. Since the city banks were usually 'overloaned' because of the high demand for credit from industry during the high-growth period of the 1950s and 1960s, they frequently had to borrow from the Bank of Japan and so submit to its guidance. Thus the central bank has been much more directly linked to the large banks in the post-war period than it was before the 1930s.

The combination of strong state commitment to economic growth and low real interest rates for bank loans encouraged high rates of corporate borrowing and led to considerable corporate dependence on the banks. For most of the post-war period, around a half of externally provided investment funds for firms has come from loans, with a substantial proportion of the rest being raised through trade credit (Hamada and Horiuchi, 1987). Equity issues and corporate bonds have been relatively unimportant until the late 1980s (Zielinski and Holloway, 1991: 14); and, although depreciation and retained earnings are more important nowadays than during the high-growth period, bank loans remain a significant source of new capital for industry (Lincoln, 1988: 148). Thus, fast growing enterprises became highly dependent on the city and long-term credit banks, as is demonstrated by the banks' ability to demand 'compensatory balances' from their customers when granting loans. These balances enabled the banks in effect to charge higher interest rates and were particularly important in the 1960s. According to Hamada and Horiuchi (1987: 237–8), the ratio of compensating balances to loans in 1964 was 11.1 per cent for city banks, 21.6 per cent for local banks, 40.6 per cent for savings banks and 41.9 per cent for credit associations, whereas these figures had dropped to 1.5 per cent, 1.9 per cent, 3 per cent and 8.9 per cent respectively in 1980. Not surprisingly, profit rates in banking were significantly higher than in the non-financial sector in the 1950s and 1960s; average after-tax profits ranged above 12 per cent per annum in these decades. These figures also indicate the preference given to the large corporate clients of the city banks relative to the small business and personal borrowers of the other banks. Thus, the larger banks and trading companies have been powerful economic actors in the post-war period, and access to bank capital for expansion plans has been a crucial weapon in the battle for market share and, in the long term, for corporate survival in Japan. As a result the close links between industrial and financial members of the zaibatsu which were broken by the occupation authorities have been renewed, albeit in a different form.

The final feature of state–business relations in Japan to be noted here is the continuing and substantial support of the agricultural system and the strong political concern to limit the impact of industrialization on rural households in the post-war period. Principally through price support schemes and control of imports, the state has ensured a considerable rise in farmers' incomes since 1945 and removed the sharp contrast between urban and rural communities. Thus, although the number of people engaged in agriculture has dropped considerably, the number of farm households has fallen much more slowly since the war (Allen, 1981: 222–4).

Korea

As suggested above, the post-1961 military-backed state in Korea has been able to implement its economic policies effectively and gain business compliance with its wishes. Because the political executive in Korea is closely linked to the military, and took power when the business world was relatively fragmented and weak, it is much less dependent on big business than the Japanese government was after the 1880s. While it depends on the success of business to achieve economic growth and so increase the spoils of office, it does not rely on political support to the same extent as most Japanese governments have had to (Jones and Sakong, 1980: 66–9). When Park achieved power, he arrested most of the leading businessmen, many of whom had become wealthy through corruption and state-backed monopolies under the Rhee regime, and threatened them with confiscation of their assets. This threat was lifted after the business elite agreed to develop new businesses and pay some fines. However, their bank shares were seized by the state, and the banking system remains a crucial instrument of state direction of economic development (Amsden, 1989: 72–4; Haggard, 1990: 64–75). Thus, while the business community in Japan can effectively dismiss LDP politicians by withholding support in an election, in Korea they could dismiss the military-backed President only by closing their firms down and thus ruining themselves in the process. Conversely, the Korean government can ensure the failure of any business (Jones and Sakong, 1980: 68–70). As McNamara (1990: 9–18) emphasizes, this pattern of business subordination to the state in Korea was established during Japanese colonialism and has developed distinctive attitudes among Korean entrepreneurs.

A key weapon in the state's ability to dominate the private sector in Korea is its control over credit, both domestic and foreign (Jones and Sakong, 1980: 103–9). Even though some shares in the commercial banks seized by the state in 1961 have been sold to private investors, the political executive continues to retain effective control over banking operations and loan decisions. It also directly controls the allocation of scarce foreign exchange for purchasing industrial and consumer goods. While Rhee used this to reward political loyalty and election contributions, Park and his successors have tied foreign credits more to export goals and favoured industries. Because the interest of banks loans has been consistently held down to around a half of the unofficial 'curb' market rate over the period from 1963 to 1976, and has sometimes been less than the rate of inflation, demand for loans has consistently been higher than supply, and so administrative discretion has determined their allocation in favour of the export sector and other policy objectives. Given the very high dependence of the fast growing chaebol on bank credit, such that debt/equity ratios in Korean manufacturing industry since the military coup of 1961 have exceeded 300 per cent in over half of the years between 1961 and 1984 and in two years, 1980 and 1981, were over 450 per cent, this has given the state considerable control over their policies and actions (Amsden, 1989: 104). Through control over domestic and foreign loans, then, the Korean state has been able to direct leading enterprises into new fields and has also encouraged the growth of large, diversified groups by subsidizing interest rates for favoured projects.

Thus use of state control over domestic and foreign loans to influence firms' actions in Korea reflects the political leadership's general willingness to exercise 'discretionary command' over the private business sector (Jones and Sakong, 1980: 119–40; cf. Jung, 1989). In addition to manipulating firms' opportunity sets by facilitating exports and reducing windfall profits from privileged access to import licences and foreign exchange, the military regime has directly intervened in particular decisions through threatening tax investigations and the withdrawal of current or expected privileges. The downfall of the Yulsan and Jese chaebol, for example, has been attributed to political instructions to the state-controlled banks to withdraw loan facilities (Michell, 1988: 96). In the case of Yulsan, this may have been a consequence of its supporting the political opposition in 1979 (Cumings, 1987). In developing new industries the Korean state has directed particular chaebol to invest heavily and then protected them by restricting entry and granting export subsidies, as when it selected Hyundai, Kia and G.M. Korea to establish the domestic car industry as a major exporting sector. Not only did the state select the firms, it also specified the maximum size of car engines and had to approve production plans (Wade, 1990: 309–11).

While this reliance on the 'rule of men' as opposed to the 'rule of law' could be seen as typical of Confucian patrimonialism, it has been relatively successful in developing competitive export industries in Korea, according to Jones and Sakong (1980: 138–9), because of the strong leadership commitment to economic growth in a hard state where hierarchical command is rigidly enforced. As they put it (p. 139): 'Economic growth under private enterprise being well understood as the dominant system goal, officials can seldom afford to act in a manner that seriously obstructs that goal.' The opportunities for personal gain that such discretionary commands afford bureaucratic and political elites have here been substantially offset by the strong commitment to national growth and the highly centralized command system that ensures such commitment is implemented through monitoring performance. While corruption does occur in post-1961 Korea (Kim, 1979), it is limited by the overriding objective of economic development which provides a relatively straightforward measure of success. The existence of a competing regime in North Korea, and the need to justify military domination in a society where the military have traditionally had little prestige, has encouraged the institutionalization of growth as the prime goal and restricted the extent to which elites could appropriate surpluses (Haggard, 1988; Wade, 1988).

A further important instrument of state intervention in economic affairs is public ownership. This is considerably greater in Korea than in Japan and has grown since 1961. According to Wade (1988), the share of publicly owned enterprises in gross fixed capital formation between 1965 and 1980 was 23 per cent in Korea compared to 11 per cent in Japan. As well as owning the larger banks and other financial institutions, the Korean state accounts for two-thirds of value added in electricity, water and sanitation services and slightly less than one-third of value added in mining and in transport and communications (Jones and Sakong, 1980: 149–50). In addition it is active in many manufacturing industries, most notably iron and steel, where the Pohang Iron and Steel Company (POSCO) dominates the domestic market as well as exporting a considerable proportion of its output (Amsden, 1989: 293–316). POSCO exemplifies the general tendency of state firms in Korea to be highly capital intensive and operating in imperfect markets as well as often being intended to produce substitutes for imports (Jones and Sakong, 1980: 150–5). In many cases these enterprises have been used by the state to subsidize export-oriented manufacturing firms, although Amsden (1989: 297) claims that POSCO was no more advantaged as a steel exporter than its Japanese competitors by the state subsidization of loans, utilities and infrastructure. Such relative efficiency of the Korean public sector is also noted by Jones and Sakong (1980: 159–65), despite the tendency to appoint top managers from military and bureaucratic elites. Two-thirds of the presidents of public enterprises came from these groups, and 90 per cent of them had had less than five years' experience with them. Essentially they suggest that this relative success follows from the state's willingness to divest itself of low-performing businesses and to manifest public approval or displeasure on the basis of performance.

The direct impact of state intervention in firms' strategic choices in Korea can be seen in the development of general trading companies (GTCs) there (Cho, 1987: 50–8). Encouraged in 1975 to boost Korean exports, these were modelled after the Japanese sogo shosha, and state support was tied directly to export targets. By providing direct subsidies in trade, finance and foreign exchange administration, together with concessions on state-initiated projects and public prestige, this policy led to five GTCs being recognized in 1975, a further six in 1976 and two more in 1978, mostly owned by the leading chaebol. By 1983 the ten GTCs which remained accounted for 51.3 per cent of all Korean exports, compared to 18.2 per cent in 1976, and clearly dominated those in heavy industrial goods. This mushrooming of new businesses and their rapid success in meeting state objectives show the responsiveness of the private sector to particular carrots and sticks offered by the political executive.

The combination of the state's commitment to development

goals, the use of political exhortation to encourage economic growth and approval to reward success, and the close association between state objectives and support for the chaebol has made these largely privately owned enterprises attractive sources of employment for elite graduates (Jung, 1989). While the state bureaucracy has traditionally been the most prestigious employer for ambitious Koreans, the combination of inflation and relatively low wages compared with those in the larger firms has reduced the relative desirability of state employment. Together with the national prestige of contributing to growth goals and being associated with one of the largest and most powerful corporate organizations, working for the state-approved and state-supported chaebol has become more enticing for many highly educated Koreans, thus encouraging the development of a highly educated stratum of middle managers (cf. Amsden, 1989: 217–31). The expansion of engineering courses in the 1960s and 1970s also provided crucial resources for the development of heavy industry in the 1990s (Kim, 1990). This movement into private managerial hierarchies was, of course, additionally influenced by the lack of political opportunities after 1961.

In terms of the policies followed by the Korean state and their implications for the business system, the dominant feature of the military regime has been its initial focus on exports and then the development of heavy industry. While the main concern under Rhee was to restrict and replace imports with domestic production, the military regime shifted state priorities considerably to export-oriented industrialization (Mason et al., 1980: 126–32). The exchange rate was devalued on numerous occasions between 1964 and 1977; export incentives were expanded and foreign loans for machinery purchases by exporting industries guaranteed by the state and tied to export performance (Haggard, 1990: 67–74). As Deyo (1989: 172–87) had pointed out, most of these early exporting industries in Korea, as elsewhere, were labour intensive with limited capital requirements and employing large numbers of female unskilled and semi-skilled workers. The growing labour force enabled employers to keep wages down during this period, and unemployment remained high in the urban areas in the 1960s (Michell, 1988: 100–1).

In the 1970s, though, Park changed this emphasis to an ambitious attempt to establish competitive heavy and chemical industries, partly to build the basis for a domestic defence industry and to justify the Yushin constitution which gave him sweeping new powers and unlimited tenure in office (Cumings, 1988; Haggard, 1988; 1990: 130–5; Mason et al., 1980: 52–3). As a result, over half of the total industrial investment during the early 1970s went into chemicals, petroleum and basic metals, and two-thirds of state industrial loans in 1980 were directed to heavy and chemical industries (Deyo, 1989: 26), partly because of financial difficulties in these areas at the end of the 1970s.

This switch of emphasis and resources led most large chaebol to diversify their activities considerably and increased overall concentration in the manufacturing sector as the importance of small and medium sized businesses declined. While the state had to absorb much of the risk in the early days of this policy, increasing profits over the period 1972–84 encouraged the largest chaebol to become more committed to the capital-intensive sector. As they learned how to manage large-scale investments and accumulated their own resources, they began to be a more active partner with the state, according to Kim (1989a) and Amsden (1989: 80–9). Another consequence of this move to heavy industrialization in Korea was the increased need for skilled labour and a greater awareness of the importance of training and retention of skilled workers – usually male. This in turn has encouraged some of the leading chaebol to develop personnel practices more similar to those of the Japanese kaisha for particular categories of workers in heavy industry, but differentials in general between manual and non-manual workers remain high (Deyo, 1989).

Taiwan

Taiwan is similar to Korea in the degree to which private business elites are subordinated to the state and in their correspondingly limited influence on state policies compared to Japanese business leaders. The ethnic divide between mainlanders and Taiwanese has exacerbated this subordination and reinforced the traditional Chinese distrust of large concentrations of power in private hands (Gold, 1988b). The KMT has retained its dominant economic position through extension of state ownership and controls over the private sector (Wade, 1990: 175–82). Both the massacre of Taiwanese in 1947 and later political attacks on Taiwanese entrepreneurs who became too independent of the KMT have ensured that private business elites do not trespass on its preserve. Thus the translation of private economic power into political influence and control is much less marked in Taiwan than in Japan.

The importance of the state is partly manifested by its continued ownership of major industries and the banking system. The state in Taiwan dominates the steel, heavy machinery, aluminium, shipbuilding, petroleum, synthetic fibres, engineering and semiconductor industries and still provides nearly a half of Taiwan's gross domestic capital formation (Gold, 1986: 109). Essentially the KMT has retained control of the major upstream heavy industries to ensure its continued ability to dominate the economy, meet the military's needs and provide employment for mainlander followers. Unlike in Korea, the Taiwanese leadership has preferred to keep heavy industry in its own hands and leave private Taiwanese entrepreneurs to flourish in the less capital-intensive sectors, thus reducing the likelihood of local control over large concentrations of capital (Wade, 1990: 272–80).

The financial system has similarly remained under strong state control, with almost every bank in Taiwan being either wholly or partly publicly owned and all foreign exchange transactions subject to state control (Amsden, 1985b; Gold, 1986: 108). According to Wade (1988), all Taiwanese banks must report foreign transactions to the central bank on a weekly basis, and foreign banks have to report all transactions daily. As state institutions the banks in Taiwan have pursued very conservative lending policies, preferring to lend to state enterprises and large firms with large amounts of collateral. This civil service mentality and aversion to risk have earned the banks the pejorative title of 'pawnshops'. In addition to the strong desire to maintain control over the financial system, this level of state ownership has also been justified in terms of the overriding need to maintain price stability. This preference is attributed by Gold (1988b) to the perception that rampant inflation helped the KMT to lose the Chinese civil war in the 1940s and to the large number of mainlander state employees in Taiwan on relatively fixed incomes.

The high dependence on external trade after the shift to export-oriented industrialization in the 1960s has led to the internationalization of most of Taiwan's economy, with foreign trade constituting over 70 per cent of its gross domestic product in the 1970s and over 90 per cent in some years in the 1980s (Gold, 1988b). This internationalization enhanced state control over the private business sector, since imports and foreign exchange have been firmly controlled through tariffs and other devices to ensure that domestic producers are encouraged to match foreign producers' terms (Wade, 1988). However, state control of the banking system as a whole has not led to the sort of discretionary management of private firms' finances which is such a feature of Korean industrialization.

The combination of large state-owned capital-intensive enterprises, conservative lending policies and mainlander–Taiwanese rivalries has resulted in relatively low reliance on bank loans by native entrepreneurs and a rather distant attitude towards them on the part of state officials. As Gold (1986: 126; cf. Wade, 1990: 276–86) puts it:

> in Taiwan planners retained an aloof posture. They met to formulate policy and then relayed their decisions and attendant mechanisms to implement it to the business community and watched what happened. Although cadres did meet with entrepreneurs to exert some pressure and picked some favourites, Taiwan's private sector has been much more anarchical and self-directed than its Japanese or Korean counterparts.

Largely excluded from capital-intensive sectors and lacking ready access to loans from the formal banking system, Taiwanese entrepreneurs have relied heavily on family, friends, credit associations and the unregulated 'curb' market for the relatively limited amounts of capital required in light industrial sectors (Deglopper, 1978; Stites, 1982). While restricting their fields of activity, this concentration on informal personal networks has enabled successful Taiwanese business to avoid state controls and direction; and, equally, their large number and small size make official attempts at steering the strategies of individual firms extremely difficult. Thus, although overall business dependence on the state is high in Taiwan, the willingness and ability of state agencies to intervene in particular firms' decisions in a discretionary manner are much less than in Korea.

The limitations of state power in affecting family firms' strategies can be seen in the mixed success of various attempts to encourage mergers and to boost R & D spending and vertical integration in particular sectors in the past two decades. In Greenhalgh's (1988b: 242) terms:

> During the 1970s and 1980s relations between the government and the families operating these firms have at times resembled an outright struggle . . . Although the state has the advantage in legal and financial resources, the slowness of progress in resolving these issues [use of the informal money market, controls of counterfeiting, reform of accounting practices and labour management practices] is a clear sign that family enterprises have other sources of strength.

One instance of the limited extent of state direction of firms' policies in Taiwan compared to Korea is the relative lack of interest in promoting general trading companies to boost exports and the low-key response of leading business families to the 1977 and 1980 ordinances establishing guidelines for large trading companies and granting subsidies to them (Cho, 1987: 59–63). The incentives provided by the state were much less than in Korea and in many cases were also available to manufacturers who exported goods directly. Furthermore, the state sought to avoid over-concentration of economic assets by creating large trading companies (LTCs) independently of the major enterprise groups, unlike the Korean GTCs, and did not insist on adequate levels of capitalization. As a result the five designated LTCs in Taiwan handled only 1.2 per cent of national exports in 1982, and most exports continued to be traded through the Japanese (sogo shosha) or direct contact with overseas buyers (Cho, 1987: 80–1). Greenhalgh (1988b) suggests that around a half of Taiwan's exports are marketed by overseas corporations and trading firms, which could constitute considerable incentive for a developmentalist state to encourage national GTCs vigorously. However, the state's reluctance to boost the concentration of economic power in Taiwan seems to have reduced the importance of this objective, and entrepreneurs' preferences for relying on established private and informal networks have limited their interest in state-promoted trading companies.

An important contribution to business success by the state in Taiwan, as in Korea, has been its direct control and repression of the labour movement. Although enterprise-based trade unions have been encouraged by the KMT, they cannot bargain over wages, and their establishment and officials must be approved by local KMT committees (Deyo, 1989: 117–18). They are more concerned with providing member services than representing worker interests and reinforce traditional employer paternalism. In many ways they function as instruments of KMT control and to prevent independent labour organizations developing. However, unlike in Korea, this state control of the labour force has not generated large-scale violent protests and strikes for a number of reasons, in addition to memories of the 1947 massacre and martial law prohibitions of strikes.

First, many factory workers in Taiwan view employment as merely a temporary status before starting their own business, a view which rapid economic growth and the prevalence of small firms encourage (Deyo, 1989: 162; Gold, 1986: 89; Greenhalgh, 1984, 1988b). Thus, they do not identify themselves with other wage labourers or develop a strong sense of themselves as lifetime employees. Second, a substantial proportion of factory workers are young women who expect to marry or return to rural or informal-sector activities within a few years, and so have little commitment to employment or common interests with long-term industrial labourers. Third, the boundaries between urban and rural communities, and separation of the industrial workforce from rural activities and connections, are less marked in Taiwan than in Korea. Thus, many urban labourers form secondary households that are relatively temporary and remain tied firmly to primary households in rural areas by bonds of loyalty to, and identification with, their families and financial interdependence (Greenhalgh, 1984; Stites, 1982). This weakens the development of urban working-class communities and of common class interests.

The prevalence of temporary migration and residential transience in urban areas in Taiwan is linked to the considerable geographical dispersion of light industry and the continued significance of rural industry in a manner comparable to early Japanese industrialization (Allen, 1981: 66–80; Ho, 1984; Vogel, 1967). Compared to the disruptions of the colonial period and the Korean War, Taiwanese industrialization was much less destructive of traditional communities and extended family systems than in Korea, and farm incomes have been considerably augmented by 'an explosion of rural, family-run factories' (Greenhalgh, 1988b: 94; cf. Stites, 1982). Thus, the formation of large urban working-class communities has been much less marked in Taiwan than in Korea, and the degree of urban–rural disparity of incomes and opportunities has been lower.

Hong Kong

By comparison with other East Asian states, the extent of the Hong Kong government's direct intervention in business decisions and financial markets is, of course, minimal. It has not produced development plans for co-ordinating firms' strategies; it does not restrict the movement of financial assets or investments; and it does not own industrial or financial assets. There is no central bank for controlling the financial system, no direct state control over interest rates and not much over bank liquidity (Jao, 1984; Youngson, 1982: 131), although the 1986 Banking Ordinance laid down minimum capital adequacy ratios. The large banks are free to decide nearly all their major strategic choices without state control and, in the case of the Hong Kong and Shanghai Bank, can exert as important an influence on the financial system as the government. Although the state has begun to establish a few organizations to support exports, increase technological awareness and upgrade both training and machinery – and so alter entrepreneurs' opportunity sets by engaging in 'field augmentation' (Jones and Sakong, 1980: 83) – its direct impact on firms' strategies has been far less in both scope and intensity than similar efforts by the other East Asian states. Thus, the role of the state in promoting and steering economic development in Hong Kong has been much more limited than in Japan, Korea and Taiwan. It has not, however, been negligible, especially with respect to infrastructural support and maintaining low labour costs.

The major ways in which the state has impinged upon firm

growth and behaviour in Hong Kong during its industrialization concern its use of land and subsidization of wage costs. Unusually for a capitalist society, in Hong Kong the state owns practically all the land and raises substantial portions of its own revenue by selling 75-year leases at public auction. According to Castells et al. (1990: 97), land sales contributed as much as 39 per cent of total government income in the boom year of 1981–2 and have formed over 20 per cent of state income in many years between 1960 and 1985. Together with income from rates, rents and property tax, the contribution of landownership and building ownership to total government revenue rose from 15 per cent in 1947–8 to 44.8 per cent in 1980–1 and only once fell below 20 per cent between 1955 and 1985. Thus, the state has a very strong interest in maintaining property values and high land prices. However, the government has also used its ownership of land, including its ability to generate 'new' land through reclamation from the sea, to provide lower-cost facilities for industry and, of course, massive public housing (Schiffer, 1991). The early clearing of land from squatter settlements provided room for small-scale manufacturing development, and the Housing Authority also built some multi-storey factories which were let at subsidized rents (Castells et al., 1990: 114). More recently, the state has tried to encourage firms to migrate to the new towns by offering land and buildings at reduced rates. Thus, in a sense, the use of state landownership has, over the past 30 or so years, resulted in a transfer of resources from large-scale commercial and financial firms which have bought land leases at high prices to small manufacturing firms operating in very small industrial premises or their owners' publicly subsidized flats. According to Castells et al. (1990: 72), as many as 40 per cent of these small firms operated from domestic premises in the late 1970s.

The massive public housing programme in Hong Kong, together with substantial control over private sector rents, represented a transfer of resources in kind to the average household which was roughly equivalent to 70 per cent of the household's income and enabled manual workers in manufacturing to keep their housing costs at around 10 per cent of their income for much of the post-war period (Castells et al., 1990: 115; Schiffer, 1991). This has helped to keep wage increases relatively moderate and maintain price stability of manufactured exports, while increasing real wages in the 1960s and 1970s. According to Castells et al. (1990: 76), real wages rose by 60 per cent between 1964 and 1977 and continued to progress until 1982. The expansion of low-cost public housing provided some security for those wishing to start their own business, a factor which Castells et al. consider a major influence on the high rates of new firm starts in Hong Kong (1990: 116), although a similar factor does not operate in Taiwan, where small firms are also very important (cf. Greenhalgh, 1984, 1988b).

The second major way in which the Hong Kong government subsidizes labour costs in manufacturing industry is its control over food costs. In 1955, the state set up a Rice Control Scheme which guaranteed the supply of rice at low prices through a cartel of wholesalers. Since rice purchases constituted 15 per cent of the average manual worker's expenditure on food and 8.5 per cent of his total costs in 1963–4 (Schiffer, 1991), it can readily be seen that this subsidization is an important component of keeping living expenses down. Furthermore, the state is also heavily involved in the organization and marketing of vegetables and fish in Hong Kong, to the extent that is has successfully nurtured a highly productive local industry in these fields. Finally, as the controlling agency for buying foodstuffs from China, the Hong Kong government has been able to ensure that the staple diet of lower-income families has remained below world market prices and relatively stable in its cost. In turn, this continued low level of prices for basic foodstuffs had contributed to wage stability and hence labour costs. In total, including price control over utilities and public transport, it has been estimated that as much as 50 per cent of manual worker household expenditure in Hong Kong is subsidized by non-market forces (Castells et al., 1990: 80). This obviously benefits small labour-intensive enterprises particularly and helps to explain Hong Kong's manufacturing-based rapid economic growth over the past 40 years.

In terms of its direct control over organized labour, the state in Hong Kong is less repressive than elsewhere in East Asia. In 1949 the Illegal Strikes and Lock-Outs Ordinance forbade strikes which coerced the government or inflicted hardship on the community as well as preventing public employees from striking (Deyo, 1989: 113). However, the 1961 Trade Union Registration Ordinance granted unions full freedom to strike and picket peacefully but it also encouraged weak and fragmented unions by permitting registration for those with as few as seven members and prohibiting unionization across occupations, industries and trades, presumably to limit the possibility of widespread political unionism. Overall, as Deyo (1989: 132) suggests: 'Hong Kong's state labour regime remains relatively liberal . . . but this does not imply lack of substantial controls over workers . . . at the enterprise level.' State control over labour supply through the flow of immigrants from China and the perceived threat of being returned to China have, however, served to reduce labour activism, as has the division of the two trade union federations into politically opposed blocs representing PRC and KMT interests. In general, the state in Hong Kong has maintained a much more aloof and remote attitude to labour organizations, as it has towards the myriad of small businesses, than in Japan, Korea and Taiwan, except when they threatened to become politically disruptive. This minimal role has, of course, been facilitated by the general organizational importance of the labour movement in Hong Kong (Deyo, 1989: 114).

Turning to consider the financial system, the state neither owns nor controls the banks in Hong Kong and exerts little direct influence over their policies. Its main effect on capital markets is through maintaining low personal and corporate taxes – facilitated of course by the substantial revenues from landownership – and periodic attempts to control the exchange rate with the help of the largest banks. However, the role of the banks, especially the large ones, in funding Hong Kong's development appears to have been quite significant. Immediately after the war, the banks advanced large sums to the public utilities and reputable firms, sometimes without collateral, to restore confidence and economic activity, and later the Hong Kong and Shanghai Bank advanced HK $50 million to the Shanghai cotton spinners through the intermediation of China Engineers Ltd, which had previously had dealings with them in Shanghai (Nishida, 1990; Wong, 1988a: 117). By 1954 the two largest Hong Kong banks had lent between HK $80 and HK $100 million to the cotton spinning industry and thus played a major part in the development of the profitable textile industry (Jao, 1974: 47, 210). Overall, the banks provided much of the capital for manufacturing industry in Hong Kong – other than that raised from families and friends, who provided most initial funding for small firms – since the stock market rarely functioned as a stable source of industrial finance. As Jao (1974: 165) suggests: 'the commercial banks . . . imaginatively and boldly gave [the refugee industrialists] unstinted support . . . the mutually beneficial interactions between the banking and non-banking sectors provide one of the keys to Hong Kong's astonishing post-war economic transformation and growth'. This support tended to be in the form of short-term loans which were usually rolled over and continued. The Hong Kong banks did not typically take equity stakes in the firms they supported.

Overall, then, the business environment faced by Hong Kong's entrepreneurs was much less dominated by the state than that elsewhere in East Asia, in terms both of providing support and sharing risks and of being a powerful agency controlling access to

Table 5.2 *Differences in state–business relations in East Asia*

	Japan	Korea	Taiwan	Hong Kong
Business subordination	Medium since 1930	High	High	Low
Discretionary state intervention	Considerable after 1945	High	Low	Low
State ownership of industry	Low	Medium	High	Low
State ownership of banks	Low	High	High	None
State control of financial system	High after 1945	High	High	Low
State promotion of heavy industry	High after 1930	High	Limited	Low
State promotion of GTCs	High	Medium	Low	None
State control and suppression of organized labour	Low after 1945	High	High	Limited
State support for agriculture and rural industry	Considerable	Low	Medium	n.a.

key resources such as capital, foreign exchange and technology. Instead, it was more institutionally pluralistic with a relatively well-developed commercial and financial infrastructure dominated by external, that is, colonial, elites and practically no restrictions on trade or financial flows across territorial boundaries. Thus, with the important exception of the Commonwealth preference system, and later arrangements for limiting textile exports which protected existing firms through the quota system (Wong, 1988a: 120–1), manufacturers in Hong Kong were exposed to international competition and market forces from the beginning of its industrialization. Risk and uncertainty were not mediated or controlled by the state beyond the textiles industry, and as a result flexibility was at a premium.

These variations in state–business relations are summarized in Table 5.2. The greater levels of state autonomy in Korea and Taiwan compared to Japan and Hong Kong are, of course, reflected in the greater degree of business subordination to political goals and strategies in the former countries. However, this subordination does not necessarily lead to state intervention in firms' strategic choices in a discretionary manner, as the example of Taiwan illustrates. Equally, greater business independence and influence need not prevent the state attempting to steer and manipulate those choices, as the activities of MITI in post-war Japan show.

State ownership of economic assets is, of course, a traditional indicator of state domination of business interests and economic outcomes, and, as we have seen, its extent varies considerably between East Asian societies. Of particular importance here are the ownership and control of banks, given their crucial role in the industrialization process in credit-based financial systems, and the overall role of the state in the financial system. In Korea and Taiwan the state clearly dominates the financial system as a whole and the major banks in particular, although the informal 'curb' market remains somewhat beyond the authorities' control. In contrast, state ownership of banks in Japan has been low, but since the 1930s the Ministry of Finance has exerted considerable control over the structure and operation of the financial system, and, of course, MITI has used its control over access to foreign exchange as an instrument of industrial policy.

Important differences in the policies followed by the state in these four countries concern: (a) the development and control of capital-intensive industry; (b) attitudes towards large concentrations of economic assets in private hands; (c) the development of general trading companies for overseas trade; (d) control over the labour movement; and (e) the management of the agricultural system. The direct support of privately owned capital-intensive industry by the state in Japan and Korea had major consequences, not only for the firms concerned but also for the financial system and linkages between the state, bank and large-scale industry. Equally, the lack of such support in Taiwan and Hong Kong affected the sorts of businesses that came to dominate the private sector and the need for large sums of capital from the official banks. The early encouragement of the general trading companies in Japan was another feature of state–business relations that had major consequences for Japanese firms in terms of the activities they concentrated on and how they managed their foreign trade. Similar efforts by the Korean state in the 1970s had rather less impact, because the chaebol were already established as the dominant form of business organization, and the state did not try to break them up.

State control over organized labour has, of course, been a feature of many industrialization processes, from the prohibition of unions and strikes to the total incorporation of workers' organizations into the dominant political apparatus. In the post-Second World War period, the Japanese state has not controlled and suppressed labour organizations to nearly the same extent as it did in the earlier twentieth century, although it did support employers' attacks on industrial unions in the early 1950s and their development of enterprise unions. The Korean and Taiwanese

Table 5.3 *Consequences of differences in political systems and state–business relations*

	Japan	Korea	Taiwan	Hong Kong
Importance of state approval and support	High after 1930	High	Medium	Low
Bargaining power of firms	High	Low	Low	Low
Dependence on banks	High	High	Medium	Limited
State risk sharing	High	High	Medium	Low
Encouragement of large firms	High	High	Low	Indifferent
Dependence on GTCs	High	Low	Low	Low
Strength of organized labour	Medium after 1945	Low	Low	Low
Urbanization and concentration of workers	Medium	High	Medium	High

states have, of course, both exercised highly repressive control over their labour movements, although perhaps rather more overtly in Korea. The Hong Kong government has tended to be more concerned with political threats from labour organizations than their economic power and has exhibited relatively liberal attitudes.

Finally, the degree to which the state tried to mitigate the harshness of the transfer of economic surpluses from the agricultural sector to industry and retain the support of the peasantry was clearly greater in Japan and Taiwan than in Korea. Thus, urban–rural disparities have been greater in Korea, and the involvement of rural families in the industrialization process has been more apparent in Japan and Taiwan. Family structures have tended to be more extended and continuous in the latter countries than in Korea, where the nuclear urban family has become the dominant form.

These differences in political institutions and state–business relations have had significant consequences for the sorts of business systems that became established during industrialization in these countries. These are summarized in Table 5.3. Perhaps the most important of these concerns the need for firms to obtain state approval and support for their activities, and hence develop close ties to political and bureaucratic elites. Allied to this varying dependence is the relative bargaining power of dominant companies, which is considerably greater in Japan than in the other three economies here. In the case of Korea, dependence on the state is reinforced by high levels of bank borrowing from state-controlled banks, whereas in Taiwan privately owned businesses rely less on bank borrowing, partly because of their lower capital requirements and partly because of their suspicion of Nationalist-controlled institutions.

This suspicion reflects the ethnic divide in Taiwan, as well as traditional Chinese distrust of state officials, and inhibits the establishment of large businesses within dominant market positions. Such concentrations of economic assets under Taiwanese control are seen as involving considerable political risk, and so the degree of private economic concentration is much lower in Taiwan than in Korea. This is, of course, also the result of major differences in risk sharing between the state and private business, and overall levels of state support for indigenous firms. This has been greatest in Korea, significant in Japan, more limited in Taiwan and rather tenuous and indirect in Hong Kong except in textiles, at least in terms of controlling and mediating world competition.

An important consequence of the early establishment of general trading companies in Japan with state support and encouragement was the high level of business dependence on them for purchasing raw materials from abroad and for distributing and marketing their products abroad. As major sources of trade credit and loans, they have also supported small and medium sized enterprises, particularly those involved in the export trade. This dependence on indigenous GTCs has been less in Korea because they were established much later in its industrialization. In Taiwan, the combination of the large Japanese sogo shosha, direct connections to large-scale purchasers in the USA and Europe and existing networks of trading relations among Chinese businesses in Asia and elsewhere have limited the growth of GTCs. In Hong Kong, of course, the commercial and trading networks were already well established before industrialization took place, and so there was little scope for large-scale GTCs.

In general in East Asia, labour movements have not been as strong or as structured around occupations or skills as in Europe and North America; but unions have clearly been more important in Japan since the SCAP reforms than in Korea, Taiwan or Hong Kong. Thus, firms have had to take more account of worker-based organizations in Japan than elsewhere in East Asia since the war, and have not been able to sack core workers when demand declined. The relative tractability of the workforce in Japan and Taiwan during industrialization may be partly due to the continuing connections between urban centres and the countryside, and the continued significance of rural industry. In contrast, the large-scale movement of people in Korea since the 1930s and bias of state policies and investment towards urban centres, especially Seoul, has weakened urban–rural ties and generated relatively large masses of urban workers cut off from family ties in the countryside. Despite strong state control over labour movements, this concentration of workers in urban centres has helped to produce periodic large-scale disturbances and, recently, massive pressure for wage increases. An additional factor limiting the power of organized labour in many East Asian countries has been the considerable labour surplus during early industrialization, particularly in Korea where the population in the early 1960s was growing at a rate of nearly 3 per cent per annum (Michell, 1988: 101).

These consequences of institutional differences between East Asian societies can be combined to explain some of the major differences in business systems identified in Chapter 3. For example, the high level of dependence of Korean businesses on state approval and bank borrowing, coupled with their relatively low bargaining power, has meant that entrepreneurs have to adapt their policies to state plans and devote considerable energies to ensuring political support. Given the centralized nature of the Korean state and its domination by the political executive, this encourages centralized control over firms' activities and makes high levels of trust between managers a critical factor.

Similarly, the combination of state domination of the economic system, its suspicion of private concentrations of economic power and limited support for capital-intensive industry in Taiwan's private sector has restricted the growth of large firms in heavy industry in Taiwan and the overall development of heavy industry in export markets. Thus Taiwanese and Korean industrial structures differ significantly, especially in terms of their relative importance in world markets (Levy, 1988). However, these sorts of differences need to be combined with those identified in Chapter 4 if we are to arrive at a more complete understanding of the differences between East Asian business systems, and this will be done in the next chapter.

6

The Effects of Institutional Environments on East Asian Business Systems

In the last two chapters I have summarized the major features of pre-industrial Japan, Korea and China and of industrialization processes in East Asia which have affected the development of different kinds of successful business systems in Japan, South Korea, Taiwan and Hong Kong. Here I focus on the processes by which these institutional features have helped to generate and reproduce the distinctive characteristics of the Japanese kaisha, the Korean chaebol and the Chinese family business which were highlighted in Chapters 2 and 3. Initially, I shall consider how these characteristics can be understood as the outcome of particular combinations of pre-industrial institutions and key features of industrialization patterns for each type of business system, and then the three types will be compared to identify common processes and relations.

For each business system its distinctive characteristics, as discussed in Chapters 2 and 3, will be summarized and then discussed in terms of the major institutional influences which have facilitated or constrained their development and effectiveness. These influences derive from the key features of pre-industrial Japan, Korea and China identified in Chapter 4 and of the industrialization processes discussed in the previous chapter. Where the features listed in Tables 4.2 and 5.3 have had similar consequences for the sort of business system that became established in a particular economy, they are combined into a single institutional influence. For example, the lack of economic autonomy and decentralization in patrimonial Korea and China is combined with the pervasive sense of insecurity among merchants in those countries because both features have limited the development of trust between officials and merchants as well as the development of stable relations between unrelated economic agents.

A further simplification can be made by considering the overall legacy of pre-industrial Japan, Korea and China for industrialization processes in terms of three major clusters of institutional features: the level of trust between business partners and non-kin; the extent of collective loyalties and commitments beyond families; and the degree of formalization and depersonalization of authority relations and administrative procedures. Similarly, many of the distinctive characteristics of the three business systems can be reduced to three major interrelated clusters because they seem to have resulted from similar combinations of institutional influences. These are: (a) firm type and market organization; (b) ownership, authority and control systems; and (c) levels of employer–employee commitment and interdependence and conceptions of the managerial role. Major relations between these three clusters and the institutional environments that generated them, and continue to ensure their effectiveness, are summarized in figures at the end of each section on the individual business system.

The Japanese Kaisha

As mentioned earlier, the key features of the modern Japanese kaisha are closely interrelated and mutually supportive. Relational contracting and long-term commitments between exchange partners, for instance, are echoed in the development of long-term employer–employee commitments, and business specialization is associated with managerial homogeneity, incremental strategic change and risk sharing with industry partners, core workers and the state. However, the modern Japanese business system is not entirely a seamless web, and many of the distinctive features listed in Table 3.5 can be examined separately. As the comparison of the kaisha with the Chinese family business shows, for instance, specialization is compatible with both extensive mutual dependence and commitment between business partners and much more limited commitment to preserve flexibility. Thus, effective risk management strategies do not automatically follow from managerial specialization and homogeneity but depend on institutional contexts, in this case the presence or absence of strong trust-building and trust-maintaining institutions.

In considering how the major features of Tokugawa Japan and patterns of Japanese industrialization identified in Chapters 4 and 5 combined to generate the distinctive characteristics of the post-war kaisha, 13 distinct institutional influences can be derived which affect different aspects of the Japanese business system. While a few of these are similar to those listed in Tables 4.2 and 5.3, most are combinations of institutional features. Thus, political differentiation here includes both the long-standing separation of reigning from ruling and the considerable extent of local autonomy and political decentralization found in Tokugawa Japan. Likewise, economic decentralization and merchant security can be combined since they both granted merchants a legitimate, albeit low, status and enabled them to form strong guilds and enter into long-term

Table 6.1a *Institutional influences on the development of the Japanese kaisha: the nature of the firm and market organization*

	Distinctive characteristics				
	Separation of ownership from control	Business specialization and managerial homogeneity	Risk management by mutual dependence	High levels of market organization	Collective inter-firm commitments
Pre-industrial institutions					
Political differentiation	X				X
Integrated vertical loyalties	X				
Rule formalization					X
Economic decentralization and merchant security	X	X	X	X	
Competence-based merit	X				X
Village cohesion, co-operation and autonomy	X		X	X	X
Family structures	X				
Industrialization					
Growth of state bureaucracy and intervention	X	X	X		X
Sogo shosha		X	X	X	
Dependence on banks	X	X	X	X	
State risk sharing		X			
Skilled worker shortage					
Strength of labour movement and enterprise unions		X	X	X	

Table 6.1b *Institutional influences on the development of the Japanese kaisha: employment practices and authority systems*

	Distinctive characteristics			
	Formalization of procedures and authority	Employer commitment and dependence on core employees	Delegation to middle management and groups	Facilitative managerial role
Pre-industrial institutions				
Political differentiation	X			
Integrated vertical loyalties		X	X	X
Rule formalization	X		X	
Economic decentralization and merchant security	X		X	
Competence-based merit	X	X	X	X
Village cohesion, co-operation and autonomy	X	X		X
Family authority structures	X	X		X
Industrialization				
Growth of state bureaucracy and intervention	X		X	
State sharing of risks		X		
Skilled worker shortage		X	X	X
Strength of labour movement and enterprise unions	X	X	X	X

commitments. Village cohesion, autonomy and co-ordination here summarize the key features of the Tokugawa village highlighted by Smith (1959) which limited the individual power of the headman and developed high levels of inter-family collaboration. Similarly, family authority patterns combine the relative differentiation of paternal and maternal authority, the importance of the latter and the limited nature of the father's authority in the Japanese family.

Turning to the key features of Japanese industrialization, the importance of the trading companies and banks was clearly linked to the development of the zaibatsu, which in turn influenced the establishment of the inter-market groups after Japan recovered its independence in 1952, although they also played a major role in the development of the textile industry and other non-zaibatsu-dominated sectors. The growth of the state bureaucracy and intervention refers here to the combination of: (a) the Meiji state's adoption of Western organizational forms, which served as models for private organizations (Westney, 1987); (b) the general growth of the central bureaucracy at the end of the nineteenth century; and (c) the greater degree of state commitment to, and involvement in, industrial development during the 1930s. Finally, the strength of the labour movement and development of the labour unions cover the general impact of the SCAP reforms and employers' responses to the expansion of trade unions in the 1940s and 1950s.

Tables 6.1a and 6.1b summarize the connections between nine distinctive characteristics of post-war Japanese kaisha and key features of the institutional environments in which these developed. The ten characteristics listed in Table 3.5 have been reduced to nine by combining the formalization of personnel procedures and employment practices with the depersonalization of authority relations, since in practice these overlapped considerably. They suggest that the particular kind of business system as a whole that has become established in Japan reflects the combination of both pre-industrial Japanese society and patterns of industrialization. While some characteristics, such as strong inter-firm obligations, are partly explicable in terms of particular features of the industrialization process, they would not have become established without antecedent institutional developments, such as relative stability and security of private merchant wealth and guilds in pre-industrial Japan. Thus, the more proximate institutional factors, such as the autonomy and significance of trading companies and banks, combined with longer-established features of Japanese society to encourage the development and continued effectiveness of distinctive characteristics of the Japanese business system and would not have had such consequences if pre-industrial Japanese society had been significantly different. Indeed the process of industrialization itself and the success of, say, the sogo shosha would have been quite different if key features of Tokugawa Japan had varied markedly. The particular ways in which these features combined to generate the modern Japanese kaisha and form a supportive environment for it will now be briefly explored under the headings used earlier for comparing business systems, combining employment practices with authority and control systems.

The Nature of the Firm
The strong separation of ownership from control in large Japanese kaisha reflects the combination of integrated vertical loyalties, political and economic differentiation and decentralization and patterns of village organization in Tokugawa Japan, together with the expansion of the central state bureaucracy in the Meiji period and its increasing intervention in the economic system in the 1930s. The long separation of reigning from ruling, and growing emphasis on competence as an important criterion of merit in addition to personal loyalty during the nineteenth century, encouraged the relative depersonalization of power and facilitated the development of loyalties to collective entities, as did the strong collective traditions of the Tokugawa village which constrained the personal power of the village headmen. In addition, the relatively stable and entrenched system of vertical loyalties and obligations in Tokugawa Japan, together with considerable merchant security and stability of the economic system, developed trust between owners and managers and formed the basis for the rapid establishment of the new cadre of college-educated salaried managers at the top of the zaibatsu in the early twentieth century. Without these institutional factors it is unlikely that owning families would have been willing to delegate responsibility and control to non-family managers.

Such delegation was, of course, facilitated by the flexibility of the traditional Japanese family which enabled merchants and samurai to adopt non-blood-related people into their families and led to unrelated clerks being given senior posts in some Tokugawa merchant houses. Together with the more differentiated and shared system of parental authority in Japanese families, and growing significance of collective identities and loyalties rather than personal ones, this flexibility encouraged the institutionalization of collective loyalty to the merchant 'house', as distinct from the individual patriarch, and so reduced the level of dependence on purely personal forms of control (Hirschmeier and Yui, 1981: 41–6). The significance of these pre-industrial developments was, of course, greatly enhanced by the considerable continuity between Tokugawa and Meiji Japan in comparison with the disruptive effects of Japanese colonialism and war in Korea.

The growing separation of family ownership from many managerial responsibilities in pre-industrial Japan was additionally reinforced by the growth of the central state bureaucracy in the late nineteenth century and its imitation of many features from Western countries (Westney, 1987). The growing state involvement in the economic system in the 1930s and the move to a war economy further intensified this process, as the dominant zaibatsu lost much of their political influence and the bureaucracy attempted to restructure firms into vertical industry sectors and co-ordinate inter-firm flows. Although limited in their effectiveness (Udagawa and Nakamura, 1980), these attempts resulted in greater formalization and regulation of firms' operations and the growth of middle management bureaucracies (Cole and Tominaga, 1976). After the war, of course, the SCAP reforms broke up the zaibatsu and prevented the formation of holding companies through which families could control conglomerates. This removal of owning families from the zaibatsu, and separation of their component units into separate economic entities, constituted the culmination of a long process of increasing separation of ownership from control which was reinforced by the growth of inter-firm share-holdings controlled by top managers to prevent take-overs. Not only, then, has family influence based on ownership declined greatly in the larger kaisha, but institutional ownership through the stock market is also a weak constraint on managerial decisions, except of course for those within particular inter-market groups.

The high degree of business specialization and managerial homogeneity found in many large kaisha reflects the combination of pre-industrial merchant security and powerful guilds, which reduced risks and encouraged the collective organization of specialist trades, particular characteristics of the early textile industry and the role of the sogo shosha in Japan's industrialization. It is also related to the emphasis on long-term loyalty and commitment of key employees in the post-war kaisha and the institutionalization of enterprise unions. The state-supported guild system in Tokugawa Japan encouraged both artisanal and merchant specialization (Jacobs, 1958: 40) and foreshadowed the development of effective cartels in many industries, particularly textiles (Dore, 1986: 73). This cartelization was linked to specialization and considerable reliance on the new sogo shosha.

As Yamamura (1976), and Yoshihara (1982) and others have emphasized, the development of the Japanese textile industry at the end of the nineteenth century was closely connected with the rise of trading companies, especially Mitsui Bussan, which organized the purchase of raw cotton, acted as the agents for machinery manufacturers, such as Platts, and handled the export trade which constituted the bulk of the cotton spinners' early markets. Thus the leading firms in the dominant manufacturing industry in Japan for most of its early industrialization concentrated on production and did not develop multi-functional structures and skills. They formed an effective cartel that controlled production capacity and diffused technical information so that manufacturing and production practices were quite uniform in the industry and new techniques were rapidly absorbed (Nishida, 1990; Saxonhouse, 1976). This pattern of manufacturing specialization and focus on technological improvements continued into the synthetic fibres era, and even in the 1970s diversification had not been nearly as 'unrelated' as in similar firms in other societies (Dore, 1986: 215–16; Nishida and Redding, 1992).

This pattern of manufacturing firms specializing in production and technological change was echoed in many zaibatsu businesses, although the cotton spinners themselves remained distant from the zaibatsu. As Yoshihara (1982: 194–200) suggests, the sogo shosha fulfilled many of the purchasing and marketing functions for firms in new industries, because rapid economic change and ignorance of international markets created difficulties for exporting manufacturers in Japan. Similarly, the important role of banks and insurance and trust companies in financing zaibatsu firms meant that they did not need to develop extensive financial management skills. Because of the co-operative ties between the trading companies, banks and manufacturing firms within each zaibatsu, each company could concentrate its efforts on competing within its own sector rather than developing multiple managerial competences and competing against all firms in a variety of markets.

The important role of cartelization in many producer industries, which facilitated specialization, was enhanced in the post-war period by state agencies, such as MITI, both for new industries and for those in recession. Cartelization in Japan has aided technical change by reducing the risks of technological investments and encouraging the exchange of technical information, though not perhaps to the extent found in cotton spinning. It thus mitigates the risks of remaining specialized in a particular sector and makes it relatively difficult for a firm to diversify radically into remote business areas, because this would disrupt current co-operative arrangements and necessitate forging new alliances.

The post-war dissolution of the zaibatsu was partly intended to break up these inter-firm alliances and the close links between banks and industrial companies so that a more 'normal', that is, American, pattern of markets and firms would develop. However, as the rapid re-establishment of the sogo shosha and inter-market groups in the 1950s showed, the Japanese preference for specialization and inter-firm co-operative links remained strong and effective (Yamamura, 1976). This was enhanced by the growth of the trade union movement in the 1940s and the widespread development of enterprise unions in the 1950s as a way of managing this growth. Together with the increasing commitment to long-term employment for skilled workers, which began before the war in capital-intensive large firms (Aoki, 1988: 186–92), this growing significance of the labour movement resulted in 'permanent' employment for the core workforce becoming a major feature of large kaisha and the need to ensure high levels of commitment to the firm and acceptance of continuous retraining and flexible employment (Hazama, 1976). Given this policy it is not too surprising that firms are reluctant to diversify radically across sectors, since this would mean developing quite different skills and knowledge and eliciting loyalty from qualitatively different employees. Even firms in declining industries, such as textiles and steel, prefer to diversify into related sectors, since these offer the best opportunity for capitalizing on their employees' skills and maintaining competitive competences (Okimoto, 1989: 125–9).

The risks associated with sector specialization are managed in Japan by developing high levels of mutual dependence and trust with exchange partners so that shocks are not too abrupt and risks are shared. This mutual dependence is facilitated by the co-operative traditions of the Tokugawa village, in which collective responsibilities transcended individual household interests, together with the common sharing of risks and collective organization of Tokugawa guilds. The institutionalization of honesty and trust norms between Tokugawa merchants was also an important pre-requisite for the effective development of such mutual dependence relations. Again, the close and long-term relations between manufacturing firms, trading companies and banks encouraged risk sharing and mutual dependence, because the long-term growth and success of the sogo shosha and banks depended on the growth of their particular client firms and their demand for a wide range of services. In particular, the close involvement of trading companies in certain industries and firms meant that they had a strong interest in the expansion of those customers, and hence a willingness to share some of the risks. The institutionalization of strong norms of mutual obligations between partners, combined with the relatively strong commitment of sogo shosha and banks to the success of their major clients, encouraged the larger kaisha to manage risks and uncertainty by developing strong mutual dependence with particular exchange partners, including enterprise unions and their core workforce in the post-war period, because of their joint collective interest in growth and their being 'locked into' particular commitments and obligations.

Such mutual dependencies were also, of course, facilitated by state encouragement of co-operative arrangements between firms, recession cartels and relative weak anti-trust legislation and agencies in the post-war period. In general, the ability of Japanese kaisha to share risks with industry partners and other economic agents depended upon, and helped to reinforce, the tendency to develop particularistic, diffuse and long-term inter-firm relations in Japanese markets which is such a striking feature of the Japanese business system and will now be considered.

Market Organization

As discussed in Chapter 3, these links between Japanese firms occur both within vertical industry sectors and across markets and industries, although not all kaisha are equally strongly connected through inter-market groups. Accordingly, I shall consider first the institutional features which have encouraged such a high level of market organization. Second, I shall briefly discuss the processes underlying the development of relatively impersonal connections between firms, because it is a further distinguishing characteristic of the Japanese business system that such relational or obligational contracting is based more on collective, corporate identities and relations than on personal ties between individuals.

The growth of long-term commitments between business partners in Japan is the result of both long-standing characteristics of Japanese society and developments during industrialization in a similar manner to the separation of ownership from control (cf. Dore, 1983). Clearly, a crucial condition of such trust developing between enterprises is the general institutionalization of mutual obligations between non-kin, and of common expectations about appropriate behaviour, over a considerable period of time. Where trust is overwhelmingly personal and/or cannot be reasonably expected to continue over a long sequence of transactions, long-term commitments between firms are unlikely to develop on a large scale. As we have seen, village autonomy and inter-family co-ordination were high in Tokugawa Japan, with considerable group pressure being exerted to ensure collaboration between households for collective tasks and mutual assistance. A strong sense of mutual obligation developed between families, and this extended to the merchant class where demonstrating trustworthy behaviour and behaving fairly to all clients and partners were an important way of being a good citizen and showing worth (Hirschmeier and Yui, 1981: 40). Adherence to a general norm of honourable business practice was seen as crucial to justifying merchants' legitimacy in the Tokugawa period, and prevented overtly self-seeking and short-term-profit-maximizing behaviour.

Allied to this development of co-operative expectations and mutual obligations were the relative stability of Tokugawa Japan and the relative continuity of many features of that society with Meiji Japan during early industrialization (Hanley, 1986). Commitments and obligations were thus made in a stable environment where long-term benefits could be reasonably expected. The relatively high level of economic decentralization and acceptance of private wealth over some time provided a supportive environment for the development of stable trust relationships between merchants in Tokugawa Japan.

During industrialization, nationalism and the promptings of the Meiji state reinforced these tendencies for co-operation, especially for those firms engaged in foreign trade, such as the cotton spinners. The strong sense of economic inferiority and resentment against the unequal treaties imposed by the Western powers led to extensive collaboration between exporters and to the state encouragement of the trading companies in order to overcome the cartel of Western merchants (Yamamura, 1976). Strong networks of long-term obligations between firms are maintained by these trading companies, and a similar co-ordinating role is performed by the larger 'city' banks, which also have a strong interest in sustaining increasing demand for bank loans and providing a wide range of services for their industrial customers. These networks facilitate firms' expansion and investment by sharing some of the risks and uncertainties involved. They have also helped to maintain the share of small and medium sized enterprises in export trade by providing trade credit and channelling investment funds from the banks (Yoshihara, 1982: 174–83).

The strength of these long-term commitments and networks was demonstrated after the war when the financial holding companies of the zaibatsu and trading companies were dissolved by the SCAP and yet similar linkages were re-established after Japan regained its independence. Their renewal testifies not only to the strength of inter-firm loyalties and solidarity, but also to the need to safeguard access to capital through the banks and access to raw materials and overseas markets through the sogo shosha for the rapidly developing capital-intensive industries. Given the high demand for capital and for co-ordination of inputs and outputs in these newly developing industries in the 1950s and 1960s, it is not surprising that the long-term linkages between banks, trading companies and large firms became re-established.

A key agent in this process was, of course, the state, which encouraged the development of the chemicals, steel, petroleum and machinery industries and ensured that anti-trust legislation did not hinder their growth. Long-term joint planning and collaboration between the larger kaisha were partly a result of state initiatives and support in the post-war period, just as the sogo shosha themselves were partly a result of state encouragement and support in the Meiji era. This support, of course, helped to reduce investment risks and encouraged more long-term commitments than would otherwise have been the case.

Turning to the development of relatively collective, rather than individual, ties of trust and obligation between firms in Japan, this seems to reflect the gradual depersonalization of loyalties in the political system as well as the strength of the village as a collective entity that transcended individual and family interests and identities. The development of collective loyalties in villages and merchant houses has already been discussed, and clearly it would have been very difficult to establish corporate trust relations if trust between non-kin could only be established on the basis of direct personal knowledge and obligations to individuals. The 'collectivization' of loyalties and identities had been already developed in many merchant houses and it was reinforced by the growing significance of competence as a crucial element in legitimating access to authority positions in late Tokugawa Japan. It also reflects the Japanese tendency to regard family households as relatively impersonal corporations concerned with external task performance for kinship groups (Pelzel, 1970). The development of the university system in the Meiji period, and the emphasis on formal educational qualifications in the new state bureaucracy, further increased the importance of institutionalized certificates of competence, although personal knowledge and contacts remained significant in zaibatsu careers.

The developing system of administrative rules and regulations before and after the Meiji restoration additionally depersonalized loyalties and obligations in large bureaucracies and helped to institutionalize separate, formally specified ranks in them, although not to the same extent as in the West of course. Position and status became less a matter of personal choice of the leader of enterprises and more formally specified through bureaucratic procedures.

Thus, personal ties between firms gradually became less tied to individuals and more collective and corporate (Dore, 1986: 78). This gradual bureaucratization of posts in zaibatsu firms was reinforced by the militarization of the economy in the 1930s and the concomitant growth of state regulation and attempts at industrial restructuring. Together with the separation of ownership from control, this further reduced the importance of purely personal loyalties and commitments.

Employment Practices and Authority Systems
These developments towards greater formalization of relationships and reliance on formal educational achievements as recruitment criteria also affected both personnel practices and the use of formal co-ordination and control systems in Japanese corporations. The relatively formal and impersonal procedures for recruiting employees, evaluating their performance and promoting them clearly would not have developed without the general growth in formalization and non-personal ways of assessing individual behaviour throughout Japanese society during industrialization. A further important factor in the post-war formalization of personnel practices was the growing importance of trade unions and the corresponding need to be seen to be systematic and impersonal in making personnel decisions. Thus the SCAP labour reforms, and subsequent ability of the labour movement to encourage seniority-based promotion procedures and extended employment commitments, were significant influences on the institutionalization of formal personnel practices and the reduction of personal discretion among supervisors and managers.

The general depersonalization of authority relations in large Japanese kaisha relative to that apparent in Korean chaebol and the Chinese family business can thus be seen as the outcome of the combination of particular features of pre-industrial Japan, of the early industrialization process and of the post-war reforms. As well as the general separation of reigning from ruling and the significant level of merchant security, the growth of administrative rules and regulations governing official actions and the establishment of a formal system for resolving disputes during the Tokugawa period restricted the autonomy and discretion of individual officials. Additionally, the strong collective organization of the Japanese village limited the individual power and claims to personal loyalty of village headmen. Together with the lack of a military role for the daimyo, and the related decline in their ability to demand strong personal loyalty from their administrators, these features sharply limited the significance of purely personal authority in nineteenth-century Japan.

The abolition of feudal statuses and ties by the Meiji oligarchs further reduced the importance of personal authority, as did the growth and prestige of the central bureaucracy and its successful extensions of formal, central administrative control throughout Japanese society. As Westney (1987) has shown, the development of the national army, police force, school system and similar institutions in Meiji Japan based on various models from Western countries helped to define significant features of formal bureaucracies and provided models for other organizations. The speed of adoption of these features reflected the characteristics of Tokugawa Japan discussed above, and the new model state organizations encouraged similar features in the emerging private sector, especially the standardization of co-ordination and control procedures, formalization of official statuses into hierarchies and use of competence as an important criterion of appointment and promotion. While not leading to the institutionalization of fully fledged formal bureaucracies in the Western mode, as we have seen, the Meiji state undoubtedly hastened the replacement of purely personal forms of authority and control with more formal and standardized procedures and a greater reliance on formal hierarchical position as the basis for eliciting compliance. The post-war break-up of the zaibatsu, reform of the legal system and greater involvement of the state bureaucracy in economic growth further intensified these processes – as did, of course, the growth of the union movement, which sought control over managerial behaviour through the development of agreed rules and procedures.

Similar factors underlie the development of 'lifetime' employment patterns in the larger kaisha and consequent high mutual dependence between firms and core workers. Without, first, the generally widespread commitment to norms of mutual obligation and reciprocity between economic partners, second, the importance of collective commitments and, third, acceptance of competence-based hierarchical authority over work allocation and performance evaluation, it is improbable that such long-term commitments would have been institutionalized or have elicited such high levels of flexibility and commitment to the enterprise. More direct reasons for large firms committing themselves to such dependence on their core workforce were the growing shortage of skilled male workers in the more capital-intensive sectors and the pressure from the influential trade unions in the late 1940s.

The relatively high levels of delegation of task performance to work groups, and the importance of middle management in the larger Japanese kaisha, reflect the general institutional factors already mentioned that generated vertical loyalties to collective entities and considerable trust between owners, top managers and employees. Just as the combination of political and economic decentralization in Tokugawa Japan, the growth of competence-based merit and the development of collective identities and loyalties encouraged the delegation of control from owners to managers within the zaibatsu, so too these factors combined with others to facilitate further delegation in later periods. Among these additional factors were the general growth in rule-governed behaviour and depersonalization of authority, which meant that direct personal control of task performance became less necessary, the growth of middle management ranks and greater formalization of hierarchies in the 1930s as the result of increasing state involvement in market structures and processes, and the post-war labour reforms which encouraged the growth of the labour movement.

The growth of the unions, together with the skilled labour shortage in capital-intensive industries, and the development of enterprise unions as a way of managing it, led to the 'white-collar-ization' of the core labour force in large kaisha (Koike, 1987), as we have seen. This in turn enabled firms to rely more on work group commitment to, and dependence on, employers than on formal control over how work is performed. Such delegation to groups is of course additionally effective in Japan because of the strong tradition of collective responsibility in the Tokugawa village and the importance of group performance and success (Hirschmeier and Yui, 1981: 47–51). In sum, the high level of long-term commitment to the core workforce, which was a response to both the shortage of skilled labour and the post-war growth of the labour movement in Japan, encouraged substantial delegation of control over task performance to work groups, which was effective because of the continuity of particular features of pre-industrial Japanese society. Thus, the development both of mutual employer–employee dependence and of delegation to middle management and skilled workers depended upon key institutional factors which continued from Tokugawa Japan.

Finally, the distinctive conception of the managerial role common in the larger kaisha, which emphasizes managers' abilities to produce high group performance through close involvement in groupwork and does not insist on their total superiority over subordinates, can be seen as the result of the strong collective organization of the Tokugawa village, together with the differentiated family authority structure, the importance of mutual obligations and some reciprocity in vertical authority relations, and the strength of the labour movement in post-war Japan. As Smith

(1959) has emphasized, leadership in pre-industrial Japanese villages was not a top-down, authoritarian and personal phenomenon but a much more collective, conciliatory and discrete activity in which headmen had to manage the leading families into a consensus for their policies and actions. They appeared to follow the collective consensus rather than dictate it, and their authority rested upon collective consent as much as delegated powers from the daimyo or tradition.

Similarly, the major role of the mother in bringing up Japanese children, and consequent differentiation of paternal from maternal authority, has accustomed them to dual systems of authority in which male children can expect relatively independent treatment from their mothers. Furthermore, paternal authority is more emotional and less omnipotent than in the Chinese family, so that Japanese children, or at least males, expect to be supported and share emotional commitments with their parents. Attitudes to superiors in large organizations thus combine obedience with expectations of managerial support and concern, what Pye (1985: 163) sees as the nurturing style associated with maternal authority. Such expectations are not, of course, always met, as the history of early Japanese industrialization shows; but when most key workers in large firms are unionized, skilled and long-term employees, as in post-war Japan, they encourage a more supportive and emotionally involved managerial style than occurs in Chinese or Korean enterprises. Furthermore, because the Japanese manager, like the Japanese father, can admit he needs the support and ideas of his subordinates without thereby losing his authority, he is much more able to encourage group involvement in problem solving and to provide support for group activities than his Chinese or Korean counterpart.

Equally, the greater extent of pre-industrial vertical integration of loyalties and political hierarchies in Japan, together with the need to legitimate authority through some collective service, such as maintaining order, and demonstrable competence have encouraged the development of reciprocity in managerial authority relationships. This means that Japanese managers are highly concerned to assist group performance and elicit commitment through close personal involvement with subordinates. Again, this becomes more important when the labour movement has developed some power and independence and firms are committed to long-term dependence on the bulk of the workforce, so that obtaining employee commitment to both their current jobs and the future of the firm becomes a crucial managerial function.

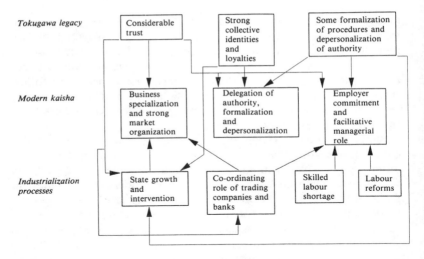

Figure 6.1   *The Tokugawa legacy, industrialization and the modern kaisha*

As mentioned earlier, the overall legacy of pre-industrial Japan can be summarized in three broad institutional features which influenced both the pattern of Japanese industrialization and the establishment of key characteristics of the kaisha. These are: first, the relatively high level of trust and mutual obligation between business partners and between superiors and subordinates; second, the strong sense of collective identity and loyalty; and, third, the growing formalization and systematic use of rules, procedures and performance standards. These phenomena laid the foundations for the establishment of public and private bureaucracies during the Meiji era and, together with the particular features of Japanese industrialization identified above, helped to develop the modern kaisha. Without them it is highly unlikely that the modern Japanese business system would have developed as it did or that its distinctive features and practices would be effective. As suggested in Figure 6.1, their influence affected the growth of the Meiji state and the co-ordinating role of the trading companies and banks, as well as the core characteristics of modern kaisha.

This figure attempts some heroic simplifications to highlight the key relationships summarized in Table 6.1a and 6.1b. The nine characteristics of the modern Japanese business system are reduced to three major components on the basis of their interrelationships and links with similar institutional influences. First, business specialization, market organization and managing risks through mutual dependence are combined. Second, the separation of ownership from control is linked to the delegation of authority to middle management and work groups, and to the formalization of procedures and depersonalization of authority and of commitments between economic agents. Third, employer commitment to core employees is connected to the facilitative managerial role. Although these three components are interrelated to some extent, their internal interdependence seems greater than those between them. Finally, the growth of the modern state is combined with its assuming a leading role in the 1930s and sharing investment risks in capital-intensive sectors, and the co-ordinating role of the trading companies is linked to that of the banks. By these reductions Figure 6.1 emphasizes the combined impact of the legacy of pre-industrial Japanese society and its industrialization path. As we shall see, these connections were quite different in Korean and Chinese societies.

The Korean Chaebol

As discussed in Chapters 2 and 3, the large, conglomerate chaebol which dominate the South Korean economy share some characteristics with Japanese kaisha but are more similar to the Chinese family business in many of their employment practices and authority patterns. They are like the modern kaisha in being large and active in capital-intensive sectors as well as in light industry and service businesses but differ in being much more vertically integrated through authority hierarchies and diversified across a variety of industries. They are also unlike Japanese firms in not being enmeshed in long-term, diffuse alliances with particular business partners, and the Korean business system exhibits a relatively low level of overall market organization. Similarly to the Chinese family business, the chaebol owners exert strong personal central control over their businesses and rely heavily on family members to fill top management posts. Thus delegation to middle management is limited and authority within enterprises is more personal and less governed by formal rules than in Japanese kaisha. Employer commitment to, and dependence on, skilled workers is also much less than in large Japanese firms and, indeed, is sometimes less than in Taiwanese family businesses. Equally, despite formal commitment to Confucian paternalism, the dominant management style in the chaebol is directive and rather authoritarian. Work group autonomy is correspondingly low. In contrast to many Chinese family businesses, though, the chaebol have developed some formal co-ordination and control systems and

Table 6.2a   Institutional influences on the development of the Korean chaebol: the nature of the firm and market organization

	Distinctive characteristics			
	Strong owner control	Hierarchical integration of diverse activities	Risk management by vertical integration and diversification	Low inter-firm mutual dependence and obligations
Pre-industrial institutions				
Political centralization	X	X	X	X
High level of personal and factional conflicts at centre	X			X
Low integration of vertical loyalties	X			
Strong consciousness of rank and status		X		
Low rule formalization	X			X
Merchant insecurity	X			X
Merit based on moral worth	X			
Patriarchal authority	X			
Industrialization				
Authoritarian colonial regime	X	X		X
Militaristic, dominant state	X	X	X	X
State risk sharing and support for diversified large firms		X	X	X
Weak labour movement		X	X	
Wartime disruption and rapid urbanization	X			X

Table 6.2b *Institutional influences on the development of the Korean chaebol: employment practices and authority strictures*

	Distinctive characteristics			
	Low formalization of procedures and authority	Low employer–employee commitment	Low delegation to middle management and work groups	Directive management role
Pre-industrial institutions				
Political centralization	X		X	
Personal and factional conflicts	X		X	
Low integration of vertical loyalties		X	X	X
Low rule formalization	X		X	
Merchant insecurity		X	X	
Merit based on moral worth	X	X	X	X
Patriarchal authority	X	X	X	X
Industrialization				
Authoritarian colonial regime	X	X	X	X
Militaristic, dominant state	X	X	X	X
Weak labour movement	X	X	X	X
Wartime disruption and rapid urbanization		X		X

use more formal recruitment and other personnel procedures, although personal connections and attitudes remain important. Additionally, in the capital-intensive sector a distinctive cadre of middle management has developed which has some operational autonomy, although not nearly as much as in the kaisha.

Many features of pre-industrial Korea can be summarized in terms of comparable dimensions to those used to characterize Tokugawa Japan, albeit at different ends of the spectra. Thus, the degree of political centralization was high, as was that of merchant insecurity, and vertical loyalties were weakly integrated. The intense personal and factional battles within the centralized political system do, however, require separate emphasis since they remained an important feature of the Korean political system after independence. Similarly, the highly authoritarian and centrally directed nature of early industrialization under Japanese colonial rule also needs to be highlighted, as does the critical role of the military during industrialization and the high level of disruption caused by industrialization and the Korean War. The dominant role of the political executive within the state and its ability to implement its economic policies are key additional factors. In contrast to Taiwan and Hong Kong, the Korean state has encouraged private concentrations of economic resources under its influence, and employment in these large state-supported enterprises has become quite desirable for the graduates of prestigious universities.

Tables 6.2a and 6.2b summarize the relations between these features of the institutional environment and the distinctive characteristics of the Korean chaebol. While many of the latter reflect the combination of pre-industrial institutions and particular features of the industrialization processes as in Japan, the major discontinuities of colonialism and the Korean War have meant that the role of the modern, military-dominated state has been especially important, albeit in conjunction with the traditional form of Korean patrimonialism emphasized by Jacobs (1985). Colonialism and war have also reduced the significance of earlier patterns of village organization relative to the Japanese case and increased the importance of urbanization as a factor weakening traditional norms of collective obligations and reciprocity (Brandt, 1987). These connections will now be explored in a little more detail under the three main headings used earlier.

The Nature of the Firm
The domination of the chaebol by their owners and their families reflects the combination of the historical insecurity of officials and

merchants which continued through much of the twentieth century, the lack of strong institutions for establishing and maintaining trust between non-kin and strangers and their high level of dependence on personal connections with the political leadership during the industrialization process. As described in Chapter 4, Korean society under the Yi dynasty was characterized by a high degree of political centralization in the capital, with little toleration of local power groups or concentrations of economic power in private lands. The aristocracy competed for state offices and engaged in bitter personal and factional battles over these positions.

Centralization, then, meant that power was concentrated in Seoul but did not imply that it was concentrated in the hands of the monarch. On the contrary, it was the focus of the continuing conflicts between the King, his family and different factions in the central bureaucracy which frequently resulted in political paralysis. Thus political stability at the centre was low, and privilege depended on personal ties to currently dominant families and groups. Unlike in Tokugawa Japan, formal rules and procedures did not become established as the basis for administrative behaviour, and personal, especially family and lineage, connections remained the dominant means of organizing loyalties and obligations. As the number of yangban grew during the Yi dynasty, competition for state offices became more intense and encouraged opportunistic changes of allegiance. Families remained the major source of stability in these struggles.

Political and official insecurity was mirrored by merchant insecurity in this patrimonial Confucian society where private wealth was regarded with suspicion and subject to official exactions. The lack of legitimacy as an independent, separate activity and status meant that commerce was always liable to state demands and capricious interventions, so that merchants sought to ally themselves with dominant factions and families. They thus relied heavily on personal ties to leading officials in Seoul to protect themselves, focused on relatively short-term gains and failed to develop co-operative alliances between merchants to stabilize markets and ensure continuity of obligations and trust (Jacobs, 1985: 132–5). Trust relations remained dependent on personal, usually family, connections, a phenomenon that was reinforced by the lack of integrated loyalties and reciprocal obligations between superiors and subordinates in pre-industrial Korea.

This pattern of dependence on the goodwill of the political executive and pervasive insecurity was maintained during the period of Japanese colonialism when some of the early chaebol owners first began their business activities. The authoritarian and alien state was often hostile to Korean enterprises, and so 'networks among kin and close associates became even more acceptable' (McNamara, 1990: 135). The disruption and upheaval that followed the Japanese defeat and later accompanied the Korean War further intensified economic instability, and the patrimonial character of the Rhee regime encouraged dependence on personal ties to the political executive. In these circumstances the development of trust and mutual commitment between owners and managers who were not related, and of formal procedures for ordering such interrelations, was, to say the least, unlikely.

The military coup in 1961 and subsequent commitment to export-oriented industrialization continued this pattern of strong business dependence on the state, especially through political control over access to relatively cheap credit. Although the status of business owners was considerably higher and more legitimate than during the Yi dynasty, their success and, indeed, survival depended greatly on continued political beneficence and favour. These in turn depended on achieving state objectives and maintaining good personal relations with political leaders. Thus chaebol owners remained subservient to the political executive and could not easily delegate the management of their political connections to non-kin salaried managers. Despite their growth in prestige and importance, they were still subject to political displeasure and withdrawal of favours and could not develop the sort of autonomy and independence enjoyed by the Japanese kaisha. As a result, direct personal control of major resources and choices remains a key characteristic of the modern chaebol, and high personal trust between top managers is crucial to their effective operation, typically assured through family membership.

The much greater degree of diversification and heterogeneity of economic activities controlled through managerial hierarchies in the chaebol relative to Japanese kaisha resulted from both the strong state pressure to move into new sectors, especially heavy industry in the 1970s, and the lack of strong, autonomous trading companies to provide quasi-contractual forms of vertical integration. The 'internalization' of risk probably also stems from the need to maintain strong central control over economic activities where political risk is so considerable, and the relative difficulty of establishing long-term diffuse ties between firms in Korean society where trust levels have been much lower than in Japan.

The establishment of large managerial hierarchies to co-ordinate and control these diversified enterprises reflects three features of pre-industrial and twentieth-century Korean society. First, the importance of yangban status, its elaborate grading system and its considerable broadening in the later periods of the Yi dynasty helped to develop widespread and intense concern over, and consciousness of, relative status in formal ranking systems, at least among the ambitious (Jacobs, 1985: 190–202). This has encouraged considerable competition for high-ranking posts and thus a greater acceptance of formal hierarchies of managerial positions, if not of purely formal bases of authority, than in Chinese society (Brandt, 1987). This greater acceptance of formal ranks in Korean society may also be due to the more important economic role and authoritative status of eldest sons in Korean families compared to Chinese ones (Brandt, 1987: 137–8; Jacobs, 1985: 209–10). In this respect, sibling hierarchies appear to be intermediate in significance in Korea between Japan and China.

This concern for formal rank and status has been reinforced by a second feature, the militarization of Korean society. The pervasiveness of the military model of organization in Korea, and the extensive subjection of Korean males to military discipline and activities since the 1950s, have reinforced the effects of Japanese colonial rule which inculcated military conceptions of obedience to superiors and formal rules (Kim, 1988). Although, then, authority is more personal in Korea than in Japan, obedience to rules and procedures and respect for formal positions in hierarchies are stronger in Korea than in Taiwan or Hong Kong and so have enabled chaebol owners to establish formal authority hierarchies for managing diverse economic activities.

The third feature of Korean society which has facilitated the development of these hierarchies is the strong support for the large chaebol and public recognition of their achievements. This has made employment in them more attractive to college graduates from elite families. Despite the traditional disdain for trade and commerce among the Korean aristocracy, the new fast growing chaebol have attracted many highly educated managers in apparent preference to the state bureaucracy, partly by paying relatively high wages and providing expanding promotion opportunities, but partly also by being acclaimed as national institutions contributing to Korean development (Brandt, 1987; Kim, 1988). This ability to attract and retain highly educated managers despite being family dominated increased the capacity of the chaebol to manage diversity and rapid growth through managerial hierarchies compared to the Chinese family business. An important characteristic of these managers is their transferability across sectors and member firms of the chaebol (Amsden, 1989: 128). This may well reflect the general lack of specialization in particular skills and roles in pre-industrial Korea and the low status of specialist expertise and knowledge in Korean society. According to Henderson (1968: 226–44) and Jacobs (1985: 20–1), technical specialism has not been highly regarded either in villages and towns or in the central bureaucracy, and so Korean managers are more likely to see themselves as generalists – in both functional and sector respects – than are Japanese ones. They are thus more willing to diversify into new fields.

Finally, it should be noted that the weakness of the labour movement, and the limited need of employers to obtain the commitment of manual workers, meant that the chaebol could diversify into new fields of activity without being restricted by current skills and capacities. Specialization was thus not encouraged by the need to maintain a cohesive and relatively homogeneous culture and identity. Instead, diversification was facilitated by the considerable level of labour turnover among manual workers in Korea and the low degree of employer–employee commitment compared to the kaisha (Brandt, 1987).

Similar factors have encouraged the chaebol to manage risks by integrating diverse activities through authority hierarchies. This presumably reflects the general preference for large size to reap the benefits of bank and state support. Because the primary risk in Korean big business is losing political support, and this is linked to overall size and success in meeting state priorities, chaebol owners are encouraged to control a large number of businesses directly. Equally, of course, the high level of state support for risky new investments in priority industries has encouraged the chaebol to diversify more widely and more quickly than their Japanese counterparts. The relative ease with which manual employees can be laid off when markets contract or new ventures are less successful than expected additionally facilitates diversification and investments in new kinds of activities.

Market Organization
The low level of reciprocal obligations and long-term commitments between large firms and their subcontractors in Korea is echoed by the absence of long-term alliances between firms in different sectors. This is partly because the important co-ordinating businesses in the zaibatsu, and later in the inter-market groups, the banks and the sogo shosha, do not perform similar roles in Korea. The banks, as we have seen, are state controlled and implement state policies rather than contribute to the long-term development of particular business groups, and the trading companies are simply chaebol subsidiaries concerned with facilitating exports and have little or no autonomy.

More generally, the low level of market organization in Korea can be seen as the outcome of traditional patterns of political and economic centralization, reinforced by Japanese colonialism, which prevented the establishment of roughly equivalent economic enterprises that could negotiate common activities and alliances while retaining their independence. The dominant role of the central state, and its reluctance to permit independent private accumulations of wealth and control over economic activities, inhibited the development of substantial firms that could work out their own pattern of competition and co-operation. Instead, like many collective entities in Korea, their survival and growth depended, and still depend, on their links with political leaders and bureaucrats at the centre, links which were essentially antagonistic between rival enterprises. Thus, the limited degree of autonomy of the market system from the state before, during and after the colonial period meant that firms competed with each other indirectly through the central state as much as directly through the market; and so establishing long-term links with industry partners was subsidiary to seeking political allies and influence. Furthermore, since the state was often suspicious of private alliances and networks which threaten its dominant role, they were not encouraged, although the cotton spinners and weavers did manage to establish a successful cartel (Amsden, 1989: 64–8).

The Korean preference for central authoritative control of different economic activities, rather than mutual obligations and particularistic, diffuse commitments between exchange partners, also reflects the slow economic development of rule formalization and lack of long-term security of economic owners during the pre-industrial and industrializing periods. As mentioned above in the discussion of Japan, the development of long-term commitments between firms depends on relative stability and assurance that such commitments will be reciprocated in the future. Where private wealth is subject to expropriation and future success is liable to the outcomes of palace intrigues, short-term advantage is likely to be pursued at the expense of long-term gains. Equally, the rapid pace of economic and social change during Japanese colonialism, the Korean War and the unpredictability of the Rhee regime emphasized the critical importance of personal control over assets and the difficulty of ensuring long-term stability and mutual benefit. As Brandt (1971) suggests, the strong norms of reciprocity and mutual obligation characteristic of the relatively egalitarian village he studied were not echoed in the city or in the more hierarchical, yangban-dominated villages. There, individual family interests were pursued at the expense of more collective obligations, and reciprocity between unrelated exchange partners was difficult to sustain over time.

Employment Practices and Authority Systems
The continuing importance of personal authority relations and personal discretion in allocating rewards, posts and resources in Korean chaebol is the outcome of institutional influences similar to those which ensure the continuation of control exerted by owners and their families. In a society where the political executive is not governed by an abstract legal system, and formal rules are more a means of exercising control over inferiors than of justifying authority and ordering hierarchical relations, authority within enterprises is unlikely to be based on formal rules and procedures. Rather, the long tradition of dependence upon the central power, together with high levels of factional and personal competition for central favours and reliance on personal connections with leading factions, strengthened during colonial rule and by the military-backed strong state, have encouraged similar patterns of dependence and authority within large enterprises. The Confucian justification of authority in terms of moral worth demonstrated by educational success permits it to be unconstrained by reciprocity norms and emphasizes the personal qualities of leaders rather than their fulfilment of formal roles. The strength of this conception of authority in the Korean political system, and of the institutional arrangements which it supports and expresses, has thus limited the development of more rule-governed and impersonal forms.

A further factor limiting this development is the weakness of the labour movement. Until the last few years, the state has systematically controlled and manipulated labour organizations in Korea in support of the export-oriented industries, so that the chaebol owners have not had to take much account of their demands or obtain their commitment for firms' policies and practices. As a result, the formalization of reward and promotion procedures has not been encouraged by union pressure, and supervisors have been able to exercise high levels of personal discretion. The replacement of individual competition for favours and rewards by collectively agreed rules and procedures has not, therefore, developed to a significant extent in the chaebol.

The dominant role of the military and their recruitment to top management posts in many chaebol have, though, encouraged the use of formal control procedures and a considerable reliance on formal performance measures for managerial assessment (Chung et al., 1988). This has also been facilitated by the expansion of US-influenced training programmes in business and management (Lee,

1984). As Henderson (1968: 350–7) has indicated, the reformed military training system developed administrative skills and techniques which were transferred to civil society after Park took over in 1961. The growing significance of a military career attracted many ambitious Koreans, who thus acquired 'modern' methods of decision making and control and later applied these to public and private enterprises (Jacobs, 1985: 178). Together with the recruitment and retention of college graduates as a core managerial cadre which was highly rewarded, this enabled the chaebol to grow at a fast rate without fragmenting into separate businesses. It should be noted, however, that most personnel decisions at management levels remain highly centralized and are often the personal preserve of the owner. Thus, although the chaebol have imitated some of the formal recruitment and selection procedures of the kaisha, and emphasize seniority in promotion decisions, many aspects of their personnel management practices remain essentially patrimonial (Brandt, 1987).

The low level of commitment to employees, and of dependence on them, can be attributed to the combination of traditional conceptions of authority, the limited extent of village cohesion, and autonomy and integration into the political system, together with the weakness of the labour movement during industrialization. The traditional emphasis on moral worth as the basis of authority and lack of reciprocity between superior and subordinate in Confucian Korea have not encouraged chaebol owners to share authority with workers or commit themselves to long-term support for them. This reluctance has been reinforced by the dominant pattern of patriarchal authority in the Korean family which ascribes omnipotence and omnicompetence to the father and hence makes it difficult for him to admit dependence on other family members.

It is also the result of limited village cohesion and co-operation in traditional Korea and the weak integration of vertical loyalties compared to Tokugawa Japan. Although collaboration and reciprocity in agricultural and construction activities did, and do, occur across kinship boundaries in some Korean villages (Brandt, 1971: 154–61), such egalitarian co-operation between households was less evident in richer villages and/or where particular aristocratic clans predominated. Here, mistrust between clans and the primacy of lineage boundaries seemed strong, according to Brandt (1971: 238). Thus the overall extent of collective loyalty to the village as a whole and the importance of its collective identity and success appear less marked in Korea than in Japan. Furthermore, of course, the degree of village autonomy and ability to resist outside demands was less in Korea, and local officials were seen more as alien state agents than as representing village interests. Loyalty to them, and through them to superior ranks, was therefore not high and could not serve as the basis for loyalty to authority hierarchies in firms. The level of collective organization and its integration into vertical hierarchies were not, then, considerable in Korea, and the disruption of rapid urbanization, industrialization and war reduced them further, especially as competition for access to central power holders grew after the Japanese defeat. As a result, eliciting collective employee commitment to particular employers on a long-term basis remains more difficult in Korea than in Japan, even when chaebol owners see the need for it because, for instance, of a shortage of skilled labour.

Another major difference from Japan, of course, has been the weakness of the labour movement as a result of state oppression and control. This has meant that employers have not had to gain the co-operation of trade unions or to elicit workers' commitments to enterprise goals. By and large, the large-scale movement from rural areas to the cities and growth of the population since the war have maintained a labour surplus for most jobs and enabled the chaebol to hire and fire as they have wished (Michell, 1988: 106–79). Long-term commitments have thus not been necessary, except perhaps in a few cases for skilled workers.

The low level of delegation to middle management and of task autonomy among work groups can similarly be seen as the result of merchant insecurity and dependence on the state in traditional Korea, reinforced by the colonial and military regimes, coupled with the prevalent conception of authority, the limited extent of formalization and the weak labour movement. Delegation of control within businesses requires trust and the ability to ensure commitment to the enterprise in a similar way to delegation from property owners to salaried managers. Where the traditional level of political and economic insecurity has been high, and dependence on the personal decisions of political leaders remains considerable, such trust is likely to be limited to those with strong personal ties to the owners, and collective commitments to the firm as a formal entity cannot be assumed to be high (Brandt, 1987). The traditional justification of authority does not, of course, encourage Korean chaebol owners to elicit commitment by developing relations of mutual dependence with their middle managers, nor does the adoption of military administrative systems.

Finally, the directive, not to say authoritarian, approach to management and supervision in the Korean chaebol results from the traditional authority patterns combined with the dominant role of the military since 1961 and, again, the weakness of trade unions. The adoption of Confucian conceptions of merit and authority by the Korean aristocracy meant that they did not have to demonstrate their competence through competitive struggles or elicit support from the peasantry by providing reciprocal services. Obedience to them was claimed on the basis of their moral superiority and so did not require them to be closely involved with the work of others or to perform any useful function. The centralization of power in the capital and lack of local intermediary institutions which could link village activities and authority to the central power additionally meant that authority was seen as remote, incomprehensible and disconnected. This conception of managerial authority also echoes the patriarchal form of family authority in Korea, where the father is omnipotent and regarded as omnicompetent. Unlike his Japanese counterpart, he cannot display emotional dependence on the family or ask for its help without compromising his authority (Pye, 1985: 75).

This remote and patriarchal conception of authority was reinforced by the militarization of the political system and the experience of military service for many Koreans. The transfer of military systems of organization and control to many parts of the state bureaucracy after 1961 was echoed by their influence on private business organizations, not least through the recruitment of military officers. Military styles of management thus became important models in the rapidly expanding chaebol and matched traditional patterns of authoritarian supervision. The lack of a strong labour movement, of course, meant that there was no collective organization to challenge this pattern and little need to modify it to elicit greater worker commitment.

In summarizing these relationships in Figure 6.2, it seems clear that many characteristics of the Korean chaebol can be seen as the product of historical insecurity and dependence on capricious central officials and leaders, coupled with traditional conceptions of authority, both of which were reproduced and reinforced by the Japanese colonial regime and the militarization of Korean society. These factors have resulted in personal trust and loyalty being very highly valued by business owners and typically restricted to family members and close personal associates. They thus restrict delegation and encourage strong central and personal control of economic activities. Continued dependence on the central power and competition with other business owners for political patronage have likewise restricted the development of strong inter-firm connections and so of high levels of market organization. The same

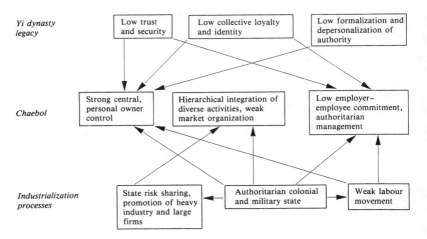

Figure 6.2   *The Yi dynasty legacy, industrialization and the Korean chaebol*

combination of factors has limited the level of commitment to employees and encouraged a directive, authoritarian management style. They can be summarized as leading to low levels of trust and security.

A second set of factors has led to weak collective commitments and identities beyond kinship groupings compared to those in Japan. The varied extent of village communication and cohesion in pre-industrial Korea, coupled with the fiercely competitive struggles over access to state posts among the elite and the lack of inter-mediate institutions which could have integrated vertical loyalties, limited the development of collective loyalties to non-family institutions. The upheavals of Japanese-induced industrialization, the Korean War and rapid urbanization further limited the transfer of village-based obligation patterns and loyalties to modern enter-prises. As a result, mutual employer–employee commitment has not developed very strongly, and delegation of control to work groups and middle managers has not been encouraged. Finally, the comparative lack of institutionalization of formal rules and procedures for administering state affairs in Yi dynasty Korea inhibited the native formalization of hierarchical relations during industrialization and so the depersonalization of authority, a gap which was only partly filled by Japanese colonialism.

During industrialization, the authoritarian nature of the Japanese colonial state and its military-backed successors constituted a key factor which continued the pattern of high dependence on the political executive and insecurity, together with the large-scale mobilization of the population and their subjection to military discipline. This reinforced the chaebol owners' concern with personal reliability and control, limited their need to elicit the co-operation of labour organizations by repressing them and helped to establish large-scale authority hierarchies in the private sector. The high level of state risk sharing and promotion of heavy industry, together with support for the large chaebol, encouraged diversification and high growth rates as well as legitimating employment in them for elite sons. Diversification and discontinuous growth by acquisition were also facilitated by the weak labour movement, which, of course, additionally did not seriously challenge the strong centralized and mostly personal authority structures.

The Chinese Family Business

The third form of business organization considered here, the Chinese family business, differs substantially from the Japanese kaisha on most dimensions and from the Korean chaebol on some. Perhaps the most striking differences are its limited size and lack of involvement in heavy manufacturing industry, together with its strong reliance on personal authority and personal obligation networks between firms. The Chinese family business also differs from the kaisha in its management of risks through limited commitments to business partners rather than by building strong organizational relations of mutual dependence with them. This limitation facilitates flexibility and means that market relations are less stable and reciprocal than in Japan, especially with subcontractors. Where long-term commitments are developed between Chinese family businesses, they are based on close personal ties between their owners and are rarely generalized beyond these to the firms as distinct collective entities.

The importance of personal relationships and trust is also reflected in the internal authority systems of Chinese family businesses. Just as owners rarely delegate overall control to non-family managers, so too authority within enterprises tends to be highly personal and centralized. Personnel procedures and employment practices are also informal and tied to the personal decisions of the owner. Commitment to core employees is similarly personal and rarely implies mutual dependence and reciprocity, at least overtly. It is thus discretionary and limited compared to that common in the larger Japanese kaisha. Equally, task autonomy is limited and depends on establishing personal trust relations between individual workers and the owner. Finally, as was emphasized in Chapter 3, managerial authority is paternalist and didactic, with the managerial role seen as more remote and omniscient than in Japanese firms.

Some of these features stem from the patrimonial nature of preindustrial China and the dominant forms of commercial organization that developed there. Many aspects of this patrimonial system were similar to that in Korea, such as the lack of local power centres, the emphasis on moral worth as the basis of authority, the low integration of vertical loyalties and considerable merchant insecurity, but there were some important differences. Perhaps the most significant of these for our purposes were the importance of aristocratic status and rank in Korea, coupled with intense factional disputes and conflicts at the centre, and the more unequal inheritance principle in Korean families. The former has encouraged a much stronger concern with formal status and position in Korean organizations than in Chinese ones, while the emphasis on equal division of family resources has been seen as an important factor in the strong drive to self-employment among Chinese males (Wong, 1988a). This equality of status and expectations between male siblings generates considerable fraternal rivalry and limits family cohesion and integration (Freedman, 1966: 45–8).

Turning to consider industrialization patterns and the institutional environment in which the Chinese family business developed in Taiwan and Hong Kong, there are, of course, some important differences which were summarized in Tables 5.1 and 5.2. However, these differences do not seem to have had major effects on the sort of competitive export-oriented business that has become established in these two countries, because there are also important common elements which combined with pre-industrial features of Chinese society to generate remarkably similar principles of business organization. First, in both societies the bulk of the population was excluded from elite positions in the state bureaucracy and political executive until recently. Second, neither state directly supported the growth of many large, capital-intensive, privately owned businesses or shared the risks of developing such firms with private entrepreneurs. Correlatively, most export-oriented firms did not need to develop the sort of strong personal links with political leaders and the ruling party as did the Korean chaebol owners. Thus, a considerable distance existed between most native business owners and the dominant groups in both societies. Third, the labour movement has been weak in both Taiwan and Hong Kong, although the state was much more directly involved in its suppression and management in the former society. As a result, its impact on firms' policies and procedures has been negligible in both systems, albeit for different reasons. Finally, the important role of Japanese firms in Taiwan, especially the sogo shosha, and the arrival of buyers from large retailers in North America compensated for the lack of strong trading networks and facilitated the development of specialized production-focused businesses there. In Hong Kong, of course, trading networks were well established, and so firms could also concentrate on production. Overall, then, many of the significant differences in the political and economic systems of Taiwan and Hong Kong had rather less impact on the dominant business system in the privately owned, export-oriented sector than might be imagined at first.

Tables 6.3a and 6.3b summarize relationships between these key features of social institutions and the Chinese family business in Taiwan and Hong Kong. As in the case of Japan and Korea, many distinctive characteristics of the CFB stem from combinations of pre-industrial Chinese society and industrialization processes, but the role of the state is less marked, except in a negative sense, and the importance of continuities in the Chinese family structure from the pre-industrial period is notable. The limited direct involvement of state agencies and banks in steering private firms' activities in Taiwan and Hong Kong has resulted in strong continuities in the overall principles of business organization of the modern CFBs from commercial businesses in pre-industrial China (cf. Deglopper, 1978; Hamilton and Kao, 1990; Redding, 1990). Certainly, the experiences of many overseas Chinese business owners seem to have reinforced traditional business practices of secrecy, reliance on personal ties and family members and a preference for flexibility and direct personal control (Wu, 1983). These relationships will now be explored in a little more detail under the three usual headings.

The Nature of the Firm

The dominant characteristic of the CFB is, of course, its strong control by the owning family and its close identification with the reputation and achievement of that family. The importance of family control, and reluctance to delegate decision making to managers who do not have close personal ties to the owners, can be attributed to the combination of traditional patterns of mistrust and insecurity beyond kinship-based obligation networks in Chinese society and to the exclusion of most CFB owners from dominant state elites in Taiwan and Hong Kong. As in Korea, the Chinese patrimonial state did not integrate vertical loyalties between the peasantry and the central monarch through a series of

Table 6.3a   *Institutional influences on the development of the Chinese family business: the nature of the firm and market organization*

	Distinctive characteristics				
	Strong personal owner control	Managerial specialization and entrepreneurial diversification	Risk management by minimizing commitments and maximizing flexibility	Limited inter-firm commitments, market organization	Personal links between firms
Pre-industrial institutions					
Low vertical integration of loyalties	X	X			X
Low rule formalization	X	X	X	X	X
Merchant insecurity	X	X	X	X	
Merit based on moral worth	X	X	X	X	X
Low village cohesion and co-operation	X				
Patriarchal authority in families	X	X			
Equal inheritance	X				
Taiwan's industrialization					
Dominant, exclusionary state	X	X			
Distant state, low risk sharing		X	X	X	X
Weak labour movement					
Discouragement of large Taiwanese firms		X	X	X	
Importance of sogo shosha for external trade		X			
Hong Kong's industrialization					
Colonial, exclusionary state	X				
Distant state, low risk sharing			X	X	X
Weak labour movement					
Subsidized housing		X			
Established trading networks		X			

Table 6.3b *Institutional influences on the development of the Chinese family business: employment practices and authority relations*

	Distinctive characteristics			
	Highly personal authority and low formalization of procedures	Limited commitment to, and low mutual dependence on, core employees	Centralized decision making and control, weak middle management	Paternalist, aloof management role
Pre-industrial institutions				
Weak vertical integration of loyalties	X	X	X	X
Low rule formalization	X	X	X	X
Merchant insecurity	X		X	X
Merit based on moral worth	X	X	X	X
Low village cohesion and co-operation	X	X	X	X
Patriarchal authority in families	X	X	X	X
Equal inheritance		X	X	
Taiwan's industrialization				
Dominant, exclusionary state		X	X	
Distant state, low risk sharing	X	X		
Weak labour movement	X	X	X	X
High urbanization and rural–urban unity		X		
Hong Kong's industrialization				
Colonial, exclusionary state		X	X	
Distant state, low risk sharing	X	X		
Weak labour movement	X	X		
Subsidized housing		X	X	X

intermediate political institutions; power was centralized, not differentiated, and not administered through formal rules and procedures. Equally, superiors did not develop obligations to subordinates or feel constrained by impersonal rules, since they justified their domination in terms of their personal moral worth. As a result, the state was viewed as a capricious external agency demanding taxes and labour services without providing any useful service in return, and political loyalties rarely extended beyond the immediate family and lineage. The 'gentry' sought to protect themselves by investing in education so that they, or a kinsman, could become an official, and/or by developing networks of personal obligations with officials. This reliance on personal networks to gain advantage and prevent state depredations remains an important feature of the Chinese political system, including that in Taiwan (Hamilton and Kao, 1990; Winckler, 1988).

The patrimonial state also, of course, was antagonistic to large private concentrations of wealth derived from commercial activities. While some merchants were granted official favours and support, the overwhelming majority were excluded from power and privilege and regarded as a source of official enrichment. As Godley (1981: 34–5) puts it: 'Merchants paid high taxes and licensing fees and their travel and trade were often subject to special bureaucratic restrictions . . . large scale corruption was the norm for, and indeed the only term for, social intercourse between the ruling and trading classes.' Additionally, the lack of a predictable system of commercial law made trading highly dependent on personal obligations and reputations. Thus, merchants feared and distrusted the state in China and developed business practices that maximized their personal control over economic activities and disguised their success and growth. These attitudes were, of course, reinforced in Taiwan by the KMT antagonism to large private enterprises controlled by Taiwanese.

The lack of a distinct, legitimate social status as merchants in Chinese society also limited their capital accumulation to that required for purchasing land and/or official positions. Because long-term wealth accumulation derived from commercial activities had little legitimacy and was likely to encourage official depredations, merchants had every incentive to invest their capital in land and education and so concentrated on short-term gains which could be transformed into more prestigious and secure resources. As a result, 'the traditional system urged successful businessmen to stop their business and, by taking part in the bureaucratic management of China's resources, to obtain merchant profits without the risk and humiliation of merchandising' (Godley, 1981: 37; cf.

Mann, 1987: 21–2). The development of continuing, collective merchant 'houses' of the type found in Tokugawa Japan was therefore not encouraged in China, and the insecurity of merchants limited their willingness to undertake long-term commitments as well as to delegate control to managers.

Strong owner control also resulted from the relatively low level of co-operation and cohesion between unrelated households in many Chinese villages. As discussed in Chapter 4, loyalties and commitments were focused much more on families than on the collective village organization in China than in Japan, and villagers were more reluctant to engage in collective enterprises which did not directly benefit their household, partly because of their being forced to compete with each other to gain access to the land and also because lower village autonomy restricted their ability to gain from such collective activities. Reciprocity and trust between non-kin was therefore less in China, and commitment to collective entities beyond family boundaries remained weak. Thus business owners could not, and usually did not, assume a strong loyalty to their enterprise on the part of the managers (cf. Silin, 1976).

An additional limitation on the development of managers' commitment stems from the widespread preference for self-employment and independence over managerial employment among Chinese managers (Greenhalgh, 1984). This results in business owners being reluctant to trust their managers, unless they have strong personal ties and obligations to them, since they are quite likely to leave when a suitable opportunity develops. According to Wong (1988a), this strong entrepreneurial desire stems from the combination of equal inheritance of the family property in Chinese families and the belief that men are naturally equal and should attempt to realize their own potential (cf. Pelzel, 1970). Each son is therefore encouraged to found his own household and seek success as an independent agent. In societies like Taiwan and Hong Kong, where elite political and administrative roles have been reserved for the minority, this search for success focuses on the accumulation of wealth, which cannot be realized as a manager. Formal status in a managerial hierarchy is less significant here than success as an independent entrepreneur.

This emphasis on strong family control also constrains managerial integration of different kinds of economic activities, since owners prefer to be able to maintain direct control of them, either through their own direction or through family representatives. This means that growth beyond the initial enterprise tends to occur through the establishment of separate firms run by the small group of trusted associates, typically of course drawn from family members (Hamilton and Kao, 1990). Thus, each individual firm remains managerially specialized, but the CFB as a whole can diversify into new areas wherever opportunities arise as long as the owner has enough closely associated 'family-type' partners to run them. The historical difficulty of developing long-term trust relations with outsiders, and lack of merchant security in pre-industrial China, thus combined with family inheritance practices and the lack of close state support in Taiwan and Hong Kong to limit firm size and the scope of managerially integrated activities.

Managerial specialization and small size were also encouraged by the KMT's hostility to large independent enterprises run by Taiwanese and the importance of the sogo shosha and large retail buyers in distributing and marketing exports. Similarly, the established trading networks in Hong Kong facilitated specialization in parts of manufacturing processes, as did the high concentration of the population in Kowloon and later on in the new state-subsidized housing estates which reduced information costs. These estates additionally encouraged small-firm growth through reducing housing costs and hence generating surplus family income for investment in family businesses. The proliferation of small firms both encourages, and is encouraged by, extensive subcontracting, which further limits the growth of managerial hierarchies. This subcontracting is not as 'relational' or 'obligational' as in Japan, because commitments beyond kinship boundaries and close personal associates are limited.

The difficulty of developing long-term relations beyond family boundaries, and pervasive insecurity of merchants in pre-industrial China, limited the willingness of Chinese business owners to engage in long-term commitments to particular exchange partners. As a result, managing risks through establishing relations of high mutual dependence, as in Japan, was not feasible in the Chinese business environment. Rather, risks were reduced by restricting the size of investments and emphasizing flexibility over long-term commitments to particular industries and resources. This focus on flexibility and ability to shift resources because of personal ownership and control has facilitated opportunistic diversification in Taiwan and Hong Kong which additionally reduced the risks associated with high levels of business specialization. By establishing separate small firms run by family members for distinct activities the CFB retains control while reducing the risks of concentrating all its resources on one area of business.

This diversification also takes place through partnerships with closely connected business associates with whom personal obligations and connections have been established. Such ties also form a way of spreading risks, although control is also, of course, shared in these cases. A further point about this preference for expansion through setting up separate firms, rather than integrating activities through a single larger managerial hierarchy, is that it helps to disguise the overall size of the CFB and so avoids attracting the attention of the central authorities. This seems to be especially relevant in Taiwan (Gold, 1986, 1988a). Overall, then, risk management through limiting commitments, restricting firm size and diversifying activities has been encouraged by low levels of trust and security in Chinese society, together with the lack of state commitment to risk sharing and promotion of particular firms in Taiwan and Hong Kong.

Market Organization
The low level of inter-family trust and its dependence on personal ties and obligations have also restricted the development of long-term inter-firm commitments, so that the level of both horizontal and vertical market organization is limited. The relatively small size and high specialization of firms in the CFB obviously imply high levels of interdependence between them; but, as discussed above, this is typically managed on a short-term contractual basis policed through reputational networks rather than by long-term mutual dependence relations. This reflects the strong preference for flexibility and lack of strong institutional procedures for generating trust – as well, of course, as the availability of efficient information networks facilitated by high population density in both Taiwan and Hong Kong.

Horizontal linkages across business sectors are also limited in scope and longevity because they are highly dependent on personal ties and specific to particular opportunities. The highly personal nature of Chinese business control and decision making means that involvement in joint ventures and risk sharing with other family businesses requires strong personal trust and recognition of mutual obligations between business owners. As a result, such commitments beyond the family are usually restricted to specific projects and rarely develop into the sorts of inter-market business groups found in Japan. Typically, Chinese business owners prefer to establish new ventures as separate projects rather than enlarge and restructure existing arrangements with partners, because these are highly personal, and it is simpler to set up new entities than to renegotiate personal obligations (Hamilton and Kao, 1990). Again, the relative lack of long-term state support and risk sharing in Taiwan and Hong Kong has limited the willingness of CFB owners to enter into long-term commitments with business partners without strong 'family-type' obligations.

The personal nature of these inter-firm connections stems, of course, from the lack of other forms of trust in Chinese society, coupled with the pervasive insecurity of merchants and traders there. The inability to rely on formal rules to ensure compliance and low levels of trust between different families, combined with business practices that reflect public insecurity mean that partnerships and joint activities require considerable personal commitments and a strong sense of mutual obligation between individual business owners. Furthermore, because each such partnership involves family assets and commitments, albeit to a limited extent, there is a sense in which inter-firm linkages involve 'family-like' connections and obligations. Because commitments and loyalties tend to be familistic rather than focused on larger collective entities, these connections depend on the personal relations between families and do not develop into long-term arrangements that transcend individual obligations.

Employment Practices and Authority Structures
The highly personal nature of authority in the Chinese family business and associated low formalization of personal procedures there reflect similar features of the institutional environment to those which encouraged a high level of owner control. The combination of low levels of trust and mutual obligation between superiors and subordinates and different families, the lack of integrated vertical loyalties and of strong collective commitments beyond family boundaries and the considerable insecurity of merchants encouraged direct personal control of activities within enterprises and prevented the growth of more impersonal forms of authority. The lack of a codified legal system and general preference for personal, informal ways of solving disputes and managing conflicts additionally restricted the development of formal rules and procedures for directing and controlling activities within enterprises.

A further feature of pre-industrial China which has encouraged a reliance on personal authority in Chinese family businesses was the emphasis on the moral superiority of those in authority, which led to obedience being owed on the basis of personal qualities rather than competence in performing some functions (Silin, 1976). Thus positional authority based on formal relationships has not developed to nearly the same extent as in Japanese, or even Korean, companies. Rather, loyalty is regarded as due to the superior worth of the business owner, who is thereby justified in controlling activities personally in a manner comparable to that of the father in the Chinese family. Formal rules and procedures which could constrain this authority reflect upon the personal merits of the owner in much the same way as criticisms of particular decisions implied the personal unworthiness of those in authority in pre-industrial China. As a result, employment practices are not governed by standardized rules but rather are highly personal and idiosyncratic to the particular relationship between the owner and individual employees.

The weakness of the labour movement in both Taiwan and Hong Kong has meant that this low degree of standardization and formalization of employment practices and personnel procedures has not been seriously challenged by workers' organizations. The personal discretion and authority of business owners have rarely been threatened by unions which, in the case of Taiwan, 'more typically function to enforce worker discipline, suppress worker demands, raise money for government projects, and administer worker services' (Deyo, 1989: 74). Equally, the considerable distance and separation between the formal bureaucracy of the state from the bulk of Chinese family businesses in these two economies have limited the diffusion of formal rules and procedures from the state to the enterprises. This separation, and sometimes antagonism, has reinforced traditional Chinese business owners' distrust of state officials and preference for maintaining personal control over major decisions, especially personnel ones.

The limited commitment to employees and weak extent of mutual dependence between business owners and employees found in most Chinese family businesses reflect the personal nature of authority and control in these enterprises and the unwillingness of owners to undertake broad, long-term commitments. In turn, these characteristics stem from the difficulty of establishing loyalty and trust between superiors and subordinates, except on a personal basis, in Chinese communities and the strong attraction of self-employment. Thus, the combination of weak vertical integration of loyalties and identities, low rule formalization, weak village cohesion and loyalty beyond the family household, traditional conceptions of authority and equal inheritance practices in pre-industrial China has been an important – if not, indeed, determining – factor in limiting business owners' development of mutual dependence relations with their employees. Where personal ties of obligation have been established, commitments are, of course, much stronger, especially to skilled male workers; but, as Deyo (1989: 160–95) points out, these typically excluded many female, unskilled workers in export-oriented light manufacturing industries. In any case, such commitment remains a matter of personal discretion for the owner reinforced by community norms rather than a jointly agreed outcome.

The lack of state risk sharing in both Taiwan and Hong Kong has reinforced this limited commitment to employees, as has, of course, the lack of legislative support for worker security. Similarly, the weakness of the labour movement in both economies has meant that employers have not had to incorporate major groups of workers into enterprise 'communities' or commit themselves to long-term employment and training. The tendency for skilled workers to leave employment and start their own businesses has also limited the development of long-term mutual commitments between employers and employees. As mentioned earlier, the high population density and, in Hong Kong, public subsidization of housing and other costs have facilitated the growth of self-employment and family mobility through entrepreneurship (Greenhalgh, 1984).

The highly centralized decision-making system of most Chinese family businesses, and the corresponding weak position of middle managers, also stems from the strong emphasis on personal authority and lack of institutions for establishing trust relations beyond family boundaries. As before, these result, in turn, from the patrimonial features of pre-industrial China which have constrained the development of collective loyalties and formal procedures for regulating authority relations and limited to mutual trust between non-kin. Clearly, where the loyalty of managers, supervisors and workers is questionable – except for those directly related to the owning family or with similar strong personal ties to them – delegation of responsibility and resource control is unlikely, and owners will be highly concerned with their personal authority and control. As Silin (1976) has shown in his account of a large Taiwanese firm, this concern is manifested in frequent bypassing of the formal authority hierarchy and a reluctance to rely on formal information systems. Equally, this lack of trust and delegation is unlikely to encourage managers to develop initiative or strong loyalties to the enterprise, and so a tendency to 'delegate upwards' is a distinctive characteristic of many middle management groups.

The authoritarian state in Taiwan has encouraged this general pattern of authority, as has the colonial state in Hong Kong, by excluding political participation and acting without consultation or much attempt to justify decisions. Additionally, the exclusion of the bulk of the population from political and bureaucratic elite positions has led to personal wealth becoming a leading goal and means of acquiring high social status, so that employment as a manager is less attractive than self-employment, as discussed above. This, in turn, limits delegation, as owners seek to reduce the risks associated with staff leaving. Again, the weak labour movement means that employers have not needed to grant high levels of task autonomy and control to work groups but have been able to control directly how work is carried out and performance assessed.

Finally, the dominant conception of the managerial role and leadership pattern reflects traditional authority relations in Chinese society and their reproduction in Chinese families, reinforced by the lack of a strong labour movement in Taiwan and Hong Kong which could challenge them. As discussed in Chapter 4, authority principles in pre-industrial China were based on the moral superiority and worth of individual leaders and their officials rather than on their competitive success in battle or providing common services for the collectivity. They thus did not need to demonstrate their superior qualities through competition once they had passed the state examinations or to elicit loyalty and commitment by performing useful functions for the morally less worthy. Rather, they were supposed to lead by their morally exemplary conduct and communicate their superior wisdom through appropriate behaviour. Leadership was conceived more as a matter of manifesting one's moral worth and superior status, to which obedience was owed, than obtaining obedience and loyalty on the basis of one's actions, competitive success and technical competence. As a result, Chinese leaders expect deference and commitment to themselves as superior people as distinct from actively seeking subordinate loyalty. They therefore maintain considerable social distance from subordinates and rarely explain or justify their decisions.

This pattern is linked to family authority relations where the father is typically aloof and distant, especially with his sons after they have reached the 'age of reason' at around six years (Wolf, 1970). Fathers are supposed not to display emotion, including open affection and pride in their children, but to represent Confucian values and the authority of the community as a formal authority figure. Obedience is owed more as a matter of duty to the patriarchal role than as emotional loyalty to the individual father (Hamilton, 1984). As a result, commitments to superiors in organizations which are based on family authority relations tend to be less strong and emotional than in Japanese firms.

These relationships can be summarized in a manner similar to those between institutional features and the distinctive characteristics of the Japanese kaisha and Korean chaebol, as is shown in Figure 6.3. A critical component of the legacy of pre-industrial China, which has been reproduced through the Chinese

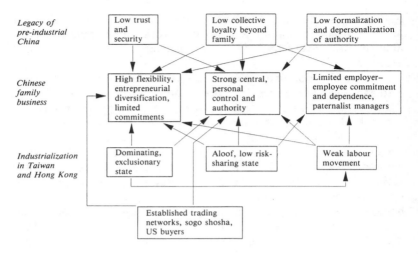

Figure 6.3   *The legacy of pre-industrial China,
industrialization patterns in Taiwan and Hong Kong and the
Chinese family business*

family and the exclusionary, dominating states of Taiwan and
Hong Kong, is the low level of trust and loyalty beyond family
boundaries. This has meant that relationships between businesses
and between superiors and subordinates within businesses that are
not based on 'family-like' ties of personal, mutual obligation tend
to be relatively short term and unreliable. Similarly, the lack of
strong collective commitments to entities beyond the family, and of
institutionalized patterns of co-operation and collaboration across
kinship boundaries, has resulted in loyalty to enterprises being
limited and conditional. This difficulty of establishing commitment
to collective enterprises has, of course, been compounded by the
low degree of formalization and depersonalization of authority.
Together, these three legacies of pre-industrial Chinese society have
encouraged a dominant concern with personal ownership and
control and with maximizing personal flexibility and minimizing
long-term commitments and an emphasis on paternalist management patterns.

These consequences of pre-industrial patrimonialism are similar
to those in Korea, except for the importance of aristocratic status
and unequal inheritance patterns there which encouraged a concern
with formal rank and perhaps mitigated the egalitarian pursuit of
self-employment. However, there were major differences in the
experience of Japanese colonial rule between Korea and Taiwan,

and in the actions and attitudes of the state in Taiwan and Hong Kong relative to that in Korea. Because Korea had considerable military significance for Japan, as well as a cohesive and autonomous culture and long-established distinctive state system, the Japanese imposed their authority in a more systematic and overtly authoritarian manner there than they did in Taiwan (McNamara, 1986). They also developed heavy manufacturing industry earlier and to a greater extent than in Taiwan, where industry was largely concentrated in the food processing sector (Cumings, 1984; Ho, 1984). As a result, Koreans gained greater experience of both state-directed industrialization and the zaibatsu's organization of industry. They were also more directly subjected to militaristic forms of organization than were the Taiwanese, whose traditional patterns of agricultural organization were less disrupted by enforced industrialization (Gold, 1986: 34–42; McNamara, 1990: 9–63).

After the colonial period the Korean state became much more directly involved in building up large private conglomerates than did the KMT in Taiwan; and, of course, the experience of the Korean War and enormous expansion of the Korean army militarized Korean society to a greater extent than happened in Taiwan or Hong Kong. Thus, although both the Korean and Taiwanese states clearly dominated their societies during industrialization, they adopted quite different relations with indigenous entrepreneurs, so that connections of state agencies and leaders with business owners were much less close and important in Taiwan than in Korea (Wade, 1990: 321–5). In both Taiwan and Hong Kong the state remained largely aloof from the bulk of private enterprises and did not provide much financial or other forms of support and risk sharing. As a result, traditional patterns of Chinese business organization have not been greatly modified in those two societies, so that, for instance, traditional distrust of state officials and unwillingness to rely on formal rules and procedures remain important characteristics of the Chinese family business. In the absence of strong state involvement in, and direction of, enterprise policies and activities, that is, traditional patterns seem to have remained significant in Taiwan and Hong Kong.

A Comparison of Institutional Influences on East Asian Business Systems

In comparing and contrasting relations between business system characteristics and social institutions in East Asia, it is clear that

Table 6.4   *Relations between institutional influences and East Asian business system characteristics*

Business system characteristics	Institutional influences			
	Low merchant trust and security	Low extra-family collective loyalty and co-operation	Low formalization and depersonalization of authority	Remoteness and omniscience of fathers
The nature of the firm				
Degree of owner control	+	+	+	
Limited size and scope	+	+	+	
Risk management through mutual dependence	-	-		
Markets				
Level of market organization	-	-		
Dependence on personal connections	+	+	+	
Authority systems				
Centralization	+	+	+	+
Formalization	-	-	-	
Commitment to core employees	-	-		
Facilitative management role	-			-

Table 6.4 *continued*

Business system characteristics	Institutional influences			
	Corporate dependence on authoritarian state	State risk sharing and support for large firms	Autonomy and support of GTCs and banks	Weakness of labour movement
The nature of the firm				
Degree of owner control	+			
Limited size and scope		–		
Risk management through mutual dependence	–	+	+	
Markets				
Level of market organization	–		+	
Dependence on personal connections				
Authority systems				
Centralization	+			+
Formalization				–
Commitment to core employees		+		–
Facilitative management role				

many of the major differences between the Japanese kaisha, the Korean chaebol and the Chinese family business result from a combination of, and interconnections between, features of pre-industrial societies and industrialization processes. This can readily be seen from Table 6.4, which summarize the key relationships between East Asian business system characteristics and their institutional contexts identified earlier in this chapter. In most instances, the influence of background institutions has been reinforced by at least one critical feature of the industrialization processes, as when low levels of trust and security among merchants in pre-industrial societies have been intensified by the role of an authoritarian, interventionist state during industrialization and generated strong owner control of enterprises and highly centralized decision making.

A second point to be noted about these relationships is their limited reversibility. Thus, while low trust and security among merchants in pre-industrial societies encourages strong owner control and centralization, it does not follow that higher levels of trust always generate managerial discretion and delegation. The extent to which this reverse relationship does occur depends on other factors, such as patterns of loyalty and co-operation, reciprocity in authority relations and the effectiveness of less personal control. Similarly, business systems with high levels of market organization, as in Japan, are unlikely to develop in societies with low trust and security, low levels of collective identity and loyalty and high business dependence on an authoritative state, but this does not mean that where these features are reversed firms will always develop strong ties of mutual dependence and support. This would depend on the existence of powerful and effective co-ordinating intermediaries, such as the sogo shosha and banks, and a supportive state committed to risk sharing. This, in turn, limits the generalizability and determinacy of these influences.

A third, related aspect of the relationships summarized in Table 6.4 is the primarily inhibiting or constraining nature of some institutional influences. Thus, business dependence on an authoritarian state inhibits the development of mutual dependence relations between firms and the management of risk through such relations. Equally, the lack of institutionalized trust relations between exchange partners and of collective loyalties beyond the family limits managerial discretion and delegation of task performance, so that, at least for these business systems, these institutional features appear to be necessary, but not sufficient, conditions for the separation of ownership from control and decentralization of decision making. For many characteristics of business systems, then, it is easier to establish necessary conditions for their establishment than to provide complete explanations of them which can be readily generalized. The interdependence and limited reversibility of institutional influences on East Asian business systems restrict the extent to which general causal connections can be identified that enable positive predictions to be made. Rather, the relationships summarized in Table 6.4 indicate how institutional contexts constrain the sorts of business systems that become established and rule out certain characteristics.

More substantively, the comparison of the development of the Japanese kaisha, Korean chaebol and Chinese family business in their institutional environments suggests six major conclusions about the development of business systems. First, pre-industrial societies where institutionalized processes for establishing trust between non-kin are weak or non-existent, and where loyalties and identities are focused on the family and lineage rather than wider collectivities, are unlikely to develop managerial hierarchies with substantial control over resources delegated from owners. Rather, the combination of merchant insecurity, weak integration of vertical loyalties and weak village cohesion and co-operation between families results in a strong emphasis on personal control by owning families, centralized authority relations and weak middle management within authority structures.

Second, the development of long-term, particularistic relations between specialized and managerially homogeneous firms, both within industry sectors and across them, is unlikely in societies where private concentrations of economic wealth and resources have been regarded with suspicion and antagonism by central political authorities and where merchants were highly dependent on their personal connections with state officials. The institutionalization of high levels of market organization seems to have required relatively stable relationships both between merchants themselves and between merchants and the state in the pre-industrial period, together with considerable autonomy from state control and domination during industrialization. In particular, of course, it grew in Japan through the rapid development of the trading companies with the assistance of the state and the co-ordinating role of banks in the zaibatsu and post-war inter-market groups. The private control of the trading companies and banks and their integration in large business groups in Japan exemplify the more reciprocal and equal relations that have developed between the private sector and the state there from 1868 to the 1950s than in Korea and Taiwan. Stable, long-term and particularistic relationships between firms do not become institutionalized in societies where enterprises are highly dependent on state support and state-controlled credit, because critical uncertainties and dependence relations are vertical rather than horizontal there.

Third, and relatedly, the development of strong ties of mutual dependence between specialized firms within and between industries as an important way of managing risk required considerable co-operation and risk sharing between households and merchants in pre-industrial societies. It was also facilitated by the growth of the trading companies and banks in Japan, which shared in the risks of long-term investments and performed integrative roles for successive stages of vertical production sequences. A further important factor was state intervention and support for particular developments, as well as the state's general willingness to permit, and sometimes stimulate, co-operative arrangements between firms. In contrast, where traditions of co-operation and risk sharing between families are weak, trust is low, and there are no co-ordinating institutions for generating long-term linkages between firms, as in Taiwan and Hong Kong, risk management is likely to concentrate on limiting commitments and maximizing flexibility. This is especially so where state agencies remain aloof from market processes and do not actively support co-operative agreements or engage in risk sharing. Thus, the more distant are enterprises from supportive agencies, and the more trust and co-operation depend on purely personal ties of obligation and loyalty, the more likely business owners will manage risks in a similar way to the Chinese family business.

Fourth, the development of formal rules and procedures for managing firms, and the depersonalization of authority relations within them, are unlikely in societies where authority has traditionally been based on the personal moral superiority of leaders and officials and local loyalties have not been integrated into larger political collectivities. This is especially so where the state does not become closely involved in firms' activities during industrialization or develop state-owned, rule-governed enterprises that serve as a model for the private sector. As in the case of owner control, the institutionalization of formal rules and procedures governing employment relations and personnel practices is aided by strong unions and the need to obtain workers' commitment to enterprise goals and, correlatively, is less likely where labour organizations are relatively weak.

Fifth, the development of strong employer–employee commitments and mutual dependence requires considerable trust between superiors and subordinates as well as traditions of strong and cohesive collective commitments and loyalty. It is aided by traditional authority relations which were based on the need to elicit commitment from supporters and actively demonstrate competitive success rather than simply demanding obedience on the grounds of moral superiority. Again, these commitments are more likely to be effective when firms can share some risks with state agencies and business partners and are more probable when the strength of the labour movement means that firms have to obtain employee support. Correlatively, where trust is low and collective loyalties beyond the family are weak, and those in authority are not accustomed to actively eliciting the commitment of subordinates, such mutual dependence is unlikely, especially if state agencies do not share the risks or permit independent unions.

Sixth, and finally, the development of different managerial roles and styles depends greatly on traditional authority relations and justification, together with the strong reproduction of family authority relations, especially those between fathers and sons. Traditional Confucian conceptions of authority coupled with patriarchal family authority patterns have resulted in distant and paternalist styles of management. Where these features have been combined with authoritarian colonial regimes and military-backed states that repressed autonomous trade unions, as in Korea, this style has become more directive and authoritarian. Conversely, the combination of more active and competence-based conceptions of authority with a more emotionally involved and support-seeking father in Japanese families has encouraged a more facilitative managerial role to develop in the larger kaisha, reinforced by the more independent and stronger labour movement after the war.

These relationships are derived from the development of business systems in societies that industrialized relatively recently and quickly, and were historically quite homogeneous and distinctive. They do not, then, necessarily apply to societies that industrialized earlier and over a longer period, or that are more institutionally pluralistic. In addition, these East Asian societies share certain features that distinguish them from most Western societies and limit the general applicability of these relationships. In the next chapter I shall briefly discuss the implications of this analysis of East Asian business systems for the analysis of hierarchy–market relations in Western societies in the light of these points.

7

East Asian and Western Business Systems

This analysis of East Asian business systems has focused on how the major differences between them can be explained by combinations of pre-industrial institutions and patterns of industrialization. The distinctive characteristics of the Japanese kaisha, the Korean chaebol and the Chinese family business developed from, and continue to be effective in, particular institutional environments. These connections between distinctive forms of business organization and dominant institutions, however, reflect certain common features of East Asian industrialization and societies which are not necessarily found to the same degree elsewhere. In particular, the speed of industrialization and its direction by powerful and autonomous state elites contributed to the more direct influence of pre-industrial institutions than in many Western societies. Equally, the relatively high level of ethnic and cultural homogeneity within these countries, and the heterogeneity between them on many dimensions, have generated strongly distinctive types of business system which can be directly related to particular institutional features of nation states. In contrast, the greater institutional pluralism within countries, and the institutional commonalities across them, found in Western Europe and North America have reduced both the distinctiveness of national business systems in the West and their explanation in terms of national divergent institutions.

In this chapter I consider the significance of these differences and their consequences for the analysis of Western business systems. Initially, I shall discuss the major common elements of East Asian societies and patterns of industrialization which distinguish them from many of those in Western Europe and North America and how these have affected business system characteristics. Second, the implications of the differences between East Asian and Western societies for the understanding of business systems in the latter will be analysed. Finally, I shall consider the major differences between nation states in these more pluralistic societies which affect forms of business organization and their consequences for hierarchy–market configurations.

Common Components of East Asian Societies and
Patterns of Industrialization

In considering how East Asian societies and their experience of industrialization differed significantly from many Western countries, I shall first discuss broad features of pre-industrial Japan, Korea and China which differentiate them from most European societies and then outline specific aspects of their industrialization which affected business systems in common ways. The major similarities in these three pre-industrial societies concern: (a) their considerable homogeneity, stability and isolation for some time before Western imperialism affected them in the nineteenth century; (b) the major role of the family as the primary unit of identity and loyalty together with the primacy of vertical loyalties and duties; (c) the weakness of formal laws and the legal system; (d) the subservience of merchants and artisans to the political elite; and (e) the importance of education as a means of legitimating domination, especially in China and Korea. Together with the common components of East Asian industrialization, these are listed in Table 7.1.

One of the most striking characteristics of pre-industrial Japan, Korea and China is the remarkable longevity and stability of their civilizations and political systems compared to most Western European states. Korea, for example, was unified in 668 AD, and the Yi dynasty lasted for over 500 hundred years (Steinberg, 1989: 16–27). Additionally, they developed in quite distinctive ways in relative isolation from each other, although Korean Confucianism was of course borrowed from China, and the Korean King was formally subservient to the Chinese Emperor. Especially in the 200 to 300 years before the arrival of Western gunboats, these three states consciously cut themselves off from outside influences. Together with their common high levels of ethnic homogeneity, those features generated highly self-conscious, distinct and uniform societies in which particular conceptions of authority, gender and role performance were strongly institutionalized and influenced the sorts of business systems that became established during industrialization.

The key social institution which reproduced these expectations and distinct identities was, of course, the family. The importance of the family as the basic unit of social identity and loyalty is a crucial feature of these three societies which not only differentiates them from Western societies in which the individual has become the basic social unit, but also from most South-East Asian societies where extended kinship links are not so significant (O'Malley,

Table 7.1   *Common features of pre-industrial East Asian societies and their industrialization processes*

Pre-industrial Japan, Korea and China
(a)   Longevity, isolation and homogeneity of each society.
(b)   Primacy of the family.
(c)   Subordination of the legal system.
(d)   Subservience of merchants to authority system.
(e)   Importance of education.

Industrialization processes in Japan, South Korea, Taiwan and Hong Kong
(a)   Autonomy of the state (less in Hong Kong).
(b)   Destruction of the landlord class.
(c)   Prestigious and highly selected bureaucratic elite.
(d)   Weak legislature.
(e)   Weak labour movement (except in Japan after the Second World War).
(f)   Credit-based financial system dominated by the state (except in Hong Kong).
(g)   Segmented labour market.
(h)   Weak development of publicly certified skills.

1988). All these 'post-Confucian' cultures share the common theme that 'individuals achieved their identity solely through family membership which carried with it not only the obligation of deferring to the collectivity in critical decision making but of acknowledging that the mortal life of the individual was less important than the immortality of the ancestral family line' (Pye, 1985: 62). While the significance of family membership and kinship organization is particularly marked in the case of the Chinese family business, it is much greater in all three societies than in Western ones and has limited the spread of individualism (cf. Brandt, 1987; Vogel, 1987; Winckler, 1987).

An important function of the family in these societies has been the reproduction of particular authority relations and respect for established hierarchies. Although significant differences in family authority structures do exist between East Asian societies, as we have seen, they none the less share a common conception of the duty of subordinates to show respect, loyalty and deference to superiors, particularly the father, and the subservience of women to men. In Korea and China, of course, this conception of family loyalty and deference was seen as the foundation of loyalty to the state and its officials. The importance of the family in pre-industrial East Asian societies has encouraged managers and owners to harness this conception of hierarchy and obedience to buttress their own authority to a greater extent than in most Western forms of paternalism.

The third common characteristic of these three societies which distinguishes them from most Western societies is the weakly developed legal system, its subordination to state elites and the relatively unimportant role of formal contracts and agreements. In particular, the Anglo-Saxon separation of legal institutions from the formal apparatus of the state and the considerable autonomy enjoyed by the legal profession are not evident in East Asia, either before industrialization or during it, with the possible exception of Hong Kong. This has meant that the 'rule of law' has not constrained the political executive very much in any of these societies and litigation is rarely used as a means of gaining redress (cf. Upham, 1987). It has also resulted in little reliance being placed on legal institutions for developing and policing agreements and trust relations. Additionally, it has restricted the development of legal-rational legitimations of authority, especially in Korean and Chinese societies. Even in Japan, authority relations are more personal and less contractual than in Western organizations (Lincoln and Kalleberg, 1990: 108–14; Rohlen, 1974: 18–20), and formal work contracts are reserved for the less favoured 'temporary' workers rather than the privileged core group of employees. The lack of a distinct and autonomous legal system in all three pre-industrial East Asian societies, then, has had major consequences for the sort of business system that has developed there, as well as for the role of the state in steering economic development.

This lack of an institutionally distinct legal system in pre-industrial Japan, Korea and China is echoed by the generally subordinate position of private economic wealth holders, especially merchants, in these societies. Even in Tokugawa Japan where merchants had a distinct and legitimate position, they were clearly subservient to, and integrated within, the feudal authority system, so that they did not develop into an independent capitalist class (Hirschmeier and Yui, 1981: 53–63). In fact, they were so integrated into Tokugawa society that many merchant houses failed to survive the Meiji reforms and certainly could not be said to have played a prominent role in their development. Thus, all three East Asian societies lacked a separate class of private, non-landed, wealth holders committed to economic development and able to mobilize capital independently of the state.

Finally, the importance of education in Confucian Korea and China has had marked effects on attitudes to formal education and certified competences in Korea, Taiwan and Hong Kong, so that both state and private investment in education have been high since 1950 (Papanek, 1988). In Tokugawa Japan, of course, formal education did not lead to state office, but the growing importance of formal educational success in demonstrating competence during the nineteenth century and the use of university degrees to justify, and filter access to, leading positions in the Meiji bureaucracy ensured that education became seen as the key to acquiring high status. As a result, East Asian societies have highly educated labour forces in terms of formal attendance at general educational institutions. However, the emphasis on formal certification of success in competitive general examinations for access to elite posts has meant that specialized technical training had low prestige, and so practical skills are not as highly developed and standardized by public institutions as they are in many Western societies.

Together these common features of pre-industrial Japan, Korea and China have meant that, relative to many Western societies, the state had an overwhelmingly dominant position and was the only agency capable of co-ordinating large-scale economic development. Furthermore, the lack of institutional checks and balances, the considerable homogeneity of the population and the traditional acceptance of, and deference to, superior authority greatly increased the ability of state elites to manage industrialization, once they became committed to it. These features have also meant that many, if not indeed most, long-term relationships between people in East Asia are organized in kinship and family-like ways, often around vertical obligations and deference (Pelzel, 1970), and horizontally based associations and interest groups, such as occupational groups, are not easily established. Equally, the Western emphasis on individual rights, duties and identities has not developed to any notable extent in these societies – as, indeed, it has not in many other countries.

Turning now to consider the major similarities in patterns of East Asian industrialization, the most notable is the dominant role of the state. In addition to the influences already mentioned, the autonomy of the state was enhanced by the effective destruction of the landlord class in Japan, Korea and Taiwan through land reform in the 1940s and early 1950s and the role of military force in ensuring executive dominance in Korea and Taiwan. The colonial regime in Hong Kong, of course, prevented democratic pressures from impinging upon economic development, although its autonomy from business elites has been less than that of the political executives in Korea and Taiwan. This autonomy of the state executive and bureaucracy has meant that economic development has taken place without involving the organized labour movement; and, in general, the labour movement has been weak as a political force.

An important feature of East Asian industrialization which

facilitated strong state influence over the economic system in Korea and Taiwan, and in post-1930s Japan, has been the credit-based financial system. The bulk of industrial development has been financed through bank and trade credit, both formal and informal, and capital markets have played only a minor role. Particularly in periods of high economic growth, this has enabled the state to exercise direct influence on firms' activities and choices (Zysman, 1983: 245–51), even in Japan where the banks are more independent from the state. A particularly important instrument of state control here was its direction of foreign exchange. Except in Hong Kong, the state has exerted considerable control over financial intermediaries in East Asia since 1945 and ensured that they supported industrial development.

Two further common features of industrialization in East Asia concern labour markets. First, they are highly segmented, particularly between men and women. Second, they are not bounded by certified skills and horizontally differentiated occupations. As Deyo (1989) has emphasized, East Asian industrialization was dominated by light manufacturing industry in its early stages, particularly textiles, in which women formed the bulk of the labour force. Typically, these workers were highly mobile, had little training and formed little attachment to particular employers (Saxonhouse, 1976). Women in general have been paid much less than men and have not been expected to become long-term employees or develop complex skills. The generally subservient status of women in these societies and the common expectation that they will leave employment upon marriage have enabled employers to develop different policies for male skilled workers and short-term female workers. They are therefore able to use women for low-paid, low-skilled tasks without committing firms to long-term employment and so have increased their flexibility. The widespread distinction between 'core' and 'temporary' workers is likewise a way of maintaining flexibility while ensuring commitment from the skilled workforce.

The lack of strong occupational identities and commitments built around standardized, certified skills is another important characteristic of East Asian labour markets. Although there were some attempts to establish craft unions and standard pay rates for standard skills in Japan before the First World War, these were successfully resisted by employers and the state (Dore, 1973: 388–97). Generally, the strong state control over the labour movement during industrialization has restricted the development of craft unions and horizontal groupings based on occupational interests, together of course with strong management resistance in many cases (Cole and Tominaga, 1976). This low level of occupational consciousness in East Asia has been further reinforced by the lack, or low prestige, of publicly developed and certified practical skills which could be owned and controlled by individuals and traded on labour markets. Technical education in general either has been neglected by the state or else is commonly viewed as inferior to success in the general educational system, and most skills are taught by firms, usually on the job, for particular purposes (Amsden, 1985a, 1989). As a result, they are not highly standardized and do not constitute the basis for separate labour markets which could be controlled by practitioners or independent training and credentialling organizations.

Overall, then, East Asian industrialization took place in societies that were quite homogeneous and relatively isolated, and had weak legal systems and few – if any – authoritative institutions beyond the state and strong family identities. It was remarkably rapid, co-ordinated by the state, which had considerable autonomy and ability to implement its policies, and funded largely through bank and family credit. It relied heavily on low-paid, short-term female labour in many industries and developed highly segmented labour markets with different conditions and terms of employment. These markets were not, though, organized around standardized, publicly certified skills and horizontally structured identities, and loyalties based on occupations are weak.

As a result, distinctive business systems have developed which share the following characteristics. First, legal and contractual forms of trust and obligation are relatively unimportant in regulating relations between business partners and between superiors and subordinates. Personal and reputational bases of trust play a much greater role in East Asia. Second, legally and financially defined and bounded firms are often not the only significant unit of economic action; rather, mutual obligation networks and alliances between owners, managers and intermediary organizations, such as trading companies, co-ordinate and share activities and risks (Hamilton et al., 1990). Thus, firms and markets tend not to be two sharply opposed and separate principles of co-ordination but rather overlap and mix. Third, task and role specialization within authority systems is limited. Typically, duties and posts are left fluid and flexible in East Asian businesses, often with overlapping responsibilities and multiple jobs held by the same person. Similarly, skills are rarely standardized and do not govern task allocations or define jobs. They are relatively firm specific, and there is little standardization of wage rates across employers and industries. Finally, employment terms and conditions differ substantially between different groups of workers, typically with a core group being granted much more favourable conditions than peripheral or 'temporary' workers.

Contrasting Features of Western Societies and their Implications

In contrasting Western societies with East Asian ones, it seems reasonable to suggest that the former are both more internally differentiated and pluralistic and less sharply different from each other than the latter. Most European societies developed secondary foci of loyalty and allegiance between the family and the state, and the various forms of feudalism institutionalized political differentiation and competition for power. The relative independence, and often considerable political influence, of religious institutions further restricted the dominance of the state in many countries. It is worth noting here that the boundaries and form of the modern state are quite recent in a number of European countries; they are often nineteenth- or twentieth-century creations. This means that many loyalties and institutions pre-dated these state systems, and so the latter cannot claim historical continuity with, and legitimacy from, long-established civilizations in the same way as some East Asian ones. The conflation of state and society is correspondingly less easy to achieve in Europe. Additionally, the guilds and urban centres exercised greater autonomy in many parts of Europe than in East Asia and facilitated the development of an independent capitalist class in some countries which fought for political authority and economic change in a way that was impossible for Japan, Korea and China (Werner, 1988). Thus, both economic and political differentiations have been considerably greater in Western societies, and the state has had to compete with a number of collective agencies and interests.

Military conflict, mercantile competition and pan-European trade routes have also resulted in a far greater mobility of people and ideas between European states than East Asian ones over the 500 years before the mid-nineteenth century. Together with the common heritage of Christianity, albeit in many different forms, and the development of relatively autonomous formal legal systems in most European countries, these interchanges meant that European states have shared many features and institutions. Consequently, the institutional context in which Western business systems have become established are neither so homogeneous and internally integrated within each country nor so strongly different between them as in East Asia.

As a result, the configurations of hierarchy–market relations which have become established in Europe and North America as effective business systems are more varied within state boundaries and less distinct between them than those in East Asia. A distinctly 'German' business system is not so readily identified and distinguished from an archetypal 'French' one to the same degree and in the same way as the post-war Japanese kaisha can be contrasted with the Korean chaebol. Rather, we find some variations between industries and sectors within countries and some commonalities across countries. For example, the differences in authority and trust relations found between East Asian business systems are not so strong in Europe because of the common heritage of legal formalism and rule-bound authority, as well as the associated development of institutional mechanisms for establishing trust. Consequently, the dimensions on which business systems vary most strongly in Western societies are not necessarily the same as those developed in Chapter 3 for contrasting East Asian business systems. In particular, the role of personal authority and trust relations is not so important in differentiating Western business systems.

A further consequence of these differences is that the institutional influences on the development and effectiveness of different business systems in East Asia highlighted in Chapters 4, 5 and 6 are not all so significant in understanding Western ones. In particular, the impact of pre-industrial political systems and patterns of rural organization has been less direct in many European countries – although not necessarily negligible in the cases of the Italian industrial districts and Danish railway towns (Brusco, 1982; Kristensen, 1989, 1990) – and more mediated by institutions that developed during industrialization. Thus, many features of pre-industrial England structured the process of industrialization in that country, which in turn has affected the sort of hierarchy-market configuration that has become established, rather than directly affecting the distinctive characteristics of modern business systems (cf. Elbaum and Lazonick, 1986; Ingham, 1984; Payne, 1990).

Furthermore, the relative detachment of the individual from the family as the basic social unit, together with the greater importance of horizontal groupings based on occupation and/or skills in many European countries, has meant that the role of the family in encouraging particular characteristics of effective business systems has been less marked in the West than in East Asia. Differences in industrialization processes and in secondary institutions of socialization and identity – such as the education and training systems, occupational associations, trade unions and forms of political association and authority – then, play a more significant and dominant role in accounting for variations between business systems in Western Europe and North America than in East Asia.

The identification and analysis of different business systems in Western Europe and North America therefore focus on less discrete and distinct configurations than in East Asia. They also involve multiple units of analysis as well as the nation state. Particular relationships between, say, the education and training system of different countries and patterns of work organization, such as those studied by Marc Maurice and his colleagues (1980, 1986), are more often the central concern than the analysis of cohesive, integrated and quite different national business systems. In addition, broad similarities on a number of dimensions may suggest the comparison of a general kind of configuration of hierarchy–market relations which occurs in, say, Anglo-Saxon societies with capital-market-based financial systems, a common legal system and strongly individualist value systems with other ones more typical of, say, continental European societies (cf. Scott, 1987).

Turning now to consider some of the specific implications of the differences between East Asian and many Western societies for the analysis of business systems in the latter countries, the greater importance of individual identities and of formal, legally defined procedures, rights and duties has obviously generated authority structures in enterprises which are less personal, more formally specified and restricted in scope and more focused on individual activities than in East Asia. Family authority principles and relations are relatively separate and distinct from organizational ones in most Western business systems. Similarly, the establishment of relatively distinct and autonomous legal systems has encouraged greater reliance on formal contracts between business partners, including between employers and employees. While the significance of legal contracts varies between Western societies, in general they are more important in organizing exchange relations here than they are in East Asia. Personal trust is correspondingly less crucial, although rarely negligible.

The lower degree of autonomy of the state, and its greater internal differentiation, in most Western countries means that state elites have been less able to generate and implement long-term coherent and consistent development policies. Political and bureaucratic elites have not dominated other elite groups in the manner of the Japanese bureaucracy, or the Korean and Taiwanese political executives, and have been more susceptible to short-term political pressures in many Western countries. As a result, business leaders are less dependent on state agencies and political leaders than in some East Asian societies, and state–business relations are more reciprocal and symmetric in many Western countries, although the closeness of these relations does of course vary between them, as is reflected in the numerous discussions of 'corporatism' in different European countries (Katzenstein, 1985: 87–133; Streeck and Schmitter, 1985). Additionally, the labour movement has played a more significant role during industrialization in many European countries, and this has had a considerable effect on labour market structures and firms' labour policies.

One of the most striking contrasts between East Asian and many Western societies, especially the Anglo-Saxon ones, lies in the much greater role of specialized, publicly certified skills and their link to distinct occupational identities in the latter countries. Among both manual and non-manual employees, horizontal loyalties to particular occupations and their organized system of representation are much stronger in the West. They are often based on distinct and separate skills which were acquired in public institutions and which structure labour markets. This results in greater specialization and standardization of jobs across enterprises and, together with the general emphasis on individualism, encourages more formal specification of individual roles and their co-ordination than in most East Asian business systems. Because practical skills are often standardized and certified by public agencies in many Western societies, they limit employers' ability to establish an idiosyncratic division of labour and to control skill definition to the same extent as in East Asian business systems. This greater importance of formally certified skills and occupational identities in Western business systems means that variations in skill formation and organization institutions between societies have more impact on work organization and control in the West than in East Asia.

Overall, then, Western societies exhibit greater institutional pluralism within states and share more common institutional features between them than East Asian ones, and so the business systems that have become established in Western European and North American countries are neither homogeneous and singular in each state nor so different between them. Additionally, the more significant development of the legal system and pervasiveness of legal-rational forms of authority in Western societies has limited the importance of personal authority and led to greater reliance on formal means of co-ordination and control procedures in Western managerial hierarchies. Similarly, the development of formal means of ensuring contract compliance and the relative reliability of institutionalized trust mechanisms have reduced the need to rely on personal knowledge and trust of business partners – and so, of course, facilitated the growth of large managerial hierarchies and impersonal trading networks. The greater emphasis on individual identities and rights, together with extensive systems of publicly certified skill development and practitioner control over skili definition in many Western countries, has limited the importance of firm-based on-the-job training as well as the ability of firms to organize and control the work process and organizational division of labour as they wish. Relatedly, the considerable significance of horizontal groupings and identities in most Western societies has made the development and integration of collective vertical loyalties less easy to achieve than in East Asia.

Institutional Differences between Western Nation States and their Consequences for Business Systems

In considering variations between business systems in Western countries, and how they can be explained, a number of studies have identified significant differences between forms of business organization across countries which have been attributed to institutional variations (for example, Granick, 1972; Lane, 1989). In particular, patterns of work organization, managerial recruitment and careers, management control and managerial specialization have been found to vary significantly between Western nation states, often within the same industry (see, for example, Gallie, 1978; Horovitz, 1980; Lane, 1987; Maurice et al., 1986), both historically and contemporaneously. The institutions invoked to explain these differences have ranged from national education and training systems to state policies and structures and the organization of labour markets (Lane, 1989: 31–8). It is clear from these and other studies that there are significant variations in modes of organizing economic activities between nation states, even if they do not form integrated business systems that differ from each other on all the major dimensions identified in Chapter 3, and that these variations are connected to institutional differences. In addition to differing on many of the dimensions discussed in Chapter 3, these systems also vary in the extent to which hierarchies systematically integrate economic activities, rely primarily on formal co-ordination and control procedures, divide individual jobs and roles into specialized tasks and separate technical from supervisory authority, and in the relative importance of different skills and managerial functions.

In analysing these differences between hierarchy–market configurations, it seems sensible to begin with the major institutions which both affect the economic system and vary significantly between states. There are at least four of these: the state and political system; the financial system; the education and training system; and the system of labour organization and control, including highly skilled white-collar labour. The critical features of the state here include its overall cohesion and integration, its ability to function autonomously and implement economic policies independently of pressure groups and established elites, its commitment to, and dependence on, economic development and growth and its correlative willingness to share economic risks and commit resources for development goals. Financial systems vary in their closeness to state agencies and to major businesses, depending on their being predominantly credit or capital market based and the major source of profits of financial organizations (Ingham, 1984; Zysman, 1983). Education and training systems differ significantly in the way they generate and organize practical skills and allocate prestige, as Marc Maurice and his colleagues have emphasized. Finally, labour markets vary in their degree of specialization around standardized skills, the strength and organization of trade unions and the overall significance of market-based wage rates and reward systems. These institutional variations are summarized in Table 7.2.

Considering first the organization and actions of the state, one of the major differences between nation states which affects their ability to develop and implement coherent policies for economic development and growth is the cohesion and integration of major state components, especially the political executive and the bureaucracy. Where state powers are separated between the legislature, the executive and the bureaucracy, and no single institution dominates the others, it is obviously more difficult to ensure that coherent industrial policies are followed than in societies where politicians and elite bureaucrats share common objectives and backgrounds, or where particular economic ministries dominate the state system, as in Japan. An important aspect of this integration is the extent of decentralization of economic powers to provincial and local governments. Where this is considerable, as in the United States, coherent central plans and co-ordination of economic activity are not likely to be particularly effective and may also, under appropriate circumstances, encourage the success of small and medium sized enterprises, as in Denmark and, perhaps, Italy (Kristensen, 1989: Weiss, 1984, 1988).

Table 7.2 *Key variations in the institutional contexts of Western business systems*

The state and political system
(a) Cohesion and integration of the political executive and bureaucracy.
(b) Influence of legislature.
(c) Differentiation and separation of major institutions and elites.
(d) Commitment to state-coordinated economic development.
(e) Extent of state risk sharing with private firms.

The financial system
(a) Capital market based or credit based.
(b) Dependence of financial institutions on individual firms' profits and growth.
(c) Segmentation of financial markets and institutions.

The educational and training system
(a) Unitary or dual education system.
(b) Involvement of employers in training and certification.
(c) Extent of practitioner control over skill training and certification.

The labour system
(a) Strength of the trade unions.
(b) Basis of union organization.
(c) Centralization of labour movement.
(d) Integration of unions with political parties.
(e) Extent of market-based reward systems.
(f) Segmentation of labour markets around skills.

The autonomy of the state and its ability to carry through policies against opposition reflect the balance of power between the executive and the legislature in democratic societies as well as the overall level of institutional differentiation and separation of elites' spheres of action. Where the legislature is relatively independent and has distinct powers of its own, as in the USA, it is clearly more of a constraint on executive action than where it is subservient to political party organizations in an electoral system that generates considerable majorities, as in the UK. Equally, the state is less likely to be able to act consistently and effectively where major activities and institutions are controlled by separate bodies such as professional institutions and independent public corporations, as tends to be the case in Anglo-Saxon societies in contrast to many continental European ones (cf. Dyson, 1980). Indeed the whole identity of this state as distinct from the government of the day tends to be weaker in the former kind of society, and so its ability to pursue coherent economic policies over an extended period of time is much less. This difference can be described as the degree of institutional differentiation and separation of elites.

The degree of state commitment to, and dependence on,

economic development and growth reflects the conditions sur-
rounding the establishment of the central state in a country,
together with the need for the political elite to legitimize its position through industrial growth. Where the dominant institutions of
the central state pre-dated industrialization, as in Britain, political
elites are unlikely to see their position depending on their successful
management of economic development. In contrast, where the
modern nation state became established after the first Industrial
Revolution and was linked to national development, as in many
nineteenth-century European states, political and bureaucratic
elites are much more likely to identify their interests with industrial
growth and commit state resources to it. Such commitment does,
of course, also depend on the availability of other sources of
economic wealth and growth and the strength of groups based on
them, such as mercantile, financial and agricultural elites.

The greater level of state commitment to industrial development,
the more likely state agencies will be willing to share risks and
information with major firms, as well as ensuring that macro-
economic policies do not inhibit or constrain such development.
Obviously this does not mean that they will necessarily become as
directly involved in the steering of firms' strategic choices as the
Korean state, but political and bureaucratic elites will probably
underwrite major investment decisions and provide considerable
infrastructural support for new developments, so that firms can
plan ahead with some confidence and assume continued economic
and political stability. Depending on the overall level of state
integration and autonomy, this may result in considerable business
dependence on the state and a strong need for firms to co-ordinate
their strategies with state policies. At the very least, such state
commitment is likely to mean that major firms will maintain close
links with members of the bureaucratic and political elites and be
more willing to undertake risky projects than where it is absent.
Clear and strong public support for industrial development is also
likely to enhance the prestige of industrial management and so
increase its attractiveness for the educated children of elite groups.
In turn, this is likely to encourage further elite integration between
industry and the state.

Second, the role of the financial system is crucial both for state
support and guidance of industrial development and for firms'
strategic choices and risk management. Where the financial system
is largely capital market based, as in Britain and the USA, the state
is limited to a predominantly regulatory role and cannot readily
intervene in firms' decisions or channel funds towards particular
sectors. Credit-based financial systems, on the other hand, enable

state agencies to play a major role in the allocation of resources and thus direct firms' choices, especially where the banking system is dominated by the state, as in France, so that it can determine the cost of investment funds and ensure high levels of demand for them, which, in turn, means that their supply becomes an administrative matter. As a result, firms are more dependent on the state where financial systems are credit based than when they are capital market based. Equally, they are more directly linked to state priorities and co-ordination plans where the state participates as an actor in the banking system than where the banks are more autonomous, as in Germany (Zysman, 1983: 55–80). As Cox (1986) points out, the nature of financial systems can change, as we have seen in the case of Japan, but none the less in any one period it does severely condition the ability of the state to implement industrial policies.

It also affects relations between banks and industrial firms and the latter's financial policies. Basically, capital-market-based financial systems have relatively specialized financial institutions competing for capital and assets through market transactions, and the prices of financial assets are largely set by competition. Here, firms raise capital in a variety of ways depending on relative costs and terms. Thus, their relationships with banks tend to be impersonal, short term and specific to particular transactions. Banks and other financial institutions on the other hand, concentrate on allocating funds on a portfolio basis to a range of activities and borrowers, so that they are less concerned with the long-term development of any single customer than with the relative attractiveness of competing projects from a variety of borrowers at any one time. As a result, firms depend more on their rating in impersonal financial markets as measured by standardized financial accounting measures when seeking to raise investment funds than on their close relations with particular banks. They therefore invest considerable resources in preparing financial accounts for the capital markets and grant more autonomy and influence to the finance function than do firms operating in credit-based financial systems. An additional consequence of operating in a capital-market-based financial system is that long-term risk sharing between financial and industrial companies is low, and so firms 'internalize' risks within their boundaries, which in turn affects their strategic choices.

In credit-based financial systems capital markets are weaker, and most investment credit is provided by banks which sometimes, as in Germany, own significant proportions of their corporate customers' shares. Financial institutions are here more dependent on the growth and success of particular borrowers, since they cannot easily trade standardized financial assets on liquid secondary markets. They therefore invest more resources in acquiring detailed knowledge of firms and industries to evaluate risks and ensure they are kept fully informed about their customers' activities and performance. This in turn encourages risk sharing, since banks have an interest in providing a wide range of financial services and larger loans for growing businesses, as well of course as acquiring more information about firms' strategies and abilities to manage risky projects. Equally, firms become more dependent on particular banks, especially in high-growth periods or when large sums are required for capital investment, since banks will only invest in firms that they already know quite well and have confidence in. As a result, public financial reporting is less important in credit-based financial systems, and the banks take on some of the functions carried out by financial managers within firms in capital market financial systems. Firms thus give up some autonomy and independence in exchange for some risk sharing and stability in their relations with financial institutions.

The third important institution which varies significantly between nation states and affects employment practices and patterns of work organization is the education and training system. Although similarities do occur across nation states, such as those influenced by the Germanic system in the nineteenth century, there are major differences in the organization and structure of formal educational institutions, and in their links to labour markets, between many countries. These differences have important consequences for firms' recruitment, promotion and training policies, as well as their organization and control of the division of labour, as Maurice et al. (1980, 1986) and others have demonstrated. Perhaps the most important difference concerns the extent to which the educational system is dominated by formal academic standards and measures of competence as opposed to incorporating systematic training in practical skills. In unitary systems, such as the French and Japanese, academic success is the crucial criterion of selection for elite institutions, and practical training is relatively poorly funded and low in prestige. Essentially, the educational system functions as a series of filters designed to select the most academically competent, who are then guaranteed access to elite positions in the state and private industry. As a result, employers are excluded from the formal system and have to provide practical training themselves which tends to be relatively task and firm specific. Practical skills are therefore not very standardized or generalizable across work organizations and industries. Firms' internal work organization and control patterns are quite idiosyncratic and not constrained by standard specialist skills.

Dual educational systems, on the other hand, of which the best example is perhaps the German one (Lane, 1989: 64–8; Maurice et al., 1980), separate technical and practical training from academic competences at quite an early stage and produce a wide range of practical skills in collaboration with employers as well as filtering the academically gifted. These practical skills have higher social prestige than similar ones in unitary systems and are quite sought after by young workers. They combine formal knowledge with practical competences and are formally taught and assessed, so that skills are broader and more standardized than in unitary systems. Because employers are involved in their determination and standard setting, they rely on them in making recruitment and promotion decisions and therefore are more constrained by publicly certified skills than are their equivalents in unitary systems. Furthermore, because practical skills here are not particularly task specific, they tend to encourage greater flexibility and accommodation to technical change than those tied to specific tasks.

These differences between education and training systems are clearly connected to the fourth major institutional arena that differs significantly between Western nation states: the structure of labour organizations and labour markets. The overall strength of labour organizations obviously affects firms' management practices and ways of structuring employee relations, as we have seen in East Asia, as does their incorporation into political movements and state bodies. The numerical weakness of French trade unions, for example, is exacerbated by their division along political lines and has tended to encourage them to seek redress through the state rather than by direct confrontation with private employers who can often afford to ignore union demands. In contrast, the strength of the Swedish and Austrian trade union movements is both symbolized and reinforced by their incorporation into the state policy-making machinery and the correspondingly centralized systems of wage bargaining (Katzenstein, 1985: 115–33). Firms in these countries have to adapt to central agreements and maintain close links with their central co-ordinating body. Many employment and personnel practices are accordingly much more homogeneous and standardized across firms than in countries where unions are weaker and unable to influence state policies.

The ways in which labour organizations are constituted is an important influence on work organization and control when union strength is high. In particular, their organization around separate craft skills and control over the definition and certification of such skills clearly restrict employers' ability to establish idiosyncratic and highly flexible systems of work organization. Tasks and skills in this situation are more standardized across firms and less firm specific than where unions are weak and/or structured around industries or form 'general' unions. Loyalties tend to be more focused on occupational identities than on particular firms, and mobility between employers is correspondingly easier. In Denmark the high degree of craft consciousness and union control of skill development and definition has meant that large firms are structured around groups of craft workers who have considerable autonomy and control over the workflow, according to Kristensen (1989, 1990). Attempts to 'rationalize' and increase direct managerial control over task definition and organization have not been particularly successful, because the competitiveness of many firms depended on the high level of craft expertise of the workforce. In contrast, the strength of the British craft unions and their concentration in maintenance functions have encouraged both the separation of maintenance activities from operations in many industries and the restriction of many operatives' skill levels, so that the co-ordination of production with maintenance has been a major managerial problem in British firms (Dubois, 1981). Thus, the extent to which, and the way in which, unions control skill definition and allocation have important consequences for patterns of work organization and control in different countries.

More generally, the extent to which labour markets are structured around publicly certified skills and occupational identities are firmly attached to specialized certified skills and competences affects employee mobility and identification with distinct expertise. As Dore (1973: 264–79) emphasized in his contrast of organization- and market-based reward systems, British managers and workers were highly conscious of their professional and craft competences and aware of their market value. Typically, loyalties and commitments to these identities were greater than those to individual employers, and wages and other rewards were more tied to such generalized, certified skills than to seniority in, and loyalty to, particular firms. Prestige and social standing in such market-oriented employment systems are more dependent on the general worth of particular specialist expertise than on the success and size of the particular employer of the moment. Identities and status are more dependent on the skill 'owned' by the individual and its value on the labour market than on the collective organization to which the individual temporarily belongs. In Anglo-Saxon societies this emphasis on specialist skills is additionally reinforced by the prestige of professional identities which fragment managerial labour markets and roles and thus increase co-ordination costs (cf. Child et al., 1983). While Western societies in general exhibit greater consciousness of occupational identities, and horizontal loyalties are stronger than in East Asia, there are, then, significant differences between them concerning the extent of labour market dependence on specialist skills and identities and their rigidity which influence work organization and managerial hierarchies.

Conclusions

This brief discussion of some of the major institutional differences between Western nation states that affect forms of business organization has highlighted the importance of national institutions in the development and continued effectiveness of particular business structures and practices. While not sufficiently different and homogeneous to generate idiosyncratic and distinct business systems, as East Asian countries are, substantial variations in hierarchy–market relations have clearly become established in different Western societies as a result of different institutional environments and patterns of industrialization. In the West, as in East Asia, effective ways of co-ordinating and controlling economic activities in market economies depend on, and are closely connected to, particular institutional arrangements of the kind just discussed and will not be as effective in situations where these differ markedly. The comparative analysis of Western business systems, then, focuses on the processes by which specific national institutions encourage and constrain specific features of business structures and managerial practices to become established and relatively effective, and how these change, within the more general context of greater institutional pluralism, commitment to legal-rational authority principles and stronger emphasis on individual identities, rights and duties throughout Western societies when compared to East Asian ones (cf. Lodge and Vogel, 1987). National configurations of hierarchy–market relations are not so distinctive and specific as in Japan, Korea, Taiwan and Hong Kong, but important variations none the less exist and can only be adequately understood in terms of major institutional differences.

These connections between particular configurations of hierarchy–market relations in Western countries, and the institutional contexts in which they developed and continue to function, raise a number of questions about the cohesion and integration of business systems, how they are to be identified and explained and how they change. Together with the earlier analysis of East Asian business systems, they also emphasize the variety of effective ways of organizing economic activities but suggest perhaps certain limitations to this variety and the ineffectiveness of some combinations of business system characteristics. A further issue raised by this analysis is the transferability of managerial technologies between institutional contexts and what effect, if any, the increasing internationalization of some markets and firms is having upon the institutional specificity of national business systems. These points will be taken up in the next chapter with some of the issues raised in Chapter 1.

8
Variety, Change and Internationalization of Business Systems

This analysis of East Asian business systems has suggested how three distinct and cohesive ways of organizing market economies became established in Japan, South Korea, Taiwan and Hong Kong as a result of particular institutional contexts. Both dominant institutions in pre-industrial Japan, Korea and China and those which developed during industrialization were important influences on the sort of business system that emerged in East Asia and are crucial to any explanation of their characteristics. As mentioned earlier, these economies are particularly appropriate for the comparative analysis of business systems in terms of their institutional contexts because of their combination of cultural homogeneity, rapid industrialization and pre-industrial isolation which together resulted in particularly cohesive configurations of hierarchy–market relations developing. This cohesion and distinctiveness facilitated the identification of the key characteristics of business systems and of the institutional features which explained them.

In this chapter I briefly discuss some of the implications of this analysis of East Asian business systems for the study of forms of business organization in market economies in general and some broader issues concerning relations between business systems and social institutions. First I consider whether the mutually consistent and reinforcing relations between some business system characteristics in East Asia imply that there are a limited number of effective combinations of these characteristics. Second, the implications of the institutional specificity of business systems for endogenous change and the interrelations between changes in social institutions and in business systems will be discussed. Third, the role of social institutions in mediating exogenous influences and of national business systems in the growing internationalization of firms and markets will be considered. Finally, I shall summarize the main conclusions of this analysis of East Asian business systems.

Interrelationships between Business System Characteristics and the Variety of Effective Business Systems

In view of the cohesive and mutually reinforcing nature of many characteristics of East Asian business systems, especially the kaisha and the Chinese family business, it is worth considering whether there are necessary, or at least very strong, relations between them which restrict the number of different business systems that can become established in market economies. For example, the combination of highly organized markets with discontinuous growth patterns seems to be inherently improbable. Thus, not all of the possible combinations of business system characteristics listed in Table 3.5 are likely to be established as effective business systems in market economies.

Dealing with this question requires the identification of the basic characteristics of business systems across market economies. This can best be achieved by returning to the three fundamental issues raised in Chapter 1. These were, first, what sorts of economic activities and resources are co-ordinated and controlled by authority hierarchies, how is discretion over them exercised and by whom? Second, how are co-operative and competitive relations between such authority hierarchies organized? Third, how are resources and skills organized and directed within dominant authority hierarchies? In principle, these issues arise in all market economies, and differences in the way they are dealt with across economies constitute the major variations between business systems. While additional differences may be significant when comparing particular business systems, such as East Asian ones, these three broad issues summarize the key ways in which hierarchy–market configurations vary in general.

The first question refers to the extent of large, private firm domination of an economy and the extent to which control over firms is delegated to salaried managers pursuing particular goals with varied capabilities. A key characteristic of any market economy is the degree of economic decentralization to private property rights owners and by them to managerial agents. As we have seen, this can vary considerably across societies as a result of differences in trust relations and institutional pluralism. Relatedly, the variety and size of resources co-ordinated by authority hierarchies also vary significantly across economies. Dominant patterns of firm growth, and discontinuities in their capabilities and resources, are further important characteristics of economic agents in market economies since they reflect and reproduce dominant logics or rationalities of economic action. Finally, firms differ greatly in their internalization of risks and the extent to which they act as independent, separate agents in making strategic choices between institutional contexts.

The second question deals largely with the extent and scope of market co-operation between firms and its basis. Economies exhibit a wide range of relations between firms, from spot market anonymous contracting to the sort of particularistic obligational contracting found in Japan. In the former case, each transaction is self-contained and focused on price, with little or no connection to other exchanges or relationships. In the latter type of economy, firms enter into relatively long-term commitments with each other, so that transactions are embedded in diffuse, particularistic and reciprocal connections between economic agents. These connections may be largely restricted to firms within individual sectors or else may range across sectors so that whole economies are characterized by elaborate networks of obligations which co-ordinate economic activities. A significant component of some market economies in which such networks are important is the existence of intermediary organizations, such as general trading companies or banks, that function as co-ordinating agencies on a quasi-contractual basis. Finally, the foundations upon which inter-firm obligations become established and reproduced differ between economies, principally in the degree to which they are tied to personal connections and relationships.

The third question can, of course, be answered in a large number of ways, as is demonstrated by the contrasts identified in Chapter 3, and not all characteristics of co-ordination and control systems are equally important in all institutional contexts. However, there are seven major ways in which dominant patterns of authoritative co-ordination and control of economic activities differ significantly between market economies. First, they vary in their degree of integration of skills and activities around common objectives from the Anglo-Saxon conglomerate, where co-ordination is largely financial, to the integrated kaisha, where interdependence between departments is high and considerable emphasis is put upon horizontal co-ordination of activities (Aoki, 1988: 32–43). Second, the basis of authority and subordination is clearly a key characteristic of any authority structure which typically varies between highly personal forms and highly formal, rule-governed ones. Third, the extent to which supervisory and hierarchical authority is coterminous with expertise and technical knowledge varies considerably across European economies, as Maurice and his colleagues (1986) have shown. This characteristic is closely

Table 8.1   *Business system characteristics*

Firms and their development
(a) Extent of authoritative control over economic activities.
(b) Extent of managerial discretion from owners.
(c) Variety of activities controlled through authority hierarchies.
(d) Extent to which strategic changes are incremental or discontinuous.
(e) Firm independence and mutual separation.

Market organization
(a) Level of market organization within and between sectors.
(b) Significance of intermediary co-ordinating organizations.
(c) Basis of inter-firm commitments.

Authority systems
(a) Degree of integration and interdependence between activities.
(b) Impersonality of authority and subordination relations.
(c) Integration of formal authority with technical superiority.
(d) Centralization of decision making and control.
(e) Specialization of tasks, roles and skills.
(f) Distance and superiority of managers.
(g) Employer commitment to employees and organization-based labour system.

connected to the overall shape of authority structures as well as to the degree of task and role specialization and individuation which forms the fourth major characteristic of authority hierarchies. Fifth, the centralization of decision making, including the ability to initiate proposals, is a further important dimension for comparing co-ordination and control structures. The sixth characteristic summarizes the extensive variations found in dominant conceptions of the managerial role and how managerial authority should be exercised in different economies. Here, I suggest that key aspects concern the distance between supervisors and subordinates in planning and carrying out tasks, together with the range and degree of managers' superiority, which affects their ability to admit ignorance and to call for subordinates' support without threatening their own authority. Finally, there are clear variations in the extent to which employers are willing to enter into long-term commitments to employees and develop organization-based labour systems which reward long service and rely on flexible, multiple and firm-specific skills. These general characteristics of business systems are summarized in Table 8.1.

In considering how these 15 characteristics may be necessarily, or very strongly, interrelated, it is important to take into account the points raised at the end of Chapter 6 about the interrelationships between East Asian business system characteristics. Three points in particular need emphasizing. First, such interconnections are not always reversible. Second, they are often not linear and continuous. Third, connections between any two characteristics often depend on their relations with other ones. As a result, they are often not readily reducible to simple correlations between arithmetic continua.

Reversibility of connections between business system characteristics here means that where we expect high values of them to occur together, so too should low values. For instance, the association between incremental growth patterns, externalization of risk and high levels of market organization found in Japan should, if generalizable and reversible, imply the association of discontinuous growth patterns, internalization of risk and low levels of market organization, as indeed is characteristic of many sectors in Anglo-Saxon economies. However, the Korean chaebol do not fit this pattern because of the high level of state risk sharing and dominance of the economy. Similarly, the Chinese family business often combines opportunistic diversification with strong interpersonal ties between economic agents which both help to reduce risk and facilitate co-operation. Equally, the strong link between owner control and centralization manifested in the chaebol and CFB does not imply that firms controlled by salaried managers typically decentralize decision making. Thus, close connections between extreme values of particular characteristics cannot be taken to imply that values at the reverse end of the continua are also highly interrelated.

The non-reversibility of connections between business system characteristics is linked to their non-linearity and frequent discontinuity, because it is often the extreme values of dimensions which are most closely interconnected. For example, the strong connections between owner control, personal authority and centralization are most notable when personal owner control is high. As it decreases, these interrelationships become less widespread and close. Similarly, low levels of market organization between firms are associated with low employer–employee dependence and a preference for market-based labour policies, but increasing inter-firm co-operative links by no means imply that employers increasingly adopt long-term dependence to their staff. In important respects, then, these connections are better viewed as threshold, either/or relationships rather than as continuous ones which can readily be dichotomized at the midpoint (cf. Ragin, 1987).

Finally, many interconnections between business system characteristics depend on the value of others with which they are also interdependent, as well of course as depending on particular features of their institutional context. An example of this point is the negative relationship between diversification and the degree of integration of economic activities. Generally, in most Western economies an increase in unrelated diversification is associated with a weakening of ties between different components of enterprises and a reduction in their interdependence. However, in the case of the Korean chaebol the highly personal nature of authority and subordination relations and centralized control of personnel decisions have enabled these firms to combine diversification with considerable integration of different activities. Here, of course, the 'strong state' has also played an important role in encouraging internal centralization of control. Similarly, business specialization is not necessarily combined with high levels of market organization, unless co-ordinating intermediary organizations have developed and inter-firm links are partially institutionalized around collective commitments rather than being dependent on purely personal obligations.

These points suggest that reducing the large number of logically possible combinations of business system characteristics to a small set of effective hierarchy–market configurations is not a simple matter, especially given the important and varied influences of dominant institutions. However, there are some general interconnections which can be readily discerned and these do rule out some combinations as being inherently unstable. In particular, three sets of strongly interrelated characteristics can be identified which imply that a high value of one characteristic has major consequences for the values of other ones.

First, high levels of owner control are closely linked to limitations on the degree of market organization found in an economy, to the highly personal nature of inter-firm connections and of authority relations within firms, and to strong centralization of decision making. These linkages imply that business systems combining high levels of owner control with strong collective ties between firms and decentralized, formal authority structures are unlikely to develop or be effective.

Second, radical discontinuities over time in the resources and economic activities controlled through authority hierarchies are strongly related to low levels of employer–employee commitment, a high degree of independence from other firms in making strategic choices and a corresponding low degree of risk sharing with them, together with a separation of technical expertise from formal authority. Thus, acquisition-based growth is unlikely to be associated with high levels of interdependence and commitment to particular business partners, or with task-continuous authority hierarchies (Offe, 1976: 25–30), because these imply relatively long-

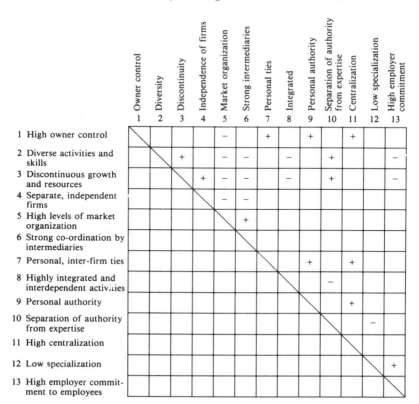

Figure 8.1 *Strong interconnections between business system characteristics*

term commitments to specific resources and skills which prevent radical changes in firms' activities and spheres of competence.

A third combination of business system characteristics, which is typified by the post-war Japanese kaisha, brings together incremental growth patterns, high levels of firm interdependence and obligational contracting, and strong and influential co-ordinating intermediaries, together with considerable risk sharing and mutual dependence between employers and employees. This suggests that high levels of employer commitment to employees and long-term investments in their skills are unlikely to develop in economies where market organization is weak and firms' growth patterns are typically discontinuous.

These relationships, and a few others, are summarized in Figure 8.1. It should be emphasized here that in most cases it is one particular value of each characteristic that is being highlighted because of the irreversibility and threshold nature of their interconnections. Firm size and managerial style are not shown in this figure because they do not seem to bear any clear and consistent relationships to the other characteristics which do not depend on other factors. Even high levels of owner control, for instance, do not preclude large firms dominating an economy, as the example of South Korea demonstrates. Similarly, dominant conceptions of managerial authority are more closely connected to general patterns of authority and subordination in the wider society than to particular characteristics of the business system.

It is clear from this figure that most connections between these characteristics cannot be derived solely from an *a priori* analysis of their mutual 'fit' and theoretical consistency. Less than a quarter of the 105 possible combinations can reasonably be inferred from general considerations, with the remaining connections depending on both multiple interdependence and the institutional contexts in which particular business systems became established. While, then, there are a number of mutually consistent and reinforcing characteristics of business systems, and some combinations are thereby unlikely to develop as effective hierarchy–market configurations, there does not seem to be a highly limited set of feasible combinations for all market economies. Given the open nature of social systems and the importance of institutional contexts, this is not of course particularly surprising, but it does highlight the varied ways of organizing economic activities in market economies as well as the changeable nature of the 'rules of the game'.

Perhaps the most important conclusion to be drawn from Figure 8.1 is that a considerable number of possible combinations of business system characteristics are unstable and unlikely to be effective. For example, high levels of market organization are not likely to develop in economies where the degree of owner control is high, because they imply the institutionalization of long-term trust relations between organizations, which in turn implies some depersonalization of inter-firm connections and a willingness to share risks and information between exchange partners. Similarly, firms embedded in long-term networks of mutual dependence and trust will not find it easy to make rapid and radical changes in their activities and skills. Equally, high levels of employer–employee commitment, which result in labour costs being regarded as fixed rather than variable in the short to medium term, encourage high levels of labour flexibility and intra-firm mobility, so that task and role specialization will be limited where such commitment is high. Thus, market economies characterized by certain features, such as high levels of owner control or highly independent firms, are not likely to be dominated by business systems with 'contradictory' features, such as long-term co-operative relations between firms, strong intermediary organizations co-ordinating resource flows, and decentralized authority relations within firms. The variety of effective business systems in market economies, considered in abstraction from their institutional contexts, is not, therefore, the total number of combinations of their characteristics but rather a more limited, though still large, set. The presence of extreme values on many characteristics rules out the occurrence of some other ones.

Institutional and Business System Changes

These interconnections and the mutually reinforcing nature of some business system characteristics suggest that, once established in particular institutional contexts, effective business systems may develop considerable cohesion and become resistant to major changes. This in turn raises the general question of how business systems do change and how changes in major social institutions in a market economy are related to changes in business system characteristics. Three general points can be made in this connection.

First, the interdependence between dominant social institutions and forms of economic organization means that, once a particular business system has become established and certain rules of the game are institutionalized, major changes in firm type and patterns of behaviour are unlikely to occur in the absence of substantial institutional changes. Thus, patterns of hierarchy–market relations established during industrialization are likely to persist as long as the dominant institutions which generated them remain largely unchanged. This is especially so where these institutions are relatively homogeneous and mutually reinforcing, so that the business system is highly cohesive. In this situation, radical external changes are often required to alter key institutions if business system characteristics are to change in significant ways. Military defeat and foreign occupation can bring about such major changes, as the examples of France, Germany and Japan illustrate, although they are never total. As a result, altering well-established patterns of business behaviour which are closely interdependent with their institutional contexts is very difficult without substantial institutional changes. The tendency of large British companies to continue to pay large dividends even when profits have fallen substantially, for example, is unlikely to alter so long as the financial system remains dominated by intermediaries focusing on portfolio management goals. Similarly, their relative unwillingness to invest in training is unlikely to change as long as high dividend payouts remain crucial to their survival and the organization of labour markets encourages 'poaching' of skills in short supply.

Second, and relatedly, the connection between institutional and business system changes varies according to the cohesion and consistency of institutions and business system characteristics. The more integrated are hierarchy–market relations with their cohesive, distinctive institutional environment, the less easy will it be for 'deviant' patterns of firm behaviour to develop and become established, and the less likely that business system characteristics will change endogenously. Contrarily, the more pluralistic and varied is the institutional context of a particular business system, the easier it is to introduce and maintain unusual features of economic organization without major institutional upheavals. This is particularly so where institutions diverge rather than mutually reinforce each other, so that deviant strategies can gain material and legitimatory support from some economic and social agents despite pressures to conform from dominant institutions. The relative institutional pluralism of Anglo-Saxon economies, for example, permits greater variation in business system characteristics and rules of the game than is feasible in more homogeneous and state-coordinated economies. Firms in the defence industries of Britain and the USA, for instance, have been relatively insulated from the demands of the financial systems and the market for corporate control by state support, and so were able, at least to some extent, to pursue 'deviant' strategic choices.

A related point about institutional and business system change is that characteristics closely linked to central institutions are less amenable to alteration than those connected to more peripheral ones. For example, the pursuit of deviant financial strategies in economies dominated by capital market financial systems, such as in the UK, is less likely to establish new patterns of firm behaviour and logics of action than pursuing deviant labour market strategies, or developing novel authority structures, where related institutions and actors are more heterogeneous and less dominating. Endogenous changes and plural logics of action are thus more likely to develop and endure in heterogeneous institutional contexts and in areas where the institutional environment is relatively open.

Third, attempts to change institutional structures and policies which impinge upon economic activities may fail where business systems are well entrenched and relatively effective, and where leading economic agents can elicit support from other groups. Thus, political efforts to change the role of the state from 'regulatory' to 'developmental' are unlikely to be effective where business elites view the changes as an infringement of their autonomy and as a threat to the rules of the game in which they were successful, particularly if they can mobilize other important elite groups to oppose it. Similarly, the deregulation of Japanese financial markets is unlikely to be as far reaching as some US pressure groups would like because it would affect established patterns of risk sharing between kaisha and could lead to a destabilizing market for corporate control developing in Japan. The strength of established ways of organizing market economies in the face of major institutional changes is exemplified by the many efforts to develop cartels in West German heavy industry after 1945 (Berghahn, 1986) and the rapid re-creation of inter-sector business groups in Japan, albeit in different form, after the end of the US occupation. While the post-war German and Japanese business systems undoubtedly display many significant differences from their pre-war predecessors, they also reveal strong continuities.

Dominant, established ways of organizing market economies, then, reflect the conditions in which they developed during industrialization and are unlikely to change significantly without major institutional alterations. Even relatively less successful and declining economies, such as the British one, do not alter important characteristics of their business system in the absence of substantial changes in their institutional contexts, especially where dominant institutions are mutually consistent. Such changes do not usually come about in the absence of substantial external pressure or large-scale internal conflict and widespread perceptions of institutional failure. Competitive pressures alone are unlikely to lead to substantial changes in business systems, especially in the larger, more self-sufficient economies.

Social Institutions, Business Systems and the Internationalization of Firms and Markets

The analysis of East Asian business systems presented in this book has emphasized the critical influences of particular social institutions in structuring and reproducing forms of economic organization. The cohesion and integration of these institutions resulted in quite distinct business systems developing, despite the important influence of Japanese colonialism in Korea and Taiwan, and limited the impact of Western rules of the game. In these cases, at least, the increasing interdependence of firms and markets in different countries and regions of the world has not standardized business system characteristics or led to a single dominant international configuration of hierarchy–market relations. Rather, business systems have become established that reflect the exigencies both of dominant local, national and regional institutions and of international markets and firms. These latter, of course, also reflect the institutional contexts in which they developed, and so markets dominated by firms from one country tend to reflect the business system that has become established there as a result of its institutions. Thus, the interdependence between social institutions and business systems highlighted in this study has generated considerable heterogeneity of managerial practices and structures in East Asia and severely limited the generalization of particular forms of economic organization. However, the degree of institutional cohesion and integration of business system characteristics does vary considerably between countries and regions, as we have seen, and these variations mean that the impact of multinational firms on business systems differs between institutional contexts, as does the transferability of managerial techniques.

The institutional dependence of hierarchy–market configurations also means that competition between firms from different business systems for domination of world markets is a struggle between different ways of structuring forms of economic organization and the dominant social institutions which generated and reproduced them. The organization of such markets at any one time reflects this struggle rather than some overriding international logic of efficiency. I will now discuss these points in a little more detail, considering first the connections between variations in the cohesion of business systems and the impact of multinational co-ordination of economic activities and then the growing internationalization of markets and its implication for national business systems.

The institutional specificity and variability of business systems implies that multinational firms from different societies follow distinctive practices and rules of the game which will govern how they set up and manage foreign operations. Thus, many multinational firms display significant differences in their organizational structures, control and planning systems, and managerial career structures, depending on their originating country (see, for example, Egelhoff, 1988: 226–9; Negandhi, 1986). Similarly, American and Japanese firms have followed different subcontracting practices in their European operations, as the growing literature on 'Japanization' makes clear (for example, Oliver and Wilkinson, 1988: 130–2). The impact of these differences on the development of business systems in 'host' countries, and in particular the ability of multinationals to transplant domestic practices to overseas subsidiaries and establish them successfully there, depend on:

(a) the homogeneity and cohesion of business system characteristics in the originating economy;
(b) the homogeneity and cohesion of institutions and business systems in the host economies; and
(c) the relative strength of the multinational firm in particular host economies and of the local institutions most related to particular procedures and characteristics.

Generally, we would expect firms from highly cohesive and homogeneous societies which have generated distinctive and integrated business systems, such as those discussed in this book, to export their successful ways of operating, and to follow the standard set of practices in all subsidiaries, to a greater extent than those from more pluralistic societies. The more a particular business system is integrated and its characteristics are mutually reinforcing, the more similar are firms and their practices in that system and the more difficult will they find it to alter established procedures and rationalities. Thus, they are less likely to adopt novel practices in foreign subsidiaries, especially where these impinge upon their domestic operations and relations. The importance of collective discussion and consensual decision-making procedures in Japanese firms, for instance, makes it very difficult for Japanese multinationals to delegate control of major decisions in their important overseas subsidiaries to native managers, or to rely on purely formal control procedures to the extent that US multinationals seem to do. Equally, it is hard to see how Chinese family businesses could rely on impersonal and formal authority relations with managers of their foreign subsidiaries any more than they do at home.

This tendency is modified by the cohesion and consistency of market institutions in host economies. Where these are mutually reinforcing and integrated, innovatory managerial practices from multinationals are unlikely to be very effective or easily established, as the fate of many US corporations in Japan illustrates. In contrast, the more 'open', pluralistic and varied are institutions and business system characteristics in a market economy, the easier it is to introduce novel procedures and ways of working. Thus, Japanese multinationals have been able to transfer some of their working practices and personnel policies more readily to their UK subsidiaries than have British multinationals in Japan. Despite the strong contrast between Japanese and British societies and ways of organizing their economies, the high level of institutional differentiation and pluralism in Britain, including the limited role of the legal system and the state in co-ordinating and ordering market relations, has facilitated the establishment of Japanese 'transplants' in Britain.

Such transfer is, of course, more likely when the firm and its home economy are considerably stronger and more powerful than the host economy and there are few established procedures to overcome. Multinational firms from dominant economies are more likely to insist on subsidiaries in smaller, weaker and developing economies following domestic procedures and, in effect, attempting to reproduce domestic patterns of economic organization in those economies than they are in larger, stronger and industrialized societies. The strength and role of the state in the host country are naturally key factors in this relationship and can often prevent the direct transfer of managerial practices and modes of organizing market relations. The capacity of some states and societies to resist the imposition of foreign conceptions of effective hierarchy–market relations is exemplified by the Japanese response to the SCAP reforms after the war.

A related point about the factors affecting the transferability of particular managerial practices is their dependence on the strength of the local institutions most closely connected with them. Where, for example, trade unions are weak and labour relations are not entrenched in legal regulations, it is likely to be relatively easy to introduce novel working practices and systems of organization. Where, on the other hand, the innovations involve changes to the more powerful institutional sectors, such as the financial system in the UK, it will be more difficult to establish and maintain them. Thus, generating new patterns of bank–industry relations in Britain along Japanese or German lines is a considerably more difficult and lengthy process than changing established patterns of industrial relations and working practices in depressed areas of the economy.

These implications of varying degrees of institutional and business system cohesion suggest that the internationalization of markets and firms is neither a simple matter of transferring managerial technologies to foreign subsidiaries, and thereby transforming 'backward' economies, nor a case of firms adapting their practices to those dominant in each host country; but it is rather a more complex and variegated set of relationships between economies, institutions and firms. Considering first the impact of multinational firms on host economies and their business system characteristics, this obviously depends on the importance of such firms in particular sectors, the strength of current practices and associated institutions and the overall cohesion of the business system. Thus, while some transfer of American and Japanese working practices to subsidiaries and imitating firms in some European countries has taken place over the past few decades, it would be quite misleading to claim that, say, the British and German economies are now run in similar ways to the US and Japanese ones (cf. Berghahn, 1986; Trevor, 1988). Rather, those practices which seemed to fit in most easily with already established ways of doing things and did not conflict with powerful institutions were easiest to transfer, while others, such as the various US attempts to reform competitive practices and break up bank–industry linkages in Japan and Europe, either were severely modified or simply remained peripheral. The growth of multinational firms, then, does not imply the standardization of business systems but rather an additional influence on their development which is most likely to affect peripheral and weakly integrated characteristics and/or those whose institutional context is most similar to that in the originating economy. The similarity of the British and US financial systems and their common tradition of independent professions, especially accountancy and law, have facilitated the transfer of financial management techniques and capital market practices between the two countries. The factors which assist the transfer of managerial technologies by multinationals are summarized in Table 8.2.

The reverse impact of multinational operations on home country business systems is unlikely to be very significant, given the typically dominant position of these economies. Thus, adapting labour policies and control systems to local practices in different subsidiaries will only affect large multinational firms substantially if these subsidiaries are relatively large and powerful with access to their own financial resources and close ties with the domestic top management. Even then such variations are unlikely to affect the domestic business system if it is fairly cohesive and strong. It is not clear, for example, that the important foreign operations of Swiss, Dutch and Swedish multinationals have directly affected the nature of their domestic business systems, although these latter are of course partly a product of major firms' international orientation and activities (Hellgren and Melin, 1992; Iterson and Olie, 1992; Katzenstein, 1985).

Turning now to consider how the internationalization of markets is related to national or regional, institutions, cultures and business systems, it is important to bear in mind that these 'global' markets are constituted by firms which have developed in particular institutional contexts. Although, then, the development of world markets in standardized commodities and of relatively small oligopolies dominating whole sectors of the world economy might suggest that

Table 8.2   *Factors facilitating the transfer of managerial technologies and ways of organizing economic activities across business systems*

Home economy
(a)   High cohesion and integration of institutions and business system.
(b)   Relative strength in world economy and of sector in home economy.

Host economy
(a)   Low degree of cohesion and integration of institutions and business systems.
(b)   Weak position in world economy and of sector in host economy.

Nature of managerial technology and associated institutions
(a)   Peripheral to business system of host economy.
(b)   Weak associated institutions in host economy.
(c)   Similarity of associated institutions in host and home economies.

---

the influence of purely national and social institutions on market structures is becoming less significant, and worldwide rules of the game are being developed by firms competing globally, this development is better viewed as a continuation of competition between national or regional business systems and institutions, because international markets are organized by firms from different economies with different organizing principles and institutions. The 'globalization' of markets and competition is thus an extension of international competition between business systems which are now, in effect, competing to establish their pattern of hierarchy–market relations as the dominant one in world markets. Even though the USA has so far appeared to dominate because of the leading position of the US economy and role of US multinational firms, this is unlikely to continue as other business systems grow in importance.

While, then, the increasing importance of international competition and impact of international 'ways of doing things' mean that purely national business systems will have to adapt some of their characteristics to the currently dominant patterns in some industries, these patterns themselves are the outcomes of competition between established business systems and the institutions that generated and support them. In the absence of genuinely international institutions which are quite distinct from national ones, there seems no reason to expect totally separate international business systems to become established. Rather, international markets and competitive logics will reflect the competitive struggle between firms and institutions embedded in national contexts which may generate novel – that is, non-national – ways of organizing economic activities on a global basis, but these will still be connected to national political, financial and social systems.

The globalization of capital markets is an example of this pattern of national dominance, since these are still largely organized around American principles of economic organization, which is not surprising given the dominant role of the US economy in the post-war period, and of US-inspired and US-dominated international financial institutions. It is important to note that participation in these capital markets is still carefully controlled by national financial authorities in many countries, notably Japan, and that trading standardized financial instruments on a worldwide basis does not mean the standardization of national financial systems. The credit-based financial systems of most European countries have not succumbed to the Anglo-Saxon model of capital market organization, and the deregulation crusade seems unlikely to transform the Japanese financial system into an imitation of Wall Street. Thus, while the growth of international capital markets has increased the variety of funding opportunities for firms in some countries, and so weakened the cohesion and integration of some national business systems, it has not generated a global financial system which organizes national ones, and has not transformed the varied patterns of bank–industry connections found in different countries.

Overall, then, the post-war growth of international firms and markets has been structured more by national business systems and institutions than the reverse, and the organization of worldwide industrial sectors is the outcome of competition between national modes of economic organization and their associated institutions. While business systems competing in world markets have to adapt to dominant patterns in those markets, this does not mean that they simply imitate and reproduce them. Taiwanese businessmen, for instance, have not adopted US business practices even though they depended heavily on the US market. Thus, business systems develop and change in response to institutional pressures and to dominant ways of doing things in their international markets. Depending on the relative strength of these exigencies, and of their own influence on international rules of the game, they display different characteristics. It is worth reiterating here that business systems with particular characteristics can be seen as 'selecting' particular markets which enable them to function effectively. As we have seen, Taiwanese entrepreneurs do not compete in capital-intensive heavy industry to the same extent that the Koreans do. Similarly, Florida and Kenney (1991) have recently argued that the Japanese way of organizing firms and markets may be more effective in technology-intensive industry than the US pattern – although this need not imply any intrinsically 'best' way of competing in this sector (cf. Sorge, 1991).

Concluding Summary

Finally, this study of how societies, firms and markets have developed in East Asia and generated three quite distinct business systems, or configurations of hierarchy–market relations, suggests a number of conclusions for the analysis of market economies which can be summarized as ten separate points.

1 There are a considerable variety of effective ways of organizing market economies, and no single one is necessarily superior; nor does temporary dominance of world markets imply continued superiority or the realization of a supra-institutional managerial rationality.
2 Effective ways of organizing market economies combine particular types of firms as authoritative co-ordination and control systems, of market organization and of authority structures in dominant firms. These combinations constitute distinctive business systems.
3 These business systems develop in, reflect and variously reproduce particular institutional contexts such that their characteristics vary between contexts and are interdependent with dominant institutions.
4 These institutions reflect the combination of pre-industrial patterns of social organization and industrialization processes. The former are especially important in societies, such as those in East Asia, where industrialization has been both rapid and recent. Key pre-industrial institutions are the political system, including the dominant set of legitimatory beliefs, the organization and control of the agricultural system and village communities, and the autonomy and structure of the commercial system. Critical proximate institutions are the political, financial, educational and cultural systems, including the family.
5 Business systems vary in their internal cohesion and consistency, and their external distinctiveness, according to the extent of integration and mutual reinforcement, and external isolation, of the dominant institutions which governed their development and establishment. Thus, East Asian systems are more cohesive and distinctive than are those in many European countries.
6 The importance of the nation state during and after industrialization, and in structuring other key institutions

impinging upon market economies, means that many business systems are nationally distinctive, although this varies according to the role of the state and the level of institutional differentiation and pluralism in different societies. Thus, some polities may develop a number of hierarchy–market configurations which share some characteristics but differ in others. Similarly, institutional commonality across national boundaries can induce similarities in certain business system characteristics.

7 Certain business system characteristics are strongly interrelated, especially at extreme values, so that some combinations of characteristics are unlikely to develop. However, the variety of feasible business systems is still considerable and reflects the variety of social institutions in market economies.

8 The impact of multinational firms on national business systems is severely constrained by the strength and cohesion of host countries' institutions.

9 Once established, effective business systems develop some autonomy and develop interdependently with their institutional contexts. Radical change in their characteristics is unlikely without major institutional change.

10 International configurations of hierarchy–market relations reflect competitive struggles between national and regional business systems and will not become distinct, separate business systems until more distinctly international and supra-national institutions are established.

References

Abegglen, J.C. and Stalk, G. (1985) *Kaisha: The Japanese Corporation*. New York: Basic Books.

Allen, G.C. (1981) *A Short Economic History of Modern Japan*. London: Macmillan (4th edition).

Amin, A. (1989) 'A Model of the Small Firm in Italy', in E. Goodman and J. Bamford (eds), *Small Firms and Industrial Districts in Italy*. London: Routledge.

Amsden, A.H. (1985a) 'The Division of Labour is Limited by the Rate of Growth of the Market: the Taiwan Machine Tool Industry in the 1970s', *Cambridge Journal of Economics*, 9: 271–84.

Amsden, A.H. (1985b) 'The State and Taiwan's Economic Development', in P.B. Evans, D. Rueschmeyer and T. Skocpol (eds), *Bringing the State Back In*. Cambridge: Cambridge University Press.

Amsden, A.H. (1989) *Asia's Next Giant*. Oxford: Oxford University Press.

Aoki, M. (1987) 'The Japanese Firm in Transition', in K. Yamamura and Y. Yasuba (eds), *The Political Economy of Japan, I: The Domestic Transformation*. Stanford, CA: Stanford University Press.

Aoki, M. (1988) *Information, Incentives, and Bargaining in the Japanese Economy*. Cambridge: Cambridge University Press.

Baechler, J. (1988) 'The Origins of Modernity: Caste and Feudality', in J. Baechler, J.A. Hall and M. Mann (eds), *Europe and the Rise of Capitalism*. Oxford: Blackwell.

Baker, H.D.R. (1979) *Chinese Family and Kinship*. London: Macmillan.

Baker, W.E. (1987) 'What Is Money? A Social Structural Interpretation', in M.S. Mizruchi and M. Schwartz (eds), *Intercorporate Relations: The Structural Analysis of Business*. Cambridge: Cambridge University Press.

Bamford, J. (1987) 'The Development of Small Firms, the Traditional Family and Agrarian Families in Italy', in R. Goffee and R. Scase (eds), *Entrepreneurship in Europe*. London: Croom Helm.

Barrett, R.E. (1988) 'Autonomy and Diversity in the American State on Taiwan', in E.A. Winckler and S. Greenhalgh (eds), *Contending Approaches to the Political Economy of Taiwan*. Armonk, NY: M.E. Sharpe.

Bauer, M. and Cohen, E. (1981) *Qui gouverne les groupes industriels?* Paris: Seuil.

Beattie, H.J. (1979) *Land and Lineage in China*. Cambridge: Cambridge University Press.

Bendix, R. (1967) 'Preconditions of Development: a Comparison of Japan and Germany', in R.P. Dore (ed.), *Aspects of Social Change in Modern Japan*. Princeton, NJ: Princeton University Press.

Berghahn, V.R. (1986) *The Americanization of West German Industry 1945–73*. Leamington Spa: Berg.

Bhaskar, R. (1975) *A Realist Theory of Science*. Leeds: Leeds Books.

Bhaskar, R. (1979) *The Possibility of Naturalism*. Brighton: Harvester.

Biggart, N.W. (1989) 'Institutionalized Patrimonialism in Korean Business', Program in East Asian Culture and Development Research, Working Paper No. 23, Institute of Governmental Affairs, University of California, Davis.

Black, C.E. et al. (1975) *The Modernization of Japan and Russia*. New York: Free Press.

Blumenthal, T. (1976) 'The Japanese Shipbuilding Industry', in H. Patrick (ed.), *Japanese Industrialization and its Social Consequences*. Berkeley, CA: University of California Press.

Bond, M. and Hwang, K. (1986) 'The Social Psychology of Chinese People', in M. Bond (ed.), *The Psychology of the Chinese People*. Oxford: Oxford University Press.

Boyd, R. (1987) 'Government–Industry Relations in Japan', in S. Wilks and M. Wright (eds), *Comparative Government–Industry Relations*. Oxford: Oxford University Press.

Brandt, V. (1971) *A Korean Village: Between Farm and Sea*. Cambridge, MA: Harvard University Press.

Brandt, V. (1987) 'Korea', in G.C. Lodge and E. Vogel (eds), *Ideology and National Competitiveness*. Boston, MA: Harvard Business School.

Bronfenbrenner, M. and Yasuba, Y. (1987) 'Economic Welfare', in K. Yamamura and Y. Yasuba (eds), *The Political Economy of Japan, I: The Domestic Transformation*. Stanford, CA: Stanford University Press.

Brossard, M. and Maurice, M. (1976) 'Is There a Universal Model of Organization Structure?', *International Studies of Management and Organization*, 6: 11–45.

Brusco, S. (1982) 'The Emilian Model: Productive Decentralization and Social Integration', *Cambridge Journal of Economics*, 6: 167–84.

Brusco, S. (1986) 'Small Firms and Industrial Districts: the Experience of Italy', in D. Keeble and E. Wever (eds) *New Firms and Regional Development*. London: Croom Helm.

Castells, M., Goh, L. and Kwok, R.Y-W. (1990) *The Shek Kip Mei Syndrome: Economic Development and Public Housing in Hong Kong and Singapore*. London: Pion.

Cawson, A., Holmes, P. and Stevens, A. (1987) 'The Interaction between Firms and the State in France', in S. Wilks and M. Wright (eds), *Comparative Government–Industry Relations*. Oxford: Oxford University Press.

Chang, S.J. and Choi, U. (1988) 'Strategy, Structure and Performance of Korean Business Groups', *Journal of Industrial Economics*, 37: 141–58.

Child, J. (1981) 'Culture, Contingency and Capitalism in the Cross-National Study of Organization', in L.L. Cummings and B.L. Straw (eds), *Research in Organizational Behaviour*, vol. 3. Greenwich, CT: JAI Press.

Child, J., Fores, M., Glover, I. and Lawrence, P. (1983) 'A Price to Pay? Professionalism in Work Organization in Britain and West Germany', *Sociology*, 17: 63–78.

Cho, D-S. (1987) *The General Trading Company: Concept and Strategy*. Lexington, MA: D.C. Heath.

Chung, K.H., Lee, H.C. and Okumura, A. (1988) 'The Managerial Practices of Korean, American and Japanese Firms', *Journal of East and West Studies*, 17: 45–74.

Clark, R. (1979) *The Japanese Company*. New Haven, CT: Yale University Press.

Cohen, M.L. (1976) *House United, House Divided: The Chinese Family in Taiwan*. New York: Columbia University Press.

Cole, R. (1979) *Work, Mobility and Participation*. Berkeley, CA: University of California Press.

Cole, R.E. and Tominaga, K. (1976) 'Japan's Changing Occupational Structure and its Significance', in H. Patrick (ed.), *Japanese Industrialization and its Social Consequences*. Berkeley, CA: University of California Press.

Cox, A. (1986) 'State, Finance and Industry in Comparative Perspective', in A. Cox (ed.), *State, Finance and Industry*. Brighton: Wheatsheaf.

Craig, A.M. (1986) 'The Central Government', in M.B. Jansen and G. Rozman (eds), *Japan in Transition: From Tokugawa to Meiji*. Princeton, NJ: Princeton University Press.

Crozier, M. (1964) *The Bureaucratic Phenomenon*. Chicago, IL: University of Chicago Press.

Cumings, B. (1984) 'The Legacy of Japanese Colonialism in Korea', in R.H. Myers and M.A. Peattie (eds), *The Japanese Colonial Empire, 1895-1945*. Princeton, NJ: Princeton University Press.

Cumings, B. (1987) 'The Origins and Development of the Northeast Asian Political Economy', in F.C. Deyo (ed.), *The Political Economy of the New Asian Industrialism*. Ithaca, NY: Cornell University Press.

Cumings, B. (1988) 'World System and Authoritarian Regimes in Korea, 1948-84', in E.A. Winckler and S. Greenhalgh (eds), *Contending Approaches to the Political Economy of Taiwan*. Armonk, NY: M.E. Sharpe.

Cusumano, M.A. (1985) *The Japanese Automobile Industry: Technology and Management at Nissan and Toyota*. Cambridge, MA: Harvard University Press.

Daems, H. (1983) 'The Determinants of the Hierarchical Organization of Industry', in A. Francis, J. Turk and P. Willman (eds), *Power, Efficiency and Institutions*. London: Heinemann.

Deglopper, D.R. (1978) 'Doing Business in Lukang', in A.P. Wolf (ed.), *Studies in Chinese Society*. Stanford, CA: Stanford University Press.

Deyo, F.C. (1987) 'Coalitions, Institutions and Linkage Sequencing – towards a Strategic Capacity Model of East Asian Developments', in F.C. Deyo (ed.), *The Political Economy of the New Asian Industrialism*. Ithaca, NY: Cornell University Press.

Deyo, F.C. (1989) *Beneath the Miracle: Labor Subordination in the New Asian Industrialism*. Berkeley, CA: University of California Press.

DiMaggio, P.J. and Powell, W.W. (1983) 'The Iron Cage Revisited: Institutional Isomorphism and Collective Rationality in Organizational Fields', *American Sociological Review*, 48: 147-60.

Dore, R.P. (1967) 'Mobility, Equality and Individuation in Modern Japan', in R.P. Dore (ed.), *Aspects of Social Change in Modern Japan*. Princeton, NJ: Princeton University Press.

Dore, R.P. (1973) *British Factory – Japanese Factory*. London: Allen & Unwin.

Dore, R.P. (1983) 'Goodwill and the Spirit of Market Capitalism', *British Journal of Sociology*, 34: 459-82.

Dore, R.P. (1986) *Flexible Rigidities*. Stanford, CA: Stanford University Press.

Dubois, P. (1981) 'Workers' Control over the Organization of Work: French and English Maintenance Workers in Mass Production Industry', *Organization Studies*, 2: 347-60.

Dunning, J.H. and Pearce, R.D. (1985) *The World's Largest Industrial Enterprises 1962-83*. Aldershot: Gower.

Dyson, K. (1980) *The State Tradition in Western Europe*. Oxford: Oxford University Press.

Egelhoff, W.G. (1988) *Organizing the Multinational Enterprise.* Cambridge, MA: Ballinger.

Elbaum, B. and Lazonick, W. (eds) (1986) *The Decline of the British Economy.* Oxford: Oxford University Press.

Encaoua, D. and Jacquemin, A. (1982) 'Organizational Efficiency and Monopoly Power: the Case of French Industrial Groups', *European Economic Review*, 19: 25–51.

Fei, H-T. (1946) 'Peasantry and Gentry: an Interpretation of Chinese Social Structure and its Change', *American Journal of Sociology*, 52: 1–17.

Fligstein, N. (1985) 'The Spread of the Multidivisional Firm', *American Sociological Review*, 50: 377–91.

Fligstein, N. (1987) 'The Intraorganizational Power Struggle: the Rise of Finance Presidents in Large Corporations', *American Sociological Review*, 52: 44–58.

Fligstein, N. and Dauber, K. (1989) 'Structural Change in Corporate Organization', *Annual Review of Sociology*, 15: 73–96.

Florida, R. and Kenney, M. (1991) 'Organizational Factors and Technology-Intensive Industry: the US and Japan', *New Technology, Work and Employment*, 6: 28–42.

Fong, P.E. (1988) 'The Distinctive Features of Two City-States' Development', in P.L. Berger and H-H.M. Hsiao (eds), *In Search of an East Asian Development Model.* New Brunswick, NJ: Transaction.

Freedman, M. (1966) *Chinese Lineage and Society.* London: Athlone Press.

Friedman, D. (1988) *The Misunderstood Miracle.* Ithaca, NY: Cornell University Press.

Fukutake, T. (1967a) *Japanese Rural Society.* Ithaca, NY: Cornell University Press.

Fukutake, T. (1967b) *Asian Rural Society.* Tokyo: University of Tokyo Press.

Futatsugi, Y. (1986) *Japanese Enterprise Groups.* Kobe: Kobe University, School of Business Administration.

Gallie, D. (1978) *In Search of the New Working Class.* Cambridge: Cambridge University Press.

Gerlach, M. (1987) 'Business Alliances and the Strategy of the Japanese Firm', *California Management Review*, Fall: 126–42.

Gerlach, M. (1989) 'Keiretsu Organization in the Japanese Economy', in C. Johnson, L. Tyson and J. Zysman (eds), *Politics and Productivity.* Cambridge: Cambridge University Press.

Godley, M.R. (1981) *The Mandarin-Capitalists from Nanyang: Overseas Chinese Enterprise in the Modernization of China 1893–1911.* Cambridge: Cambridge University Press.

Gold, T.B. (1986) *State and Society in the Taiwan Miracle.* Armonk, NY: M.E. Sharpe.

Gold, T.B. (1988a) 'Colonial Origins of Taiwanese Capitalism', in E.A. Winckler and S. Greenhalgh (eds), *Contending Approaches to the Political Economy of Taiwan.* Armonk, NY: M.E. Sharpe.

Gold, T.B. (1988b) 'Entrepreneurs, Multinationals and the State', in E.A. Winckler and S. Greenhalgh (eds), *Contending Approaches to the Political Economy of Taiwan.* Armonk, NY: M.E. Sharpe.

Goldstein, C. (1989) 'Something Must Crack', *Far East Economic Review*, 30 November: 80–1.

Goto, A. (1982) 'Business Groups in a Market Economy', *European Economic Review*, 19: 53–70.

Granick, D. (1972) *Managerial Comparisons of Four Developed Countries.* Cambridge, MA: MIT Press.

Granovetter, M. (1985) 'Economic Action, Social Structure and Embeddedness', *American Journal of Sociology*, 91: 481–510.

Granovetter, M. (1990) 'The Old and the New Economic Sociology', in R. Friedland and A.F. Robertson (eds), *Beyond the Marketplace.* New York: Aldine de Gruyter.

Grant, W., Paterson, W. and Whitston, C. (1987) 'Government–Industry Relations in the Chemical Industry', in S. Wilks and M. Wright (eds), *Comparative Government–Industry Relations.* Oxford: Oxford University Press.

Greenhalgh, S. (1984) 'Networks and their Nodes: Urban Society on Taiwan', *The China Quarterly*, 99: 529–52.

Greenhalgh, S. (1988a) 'Supranational Processes of Income Distribution', in E.A. Winckler and S. Greenhalgh (eds), *Contending Approaches to the Political Economy of Taiwan.* Armonk, NY: M.E. Sharpe.

Greenhalgh, S. (1988b) 'Families and Networks in Taiwan's Economic Development', in E.A. Winckler and S. Greenhalgh (eds), *Contending Approaches to the Political Economy of Taiwan.* Armonk, NY: M.E. Sharpe.

Gunz, H. and Whitley, R.D. (1985) 'Managerial Cultures and Industrial Strategies in British Firms', *Organization Studies*, 6: 247–73.

Haggard, S. (1988) 'The Politics of Industrialization in the Republic of Korea and Taiwan', in H. Hughes (ed.), *Achieving Industrialization in East Asia.* Cambridge: Cambridge University Press.

Haggard, S. (1990) *Pathways from the Periphery: The Politics of Growth in the Newly Industrializing Countries.* Ithaca, NY: Cornell University Press.

Hall, J.A. (1988) 'States and Societies: the Miracle in Comparative Perspective', in J. Baechler, J.A. Hall and M. Mann (eds), *Europe and the Rise of Capitalism.* Oxford: Blackwell.

Hamada, K. and Horiuchi, A. (1987) 'The Political Economy of the Financial Market', in K. Yamamura and Y. Yasuba (eds), *The Political Economy of Japan, I: The Domestic Transformation.* Stanford, CA: Stanford University Press.

Hamilton, G. (1984) 'Patriarchalism in Imperial China and Western Europe', *Theory and Society*, 13: 393–426.

Hamilton, G. (1989) 'The Organizational Foundations of Western and Chinese Commerce', paper presented to the International Conference on Business Groups and Economic Development in East Asia, University of Hong Kong, 20–22 June.

Hamilton, G. (1990) 'Patterns of Asian Capitalism: the Cases of Taiwan and South Korea', Program in East Asia Culture and Development Research, Working Paper No. 28, Institute of Governmental Affairs, University of California, Davis.

Hamilton, G. and Biggart, N.W. (1988) 'Market, Culture and Authority: a Comparative Analysis of Management and Organization in the Far East', *American Journal of Sociology*, 94, Supplement: 552–94.

Hamilton, G. and Kao, C.S. (1990) 'The Institutional Foundation of Chinese Business: the Family Firm in Taiwan', *Comparative Social Research*, 12: 95–112.

Hamilton, G., Zeile, W. and Kim, W.J. (1990) 'The Network Structures of East Asian Economies', in S. Clegg and G. Redding (eds), *Capitalism in Contrasting Cultures.* Berlin: de Gruyter.

Hanley, S.B. (1986) 'The Material Culture: Stability in Transition', in M.B. Jansen and G. Rozman (eds), *Japan in Transition.* Princeton, NJ: Princeton University Press.

Hannah, L. (1976) 'Introduction: Business Development and Economic Structure in Britain Since 1880', in L. Hannah (ed.), *Management Strategy and Business Development*. London: Macmillan.

Hannah, L. (1980) 'Visible and Invisible Hands in Great Britain', in A.D. Chandler and H. Daems (eds), *Managerial Hierarchies*. Cambridge, MA: Harvard University Press.

Hao, Y.P. (1986) *The Commercial Revolution in Nineteenth-Century China*. Berkeley, CA: University of California Press.

Hattori, T. (1984) 'The Relationship between Zaibatsu and Family Structure: the Korean Case', in A. Okichi and S. Yasuoka (eds), *Family Business in the Era of Industrial Growth*. Tokyo: University of Tokyo Press.

Hazama, H. (1976) 'Historical Changes in the Life Style of Japanese Workers', in H. Patrick (ed.), *Japanese Industrialization and its Social Consequences*. Berkeley, CA: University of California Press.

Hellgren, B. and Melin, L. (1992) 'Business Systems, Industrial Wisdom and Corporate Strategies: the Case of the Pulp and Paper Industry', in R. Whitley (ed.), *European Business Systems: Firms and Markets in their National Contexts*. London: Sage.

Henderson, G. (1968) *Korea: The Politics of the Vortex*. Cambridge, MA: Harvard University Press.

Henderson, J. (1989) 'The Political Economy of Technological Transformation in Hong Kong', *Comparative Urban and Community Research*, 2: 102–55.

Hicks, G. and Redding, G.R. (1982) 'Culture and Corporate Performance in the Philippines: the Chinese Puzzle', in R.M. Bautista and E.M. Pernia (eds), *Essays in Development Economics in Honor of Harry T. Oshima*. Manila: Philippine Institute for Developmental Studies.

Hickson, D., Hinings, C.R., McMillan, C.J. and Schwitter, J.P. (1974) 'The Culture-Free Context of Organizational Structure: a Tri-National Comparison', *Sociology*, 8: 59–80.

Hickson, D., McMillan, C.J., Azumi, K. and Horvath, D. (1979) 'Grounds for Comparative Organization Theory: Quicksands or Hard Core?', in C.J. Lammers and D.J. Hickson (eds), *Organizations Alike and Unlike*. London: Routledge & Kegan Paul.

Hirschmeier, J. and Yui, T. (1981) *The Development of Japanese Business 1600–1980*. London: Allen & Unwin (2nd edition).

Ho, D.Y.F. (1986) 'Chinese Patterns of Socialization: a Critical Review', in M. Bond (ed.), *The Psychology of the Chinese People*. Oxford: Oxford University Press.

Ho, S.P-S. (1984) 'Colonialism and Development: Korea, Taiwan and Kwantung', in R.H. Myers and M.R. Peattie (eds), *The Japanese Colonial Empire, 1895–1945*. Princeton, NJ: Princeton University Press.

Holloway, N. (1990) 'How Japan Takes Over', *Far East Economic Review*, 11 January: 40–4.

Horovitz, J.H. (1980) *Top Management Control in Europe*. London: Macmillan.

Imai, K. (1988) 'The Corporate Network in Japan', *Japanese Economic Studies*, 16: 3–37.

Imai, K. and Itami, H. (1984) 'Interpretation of Organization and Market: Japan's Firm and Market in Comparison with the US', *International Journal of Industrial Organization*, 2: 285–310.

Ingham, G. (1984) *Capitalism Divided? The City and Industry in British Social Development*. London: Macmillan.

d'Iribarne, P. (1989) *La logique de l'honneur*. Paris: Seuil.
Iterson, A.v. and Olie, R. (1992) 'European Business Systems: the Dutch Case', in R. Whitley (ed.), *European Business Systems: Firms and Markets in their National Contexts*. London: Sage.
Jacobs, N. (1958) *The Origin of Modern Capitalism and Eastern Asia*. Hong Kong: Hong Kong University Press.
Jacobs, N. (1985) *The Korean Road to Modernization and Development*. Urbana, IL: University of Illinois Press.
Jansen, M.B. (1986) 'The Ruling Class', in M.B. Jansen and G. Rozman (eds), *Japan in Transition*. Princeton, NJ: Princeton University Press.
Jansen, M.B. and Rozman, G. (1986) 'Overview', in M.B. Jansen and G. Rozman (eds), *Japan in Transition: From Tokugawa to Meiji*. Princeton, NJ: Princeton University Press.
Jao, Y.C. (1974) *Banking and Currency in Hong Kong*. London: Macmillan.
Jao, Y.C. (1984) 'The Financial Structure', in D. Lethbridge (ed.), *The Business Environment in Hong Kong*. Hong Kong: Oxford University Press (2nd edition).
Jesudason, J.V. (1989) *Ethnicity and the Economy: The State, Chinese Business and Multinationals in Malaysia*. Singapore: Oxford University Press.
Johnson, C. (1982) *MITI and the Japanese Miracle*. Stanford, CA: Stanford University Press.
Johnson, E.H. (1967) 'Status Changes in Hamlet Structure Accompanying Modernization', in R.P. Dore (ed.), *Aspects of Social Change in Modern Japan*. Princeton, NJ: Princeton University Press.
Jones, L. and Sakong, I. (1980) *Government, Business and Entrepreneurship in Economic Development: The Korean Case*. Cambridge, MA: Harvard University Press.
Jung, K.H. (1989) 'Business–Government Relations in Korea', in K.H. Chung and H.C. Lee (eds), *Korean Managerial Dynamics*. New York: Praeger.
Kagono, T., Alonaka, I., Sakakibara, K. and Okumara, A. (1985) *Strategic vs Evolutionary Management*. Amsterdam: North Holland.
Katzenstein, P. (1985) *Small States in World Markets*. Ithaca, NY: Cornell University Press.
Kim, D.K. and Kim, C.W. (1989) 'Korean Value Systems and Managerial Practice', in K.H. Chung and H.C. Lee (eds), *Korean Managerial Dynamics*. New York: Praeger.
Kim, E.M. (1989a) 'Development, State Policy and Industrial Organizations: the Case of Korea's Chaebol', paper presented to the International Conference on Business Groups and Economic Development in East Asia, University of Hong Kong, 20–22 June.
Kim, E.M. (1989b) 'From Domination to Symbioses: State and Chaebol in Korea', *Pacific Focus*, 3: 105–21.
Kim, K.-D. (1979) *Man and Society in Korea's Economic Growth*. Seoul: Seoul National University Press.
Kim. K.-D. (1988) 'The Distinctive Features of South Korea's Development', in P.L. Berger and H-H.M. Hsiao (eds), *In Search of an East Asian Development Model*. New Brunswick, NJ: Transaction.
Kim, Y-H. (1990) 'The Evolution of the College Enrollment Quota Policy', unpublished paper presented to a conference on States and Development in the East Asian Pacific Rim held at the University of California at Santa Barbara, March.
Kiyonari, T. and Nakamura, H. (1980) 'The Establishment of the Big Business

System', in K. Sato (ed.), *Industry and Business in Japan*. White Plains, NY: M.E. Sharpe.

Koike, K. (1984) 'Skill Formation Systems in the US and Japan', in M. Aoki (ed.), *The Economic Analysis of the Japanese Firm*. Amsterdam: North Holland.

Koike, K. (1987) 'Human Resource Development and Labour–Management Relations', in K. Yamamura and Y. Yasuba (eds), *The Political Economy of Japan, I: The Domestic Transformation*. Stanford, CA: Stanford University Press.

Kono, T. (1984) *Strategy and Structure of Japanese Enterprises*. London: Macmillan.

Kosai, Y. (1987) 'The Politics of Economic Management', in K. Yamamura and Y. Yasuba (eds), *The Political Economy of Japan, I: The Domestic Transformation*. Stanford, CA: Stanford University Press.

Kristensen, P.H. (1989) 'Denmark: an Experimental Laboratory for New Industrial Models', *Entrepreneurship and Regional Development*, 1: 245–55.

Kristensen, P.H. (1990) 'Denmark's Concealed Production Culture, its Socio-Historical Construction and Dynamics at Work', in F. Borum and P.H. Kristensen (eds), *Technological Innovation and Organizational Change*. Copenhagen.

Lane, C. (1987) 'Capitalism or Culture?', *Work, Employment and Society*, 1: 57–83.

Lane, C. (1988) 'Industrial Change in Europe: the Pursuit of Flexible Specialization in Britain and West Germany', *Work, Employment and Society*, 2: 141–68.

Lane, C. (1989) *Management and Labour in Europe*. Aldershot: Edward Elgar.

Lane, C. (1992) 'European Business Systems: Britain and Germany Compared', in R. Whitley (ed.), *European Business Systems: Firms and Markets in their National Contexts*. London: Sage.

Lash, S. and Urry, J. (1987) *The End of Organized Capitalism*. Oxford: Polity.

Lawrence, P. (1980) *Managers and Management in West Germany*. London: Croom Helm.

Lawriwsky, M.L. (1984) *Corporate Structure and Performance*. London: Croom Helm.

Lazerson, M.H. (1988) 'Organizational Growth of Small Firms: an Outcome of Markets and Hierarchies', *American Sociological Review*, 53: 330–42.

Lee, H.C. (1984) 'The American Role in the Development of Management Education in Korea', in K. Moskowitz (ed.), *From Patron to Partner: The Development of US–Korean Business and Trade Relations*. Lexington, MA: D.C. Heath.

Leifer, E.M. and White, H.C. (1987) 'A Structural Approach to Markets', in M.S. Mizruchi and M. Schwartz (eds), *Intercorporate Relations: The Structural Analysis of Business*. Cambridge: Cambridge University Press.

Levine, S.B. (1967) 'Post-War Trade Unionism, Collective Bargaining and Japanese Social Structure', in R.P. Dore (ed.), *Aspects of Social Change in Modern Japan*. Princeton, NJ: Princeton University Press.

Levy, B. (1988) 'Korean and Taiwanese Firms as Industrial Competitors: the Challenges Ahead', *Columbia Journal of World Business*, Spring: 43–51.

Lévy-Leboyer, M. (1980) 'The Large Corporation in Modern France', in A.D. Chandler and H. Daems (eds), *Managerial Hierarchies*. Cambridge, MA: Harvard University Press.

Liebenberg, R.D. (1982) '"Japan Incorporated" and "The Korean Troops": a comparative analysis of Korean business organizations', MA thesis, Dept of Asian Studies, University of Hawaii.

Limlingan, V.S. (1986) *The Overseas Chinese in ASEAN: Business Strategies and*

Management Practices. Pasig, Metro Manila: Vita Development Corporation.

Lincoln, E.J. (1988) *Japan: Facing Economic Maturity*. Washington, DC: Brookings Institution.

Lincoln, J.R. (1990) 'Japanese Organization and Organization Theory', *Research in Organization Behaviour*, 12: 225–84.

Lincoln, J.R. and Kalleberg, A.L. (1990) *Culture, Control and Commitment*. Cambridge: Cambridge University Press.

Lincoln, J.R., Hanada, M. and McBride, K. (1986) 'Organizational Structures in Japanese and US Manufacturing', *Administrative Science Quarterly*, 31: 338–64.

Lodge, G.C. (1987) 'Introduction: Ideology and Country Analysis', in G.C. Lodge and E.F. Vogel (eds), *Ideology and National Competitiveness*. Boston, MA: Harvard Business School.

Lodge, G.C. and Vogel, E.F. (eds) (1987) *Ideology and National Competitiveness*. Boston, MA: Harvard Business School.

MacNeil, I.R. (1978) 'Contracts: Adjustments of Long-Term Economic Relations under Classical, Neo-Classical and Relational Contract Law', *North Western University Law Review*, 72: 854–906.

Mann, S. (1987) *Local Merchants and the Chinese Bureaucracy, 1750–1950*. Stanford, CA: Stanford University Press.

Mason, E., Kim, M-J., Perkins, D., Kim, K.-S. and Kim, Q.-Y. (1980) *The Economic and Social Modernization of the Republic of Korea*. Cambridge, MA: Harvard University Press.

Maurice, M., Sorge, A. and Warner, M. (1980) 'Societal Differences in Organizing Manufacturing Units', *Organization Studies*, 1: 59–86.

Maurice, M., Sellier, F. and Silvestre, J.J. (1986) *The Social Bases of Industrial Power*. Cambridge, MA: MIT Press.

McMillan, C. (1985) *The Japanese Industrial System*. Berlin: de Gruyter.

McNamara, D.L. (1986) 'Comparative Colonial Response: Korea and Taiwan, 1895–1919', *Korean Studies*, 10: 54–68.

McNamara, D.L. (1990) *The Colonial Origins of Korean Enterprise 1910–45*. Cambridge: Cambridge University Press.

Meyer, J.W. and Rowan, B. (1977) 'Institutional Organizations: Formal Structure as Myth and Ceremony', *American Journal of Sociology*, 83: 440–63.

Meyer, J. and Scott, R. (1983) *Organizational Environments*. London: Sage.

Michell, T. (1988) *From a Developing to a Newly Industrialized Country: The Republic of Korea, 1961–82*. Geneva: International Labour Organization.

Miyazaki, Y. (1980) 'Excessive Competition and the Formation of Keiretsu', in K. Sato (ed.), *Industry and Business in Japan*. Armonk, NY: M.E. Sharpe.

Mizruchi, M.S. and Schwartz, M. (1987) 'The Structural Analysis of Business', in M.S. Mizruchi and M. Schwartz (eds), *Intercorporate Relations*. Cambridge: Cambridge University Press.

Moore, B. (1966) *The Social Origins of Dictatorship and Democracy*. Boston, MA: Beacon Press.

Morishima, M. (1982) *Why Has Japan Succeeded?* Cambridge: Cambridge University Press.

Moulder, F.V. (1977) *Japan, China, and the Modern World Economy*. Cambridge: Cambridge University Press.

Murakami, Y. (1987) 'The Japanese Model of Political Economy', in K. Yamamura and Y. Yasuba (eds), *The Political Economy of Japan, I: The Domestic Transformation*. Stanford, CA: Stanford University Press.

Mutel, J. (1988) 'The Modernization of Japan', in J. Baechler, J.A. Hall and M. Mann (eds), *Europe and the Rise of Capitalism*. Oxford: Blackwell.

Myers, R.H. (1986) 'The Economic Development of the Republic of China on Taiwan', in L.J. Lau (ed.), *Modes of Development*. San Francisco, CA: ICS Press.

Negandhi, A.R. (1986) 'Role and Structure of German Multinationals: a Comparative Profile', in K. Macharzina and W.H. Staehle (eds), *European Approaches to International Management*. Berlin: de Gruyter.

Nishida, J. (1990) 'The Japanese Influence on the Shanghaiese Textile Industry and Implications for Hong Kong', M.Phil thesis, University of Hong Kong.

Nishida, J. and Redding, G. (1992) 'Firm Development and Diversification Strategies as Products of Economic Cultures: The Japanese and Hong Kong Textile Industries', in R. Whitley (ed.), *European Business Systems: Firms and Markets in their National Contexts*. London: Sage.

Nishiyama, T. (1984) 'The Structure of Managerial Control: Who Owns and Controls Japanese Business?', in K. Sato and Y. Hoshino (eds), *The Anatomy of Japanese Business*. Armonk, NY: M.E. Sharpe.

Noda, K. (1979) 'Big Business Organization', in E.F. Vogel (ed.), *Modern Japanese Organization and Decision Making*. Tokyo: Tuttle.

Numazaki, I. (1986) 'Networks of Taiwanese Big Business', *Modern China*, 12: 487–534.

Numazaki, I. (1987) 'Enterprise Groups in Taiwan', *Shoken Keisai*, December, 162: 15–23.

Numazaki, I. (1989) 'The Role of Personal Networks in the Making of Taiwan's Guanxiqiye (Related Enterprises)', paper presented to the International Conference on Business Groups and Economic Development in East Asia, University of Hong Kong, 20–22 June.

Offe, C. (1976) *Industry and Inequality*. London: Edward Arnold.

Okimoto, D. (1989) *Between MITI and the Market*. Stanford, CA: Stanford University Press.

Okumura, H. (1984) 'Interim Relations in an Enterprise Group: the Case of Mitsubishi', in K. Sato and Y. Hoshino (eds), *The Anatomy of Japanese Business*. Armonk, NY: M.E. Sharpe.

Okumura, H. (1989) 'Intercorporate Relations in Japan', Research Program in East Asian Business and Development, Working Paper No. 27, Institute of Governmental Affairs, University of California, Davis.

Oliver, N. and Wilkinson, B. (1988) *The Japanization of British Industry*. Oxford: Blackwell.

O'Malley, W.J. (1988) 'Culture and Industrialization', in H. Hughes (ed.), *Achieving Industrialization in East Asia*. Cambridge: Cambridge University Press.

Orru, M. (1989) 'Practical and Theoretical Aspects of Japanese Business', Program in East Asian Business and Development Research, Working Paper No. 29, Institute of Governmental Affairs, University of California, Davis.

Orru, M. (1991) 'Business Organizations in a Comparative Perspective: Small Firms in Taiwan and Italy', *Studies in Comparative International Development*, 26.

Orru, M., Biggart, N.W. and Hamilton, G. (1988) 'Organizational Isomorphism in East Asia: Broadening the New Institutionalism', Program in East Asian Business and Development Research, Working Paper No. 10, Institute of Governmental Affairs, University of California, Davis.

Orru, M., Hamilton, G. and Suzuki, M. (1989) 'Patterns of Inter-Firm Control in Japanese Business', *Organization Studies*, 10: 549–74.

Palais, J.B. (1975) *Politics and Policy in Traditional Korea*. Cambridge, MA: Harvard University Press.

Papanek, G. (1988) 'The New Asian Capitalism: an Economic Portrait', in P.L. Berger and H.-H.M. Hsiao (eds), *In Search of an East Asian Development Model*. New Brunswick, NJ: Transaction.

Park, S.-I. (1988) 'Republic of Korea: Bank A', in *Technological Change, Work Organization and Pay: Lessons from Asia*. Geneva: International Labour Organization.

Patrick, H.T. and Rohlen, T.P. (1987) 'Small-Scale Family Enterprises', in K. Yamamura and Y. Yasuba (eds), *The Political Economy of Japan, I: The Domestic Transformation*. Stanford, CA: Stanford University Press.

Payne, P. (1990) 'Entrepreneurship and British Economic Decline', in B. Collins and K. Robbins (eds), *British Culture and Economic Decline*. London: Weidenfeld & Nicolson.

Pelzel, J.C. (1970) 'Japanese Kinship: a Comparison', in M. Freedman (ed.), *Family and Kinship in Chinese Society*. Stanford, CA: Stanford University Press.

Penrose, E. (1980) *The Theory of the Growth of the Firm*. Oxford: Blackwell (first published in 1959).

Pugh, D.S. and Redding, S.G. (1985) 'The Formal and the Informal: Japanese and Chinese Organization Structures', in S.R. Clegg, D.C. Dunphy and S.G. Redding (eds), *The Enterprise and Management in East Asia*. Hong Kong: University of Hong Kong, Centre for Asian Studies.

Pye, L.W. (1985) *Asian Power and Politics: The Cultural Dimensions of Authority*. Cambridge, MA: Harvard University Press.

Pye, L.W. (1988) 'The New Asian Capitalism: a Political Portrait', in P.L. Berger and H.-H.M. Hsiao (eds), *In Search of an East Asian Development Model*. New Brunswick, NJ: Transaction.

Ragin, C. (1987) *The Comparative Method*. Berkeley, CA: University of California Press.

Redding, S.G. (1980) 'Cognition as an Aspect of Culture and its Relation to Management Processes: an Exploratory View of the Chinese Case', *Journal of Management Studies*, 17: 127–48.

Redding, S.G. (1990) *The Spirit of Chinese Capitalism*. Berlin: de Gruyter.

Redding, S.G. and Wong, G.Y.Y. (1986) 'The Psychology of Chinese Organizational Behaviour', in M. Bond (ed.), *The Psychology of the Chinese People*. Oxford: Oxford University Press.

Richardson, G. (1960) *Information and Investment*. Oxford: Oxford University Press.

Richardson, G. (1972) 'The Organization of Industry' *Economic Journal*, 82: 883–96.

Rohlen, T.P. (1974) *For Harmony and Strength: Japanese White-Collar Organization in Anthropological Perspective*. Berkeley, CA: University of California Press.

Rohlen, T.P. (1979) 'The Company Work Group', in E.F. Vogel (ed.), *Modern Japanese Organization and Decision Making*. Tokyo: Tuttle.

Rosario, L. do (1990) 'Collective Fallout', *Far Eastern Economic Review*, 26 July: 20.

Rose, M. (1985) 'Universalism, Culturalism and the Aix Group', *European Sociological Review*, 1: 65–83.

Rumelt, R. (1974) *Strategy, Structure and Economic Performance*. Boston, MA: Harvard Business School.

Samuels, R.J. (1987) *The Business of the Japanese State*. Ithaca, NY: Cornell University Press.

Saxonhouse, G.R. (1976) 'Country Girls and Communication among Competitors in the Japanese Cotton-Spinning Industry', in H. Patrick (ed.), *Japanese Industrialization and its Social Consequences*. Berkeley, CA: University of California Press.

Sayer, A. (1984) *Method in Social Science*. London: Hutchinson.

Schiffer, J. (1991) 'State Policy and Economic Growth: a Note on the Hong Kong Model', *International Journal of Urban and Regional Research*, 15: 180–96.

Scott, I. (1989) *Political Change and the Crisis of Legitimacy in Hong Kong*. Hong Kong: Oxford University Press.

Scott, J. (1986) *Capitalist Property and Financial Power*. Brighton: Wheatsheaf.

Scott, J. (1987) 'Intercorporate Structures in Western Europe', in M.S. Mizruchi and M. Schwartz (eds), *Intercorporate Relations*. Cambridge: Cambridge University Press.

Shin, E.H. and Chin, S.W. (1989) 'Social Affinity among Top Managerial Executives of Large Corporations in Korea', *Sociological Forum*, 4: 3–26.

Silin, R.H. (1972) 'Marketing and Credit in a Hong Kong Wholesale Market', in W.E. Willmott (ed.), *Economic Organization in Chinese Society*. Stanford, CA: Stanford University Press.

Silin, R.H. (1976) *Leadership and Values: The Organization of Large-Scale Taiwanese Enterprises*. Cambridge, MA: Harvard University Press.

Simon, D.F. (1988) 'External Incorporation and Internal Reform', in E.A. Winckler and S. Greenhalgh (eds), *Contending Approaches to the Political Economy of Taiwan*. Armonk, NY: M.E. Sharpe.

Sit, V.F.S. and Wong. S-L. (1988) *Changes in the Industrial Structure and the Role of Small and Medium Industries in Asian Countries: The Case of Hong Kong*. Hong Kong: University of Hong Kong, Centre of Asian Studies.

Skocpol, T. (1985) 'Bringing the State Back In: Strategies of Analysis in Current Research', in P.B. Evans et al. (eds), *Bringing the State Back In*. Cambridge: Cambridge University Press.

Smith, C. (1991) 'Reforms in Store', *Far East Economic Review*, 17 January: 44–5.

Smith, T.C. (1959) *The Agrarian Origins of Modern Japan*. Stanford, CA: Stanford University Press.

Smith, T.C. (1967) '"Merit" as Ideology in the Tokugawa Period', in R.P. Dore (ed.), *Aspects of Social Change in Modern Japan*. Princeton, NJ: Princeton University Press.

Smith, T.C. (1988a) *Native Sources of Japanese Industrialization, 1750–1920*. Berkeley, CA: University of California Press.

Smith, T.C. (1988b) 'The Land Tax in the Tokugawa Period', in T.C. Smith, *Native Sources of Japanese Industrialization, 1750–1920*. Berkeley, CA: University of California Press.

Sorge, A. (1983) 'Cultured Organizations', *International Studies of Management and Organizations*, 12: 106–38.

Sorge, A. (1991) 'Strategic Fit and the Social Effect: Interpreting Cross-National Comparisons of Technology Organisation and Human Resources', *Organization Studies*, 12: 161–90.

Sorge, A. and Warner, M. (1986) *Comparative Factory Organization*, Aldershot: Gower.

Spender, J.C. (1989) *Industrial Recipes*. Oxford: Blackwell.

Steers, R.M., Shin, Y.K. and Ungson, G.R. (1989) *The Chaebol*. New York: Harper & Row.

Steinberg, D.I. (1989) *The Republic of Korea*. Boulder, CO: Westview.

Stinchcombe, A. (1965) 'Social Structure and Organizations', in J.G. March (ed.), *Handbook of Organizations*. Chicago, IL: Rand McNally.

Stites, R. (1982) 'Small Scale Industry in Yingge, Taiwan', *Modern China*, 8: 247–79.

Streeck, W. and Schmitter, P.C. (1985) 'Community, Market, State and Associations? The Prospective Contribution of Interest Governance to Social Order', in W. Streeck and P.C. Schmitter (eds), *Private Interest Government: Beyond Market and State*. London: Sage.

Suleiman, E.N. (1978) *Elites in French Society*. Princeton, NJ: Princeton University Press.

Tam, S. (1990) 'Centrifugal versus Centripetal Growth Processes: Contrasting Ideal Types for Conceptualizing the Developmental Patterns of Chinese and Japanese Firms', in S. Clegg and G. Redding (eds), *Capitalism in Contrasting Cultures*. Berlin: de Gruyter.

Taylor, C. (1985) 'Social Theory as Practice', in C. Taylor, *Philosophical Essays*, vol. 2. Cambridge: Cambridge University Press.

Teretani, T. (1980) 'Japanese Business and Government in the Take-off Stage', in K. Nakagawa (ed.), *Government and Business*. Tokyo: University of Tokyo Press.

Trevor, M. (1988) *Toshiba's New British Company*. London: Policy Studies Institute.

Udagawa, M. and Nakamura, S. (1980) 'Japanese Business and Government in the Inter-War Period', in K. Nakagawa (ed.), *Government and Business*. Tokyo: University of Tokyo Press.

Umegaki, M. (1986) 'From Domain to Prefecture', in M.B. Jansen and G. Rozman (eds), *Japan in Transition*. Princeton, NJ: Princeton University Press.

Upham, F.K. (1987) *Law and Social Change in Post-War Japan*. Cambridge, MA: Harvard University Press.

Vogel, E.F. (1967) 'Kinship Structure, Migration to the City, and Modernization', in R.P. Dore (ed.), *Aspects of Social Change in Modern Japan*. Princeton, NJ: Princeton University Press.

Vogel, E.F. (1987) 'Japan: Adaptive Communitarianism', in G.C. Lodge and E.F. Vogel (eds), *Ideology and National Competitiveness*. Boston, MA: Harvard Business School.

Wade, R. (1988) 'The Role of Government in Overcoming Market Failures: Taiwan, Republic of Korea and Japan', in H. Hughes (ed.), *Achieving Industrialization in East Asia*. Cambridge: Cambridge University Press.

Wade, R. (1990) *Governing the Market*. Princeton, NJ: Princeton University Press.

Wakiyama, T. (1987) 'The Implementation and Effectiveness of MITI's Administrative Guidance', in S. Wilks and M. Wright (eds), *Comparative Government–Industry Relations*. Oxford: Oxford University Press.

Ward, B.E. (1972) 'A Small Factory in Hong Kong: Some Aspects of its Internal Organization', in W.E. Willmott (ed.), *Economic Organization in Chinese Society*. Stanford, CA: Stanford University Press.

Weiss, L. (1984) 'The Italian State and Small Business', *European Journal of Sociology*, 25: 214–41.

Weiss, L. (1988) *Creating Capitalism: The State and Small Business since 1945*. Oxford: Blackwell.

Werner, K.F. (1988) 'Political and Social Structures of the West', in J. Baechler, J.A. Hall and M. Mann (eds), *Europe and the Rise of Capitalism*. Oxford: Blackwell.

Westney, D.E. (1987) *Imitation and Innovation: The Transfer of Western Organizational Patterns to Meiji Japan*. Cambridge, MA: Harvard University Press.

Whitley, R.D. (1984) 'The Fragmented State of Management Studies, Reasons and Consequences', *Journal of Management Studies*, 21: 331–48.

Whitley, R.D. (1987) 'Taking Firms Seriously as Economic Actors: towards a Sociology of Firm Behaviour', *Organization Studies*, 8: 125–47.

Whitley, R.D. (1990) 'Eastern Asian Enterprise Structures and the Comparative Analysis of Forms of Business Organization', *Organization Studies*, 11: 47–54.

Whittaker, D.H. (1990) 'The End of Japanese-Style Employment?', *Work, Employment and Society*, 4: 321–47.

Wilkinson, B. (1988) 'A Comparative Analysis', in *Technological Change, Work Organization and Pay: Lessons from Asia*. Geneva: International Labour Organization.

Williamson, O.E. (1985) *The Economic Institutions of Capitalism*. New York: Free Press.

Winckler, E.A. (1987) 'Statism and Familism in Taiwan', in G.C. Lodge and E.F. Vogel (eds), *Ideology and National Competitiveness*. Boston, MA: Harvard Business School.

Winckler, E.A. (1988) 'Elite Political Struggle, 1945–85', in E.A. Winckler and S. Greenhalgh (eds), *Contending Approaches to the Political Economy of Taiwan*. Armonk, NY: M.E. Sharpe.

Wolf, M. (1970) 'Child Training and the Chinese Family', in M. Freedman (ed.), *Family and Kinship in Chinese Society*. Stanford, CA: Stanford University Press.

Wolferen, K. van (1989) *The Enigma of Japanese Power*. London: Macmillan.

Wong, G.Y.Y. (1989) 'Business Groups in a Dynamic Environment: Interlocking Directorates in Hong Kong 1976–86', paper presented to the International Conference on Business Groups and Economic Development in East Asia, University of Hong Kong, 20–22 June.

Wong, S-L. (1985) 'The Chinese Family Firm: a Model', *British Journal of Sociology*, 36: 58–72.

Wong, S-L. (1988a) 'The Applicability of Asian Family Values to Other Sociocultural Settings', in P.L. Berger and H.-H.M. Hsiao (eds), *In Search of an East Asian Development Model*. New Brunswick, NJ: Transaction.

Wong, S-L. (1988b) *Emigrant Entrepreneurs*. Hong Kong: Oxford University Press.

Wu, Y-Li (1983) 'Chinese Entrepreneurs in Southeast Asia', *American Economic Review*, 73: 112–17.

Wu, Y-Li and Wu, C-L. (1980) *Economic Development in Southeast Asia: The Chinese Dimension*. Stanford, CA: Hoover Institution Press.

Yamamura, K. (1976) 'General Trading Companies in Japan: their Origins and Growth', in H. Patrick (ed.), *Japanese Industrialization and its Social Consequences*. Berkeley, CA: University of California Press.

Yoo, S. and Lee, S.M. (1987) 'Management Style and Practice in Korean Chaebols', *California Management Review*, 29: 95–110.

Yoshihara, K. (1982) *Sogo Shosha: The Vanguard of the Japanese Economy.* Tokyo: Oxford University Press.

Yoshihara, K. (1988) *The Rise of Ersatz Capitalism in South-East Asia.* Oxford: Oxford University Press.

Yoshino, M.Y. and Lifson, T.B. (1986) *The Invisible Link: Japan's Sogo Shosha and the Organization of Trade.* Cambridge, MA: MIT Press.

Youngson, A.J. (1982) *Hong Kong: Economic Growth and Policy.* Hong Kong: Oxford University Press.

Zeile, W. (1989) 'Industrial Policy and Organizational Efficiency: the Korean Chaebol Examined', Program in East Asian Business and Development Research, Working Paper No. 30, Institute of Governmental Affairs, University of California, Davis.

Zielinski, R. and Holloway, N. (1991) *Unequal Equities: Power and Risk in Japan's Stock Market.* Tokyo: Kodansha.

Zucker, L. (1986) 'The Production of Trust: Institutional Sources of Economic Structure, 1840–1920', in B. Staw and L.L. Cummings (eds), *Research in Organizational Behaviour*, vol. 8. Greenwich, CT: JAI, pp. 53–112.

Zysman, J. (1983) *Governments, Markets and Growth: Financial Systems and the Politics of Industrial Change.* Ithaca, NY: Cornell University Press.

Index